MANAGING WORKPLACE STRESS AND CONFLICT AMID CHANGE

Second Edition

Bahaudin G. Mujtaba
Timothy McCartney

ILEAD Academy, LLC
Davie, Florida. United States of America
www.ileadacademy.com

Bahaudin G. Mujtaba and Timothy McCartney, 2010. *Managing Workplace Stress and Conflict amid Change, 2nd edition*

Cover Design by: Cagri Tanyar

© 2010- Copyright by Bahaudin G. Mujtaba and Timothy McCartney
First edition, 2007 - ISBN: 1-59526-414-0;
Library of Congress Control Number (LCCN): 2006904604

ISBN-10: 0-9774211-6-3

ISBN-13: 978-0-9774211-6-9

Subject Code & Description
SEL024000 - Self-Help: Stress Management
FAM013000 - Family & Relationships: Conflict Resolution
BUS503010 - Business & Economics: Business Life - Health/Stress

Printed in the United States of America by ILEAD Academy, LLC. Davie, Florida.

Leadership Education and Associate Development Academy

Book Review Comments

Managing Workplace Stress and Conflict amid Change not only discussed the principles and theories of each subject, but it also gave practical application for managing workplace stress and conflict. I particularly enjoyed the authors' use of everyday mnemonics, or triggers like DREAM and RESPECT, to aid in remembering the steps.

Nadine L. Frazier, MBA, ACII, Managing Partner,
LIV Insurance Agents and Brokers Ltd.
Nassau, Bahamas

To achieve, synergy, productivity and innovation needed to compete in today's global environment, organization leaders of all types need to institute programs and training tools designed to address managing workplace stress and conflict management to all their employees. Mujtaba and McCartney's "*Managing Workplace Stress and Conflict amid Change*" show how to address and improve the work environment in all the following areas: Conflict – resolution and management skills, time management and problem solving and focused on the importance of making a difference through positive attitude. This unique contribution to theory and applications makes a positive impact with its easy to read style and layout. This book can be a very reliable and powerful source for today's scholars and managers to help in the management applications...It does an outstanding job of putting together resources and many years of research to provide a detail lesson in the art of achieving change management.

Dr. Claudette Chin-Loy, Program Coordinator
Nova Southeastern University

Mujtaba and McCartney have written an excellent resource for both the manager and the end user. They combine concepts of change with conflict and stress, to give the reader a better understanding of the relationship between the three interrelated topics. Individual chapters on Change Management, Stress Management and Conflict Management allow the authors to delve into these subjects in depth providing both theory and application. The Time Management and Problem Solving chapter provides useful information and helpful tools that the reader can apply to the real world of work in managing their personal stress and conflicts amid their changing world.

Dr. Daniel Sullivan, Director of Student Engagement
Nova Southeastern University

The authors' passages highlighting the influence of emotions and feelings on workplace performance and on developing the ability for self-governance are significant in light of emergent neuroscientific research. Recent brain research and emotional intelligence studies corroborate that the ability to effectively manage stress and the associated emotions, especially as they relate to change, are competencies which can be learned.

Dawn Giannoni, Education Specialist- Brain Research.

Managing Workplace Stress is directly related to one's nutrition intake and exercise regiments. You probably know that good nutrition and exercise helps you stay healthy and effectively manage your level of stress. Regardless of your stress level, good nutrition also affects how you feel both physically and emotionally which prepares one to effectively manage change and routine conflicts. Good nutrition means eating variety of foods in a balanced manner with moderation. Of course, one must remember that staying healthy requires more than just good nutrition. It is a well known fact that regular physical activity can help reduce feelings of stress, anxiety and depression. Regular physical activity boosts self-confidence by improving strength, stamina, flexibility, appearance and sense of control which are needed by busy managers in today's workforce. Good nutrition and physical activity are both important to reduce stresses of daily life because when you look good you feel good. *Managing Workplace Stress* encourages good nutrition and a regular exercise program which are important for today's busy professionals. *Managing Workplace Stress and Conflict amid Change* book is a good read and it provides effective tools for becoming aware of stress, its causes, and proactively managing it to remain healthy and in good physical shape.

Anisa Qadir, Nutritionist, MS/RD/LD
University of North Florida

It is commonly recognized among business leaders that change, conflict and time management issues are great contributors to stress in the workplace. It is nice to see a book that addresses all of these issues in a clear and usable format.

Dr. *Vincent S. Daniels, Executive*
Director, Hudson Institute

Managing Workplace Stress and Conflict amid Change by Mujtaba and McCartney is an excellent guide on coaching others through change and stress. It provides an excellent itemized list of conflict management strategies, a wonderful primer on change management, research on stress management, and a wonderful guide manager's can follow to avoid stress. It goes beyond some texts, in that it not only discusses behavioral changes in the workplace, but also talks about health and nutritional changes that can help one relieve stress, as well. It does a good job of providing tools and instruments for stress management and conflict resolution, as well as a guide for future research in the area.

Dr. *Alexander M. Pevec, Faculty*
Malaspina University-College, Nanaimo BC Canada

This book is a packed with explanations and advice for the manager or the person who wishes to understand the nature of stress, conflict and change in the workplace. It goes to some "pains" to bring together relevant information from a variety of sources to explain the real-life situations the modern worker experiences. I found it useful in explaining theories read many years ago and connecting so many bits of knowledge together in an easy to read manner.

Richard G. Adderley, Assistant Vice President-Human
Resources, The Insurance Institute of the Bahamas

Managing Workplace Stress and Conflict amid Change is an excellent bridge for contextualizing between change, conflict and stress management. It is a powerful tool for Bahamian executives. Excellent read for business executives seeking to effect change without stress and conflict.

Juliett Reid, Site Director-Bahamas Student Educational Center, Nova Southeastern University

----

This is an excellent piece of work that can help teams and management deal with routine stress and conflict situations. I encourage management to read and practice the techniques in this book. The thoughts in this book will go a long way to smooth out unnecessary organizational rancor.

Dr. Ike Udechukwu, Human Resources Specialist, Georgia State University

----

Managing workplace stress effectively is an essential part of organizational success. This book provides valuable information regarding managing organizational change and conflict, and I believe it is an asset for students, employees and employers.

Dr. Gimol Thomas, Director of Assessment, College of Dental Medicine

----

Managing Workplace Stress and Conflict amid Change is succinctly written to help the working professional manage change, stress and conflict in the areas in which they work. It is written in a practical, usable fashion which is user-friendly to those who read it and wish to apply its concepts. It is written in a practical, user-friendly manner. I highly recommend this practical book.

Barbara A. Stephens, Faculty Nova Southeastern University

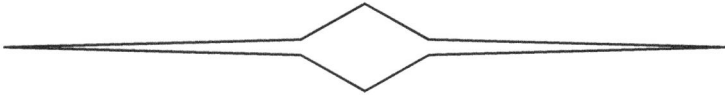

Dedication

This book is dedicated to those who set and write worthwhile
personal goals, those who deal with
and work to effectively overcome stress
and conflict in reaching their goals,
and those who encourage their
friends to do the same.

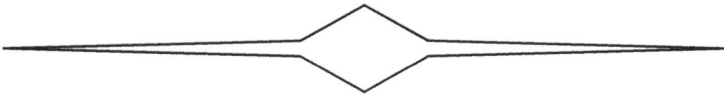

TABLE OF CONTENTS

Acknowledgements

A book cannot be completed easily and we have certainly had many colleagues and family members who helped us in the process. First, we would like to thank our Creator for giving us the ability and opportunity to make this material available. Second, we would like to thank our colleagues and family members for their contributions and guidance in preparing the content of this book. There are many individuals that have formally or informally contributed to this book and we are thankful for their generosity and friendship. Third, we thank you for reading this material.

May you always have the hindsight to know where you have been, the foresight to know where you are going, and the insight to know when you are about to go too far. Remember, if you can perceive and believe a better state of being, then you are very likely to achieve it as well.

Preface

S tress and conflict are realities of life. In July of 2009, Fox News reported that about 50% of American workers feel stressed on a daily basis. Perhaps this stress is due to the recession in the economy, job losses, more work, going to school while working, job change, more responsibilities, uncertainty, conflict, and/or too many things to achieve in a short time period. People are living in a constant period of transition, and the shelf life of solutions keeps getting shorter since what works today can become obsolete a few months later. Where is all the stress coming from in today's life? Stress is often coming from or caused by people, technology, new information, and globalization trends. Some of the commonly addressed sources of stress for businesses can include changes in nature of the workforce, economy, social trends, politics, leadership, management, organizational structures, products, services, customers, changing and conflicting demands, and location of where the firm produces or offers its products. *Managing Workplace Stress and Conflict amid Change* is about helping people effectively manage stress, conflict, and change in the workplace.

It must be acknowledged that this book is prepared as a summary to be a helpful read for busy professionals in the workplace, for those who conduct training, and for those who attend workshops on change management, time management, conflict management, and/or stress management topics. Those who wish to study this material more comprehensively can also read the 2006 book entitled *Cross Cultural Change Management* (Bahaudin G. Mujtaba, ISBN: 1-59526-568-6; by Llumina Press: www.Llumina.com). *CCCM* book is over 400 pages and covers these topics in more detail. *CCCM* also offers resources for instructors and educators who integrate the book for their workshops and academic courses. Trainers and educators who would like to use these facilitator resources for their training or teachings should contact the publisher or authors. For suggestions and questions, you can contact the authors (mujtaba@nova.edu or mccartne@nova.edu) at any time.

The topics covered in *Managing Workplace Stress and Conflict amid Change* include change management, conflict management, time management, stress management, and effective problem-solving. The book emphasizes that stress, conflict and change are realities of life in every organization. They are a natural part of evolution and human development. They have been handled for thousands of years and should be positively managed so that professionals may maximize their productivity and success in life.

Stress, conflict and change are realities of life in every organization. They are a natural part of evolution and human development. They can and should be effectively managed.

CHAPTER ONE

1 – CHANGE, CONFLICT AND STRESS

S tress, conflict, and change have always been a part of life for human beings, and perhaps more so today than ever before. Dealing with stress, conflict and change is normal, and twenty-first century professionals might as well begin seeing it as such by consciously making every day an appropriate one for themselves and their colleagues by effectively managing their own life's stress, conflicts, and changes, while also coaching others to do the same.

The fast pace of today's work environment has created many workaholics who might be successful professionally but personally they have a "bankrupt" life since they have forgotten about balancing their work time with family needs and leisure renewal. Perhaps, a busy and stressed work life is another variable playing into the high divorce rates in most countries and cultures. The fast pace of today's work world has caused changes in people's eating patterns as well. Instead of eating meals jointly with family members, friends and colleagues many families and individuals have been conditioned to eat while working. As a matter of fact, the most popular places to eat on the go were in front of the television set (60% of the respondents), in the car (42%) and at work (40%) (findings presented by USA Today, August 2005). Fifty years ago, most traditional cultures did not encourage people to eat by themselves since eating was a social time for family members to talk and converse with one another. Because of such interpersonal conversation opportunities, there was little need for psychiatrists and psychologists which are highly in demand today by many individuals because they are the only professionals who would listen to one's modern day problems, providing alternative decision-making and support. In previous centuries, when children and teenagers faced a difficult task they usually approached a family member for advice. Today, most teenagers listen to strangers on the internet and their behaviors are often driven by the actions and trends of television stars. While television icons and chat-room respondents on the internet may not always be good role models, many youngsters feel comfortable listening to them and doing what they do. These are major changes for parents and children who are brought up with traditional family values. They will have to effectively deal with these changes as well as the impact of such changes on their children and grandchildren. While many changes can be out of one's immediate control, one can be properly prepared to deal with them according to one's personal priorities and values. Even then, the most

1

prepared individuals would have to show flexibility in choosing the best course of action for moving forward and achieving one's predetermined worthwhile goals in a changing world. Changes in modern times might be a bit more challenging for those who are not brought up with them; therefore, each generation must develop skills to positively deal with new changes as they too might have been conditioned by societal or organizational cultures that do not always welcome change.

Dynamic change is a constant in today's work environment. As such, using good sense, learning the latest data, and adapting to the current facts are essential ingredients for sustainable and positive change. In the twenty-first century environment, change keeps picking up speed in all industries and professions. Today's employees and customers are living in a constant period of transition. Pritchett (1993) asks "Where is all the change coming from?" He states that "If people create change –and obviously they do – then we should expect a rapid increase in the rate of change as the population doubles in the next few decades." This growing population is armed with new technology which feeds and sustains on itself. Pritchett states that "about 80% of technological inventions have occurred since 1900." It is best to think of technological change as something that keeps multiplying on a continuous basis. Still another source of this rapid change is technical knowledge or information which seems to be doubling about every two to three years. Some of the commonly addressed sources of change for businesses can include changes in leadership, management, organizational structures, products, services, customers, conflicting demands, and the location of where the firm produces or offers its products.

Because of rapid changes, new knowledge and the doubling of information about every few years, the future promises much more change than what has been experienced thus far. What is interesting to know and keep in mind during difficult moments is that change has no conscience and it does not play favorites. Yes, it is also true that change can quickly or slowly destroy organizations that do not adapt to the new circumstances. The high-velocity change on today's workplace calls for major shifts in both thinking and behavior. Today's professionals need to think differently, prioritize, develop faster reflexes toward changing conditions, and do what works. We should welcome change with pleasure and enjoyment since it is inevitable. Enjoyment involves the use of a skill and facing of a challenge. Put more enjoyment into your life. Increase your skills, face modern challenges with an open mind. Similarly, for effective change and stress management, increase your skills and face the challenges proactively. As the saying goes, luck is simply the intersection of preparation and opportunity. Increase your luck by acquiring the relevant knowledge regarding change, conflict, stress, and their good management.

Impact of Change on Stress and Conflict

Mankind has never before experienced so many changes in such a short period of time, and this change, characteristic of our modern century, is a very pervasive one. Life itself is a process of change and adaptability. Our modern century of technological marvels and social revolutions has thrust upon us many unbearable conditions and consequences, some of which rage above our deepest sentiments and comprehension. Society today is bombarded on all sides with a series of drastic changes within all social institutions, and the degree at which these change factors and agents assault our minds and lives is overwhelmingly inexhaustible.

Managing change is a tactical and strategic affair which becomes increasingly dangerous and difficult as the number of change variables and agents increase. This is further complicated by conflict which is inherent in all human social affairs. Conflict is unavoidable, and as such, serves as the bottleneck of progress! One of the major aims in change management and conflict resolution seems to be that of eliminating conflict. This is an almost impossible task we set ourselves since our differences are individualistic. It is fully within our nature to agree and disagree with each other, and our added knowledge and information of today have both increased and decreased the threshold for disagreement under various circumstances.

Change is a frightening social and psychological experience when it requires entering new spheres and situations. Moreover, change today has a significantly wider scope than it did decades ago, as the factors of globalization and cultural diversity have become fundamental principles and paradigms upon which change is prefabricated. One must now have a variety of skills and a wider knowledge base to manage or even comprehend change as it takes place within the context of cultural and social conflicts. The cross-cultural aspects of change and conflict further complicate their management and resolution.

Change is a social process because it is the human element that gives life and significance to change in any setting. Therefore, when managers and leaders consider change within their institutions or organizations they need to take a decisively behavioral or human approach to the management of change. Change is one of the most dominant characteristics of today's hard-pressing business environment in which fast-paced technology and high level competition are pushing individuals and organizations into new situations and environments. Entering into new competitive and social arenas can be highly stressful for employees with conflicts developing internally and externally to the organization. As a result of this awareness, managers and leaders must make change and conflict management a major part of their training and responsibilities. Teaching employees about the nature of change and its significance can be a first step in the process of effectively managing change.

Change is natural and expected within our lives. It is the nature and dynamic of change that can become stressful or cause conflicts, resistance and fear in us. The problem therefore is not change itself, but unplanned change. As human beings we like to plan and be able to manage our every aspect of life and living. Planned change is the catalyst around which we approach life, our education, training, socialization, communications, etc. However, life seems to offer more of the other for which we can be wholly unprepared to manage or accept; unplanned change. The field of strategic management has offered managers and leaders considerable knowledge in the area of planning; both short-term and long-term. However, planning for change is not an easy task, and this further complicates managing change. Change in today's society can offer many advantages as well as disadvantages, and this will depend on the degree of change, the context in which change unfolds, the scope of change, the mindset, knowledge base and skills of the individual undergoing change, the type of information and education the individual possesses, the source or sources of change, and the cultural and social experiences of the individual. Culturally, change can be a very destructive force, especially when assimilation of one's values, beliefs, customs, etc., becomes the major consequence. It is this aspect of change that becomes very stressful for both individuals and groups. All forms of change have cultural and social overtones that affect organizational progress and performance. Managers and leaders must become attuned to the fact that change within organizations means change within the social contexts of employees' work and lives. The field of industrial psychology still holds great knowledge benefits for those who would examine the effects of change in work environments and change management across all organizational boundaries. Furthermore, the lack of management initiatives and programs to deal with change and conflicts in immediate organizational settings are grossly lacking in 21st century institutions. Usually, we choose to react to change only when it arrives, and this is where conflict and resistance become major issues. We must prepare for change and then we will be better able to manage it within all contexts.

Conflict is inherent in all human affairs and this seems evident even from the onset of human history when we consider life from a Creationist perspective and the evolution of adaptability. Conflict seems to be part of the imperfect mind and nature of humankind as one strives to make decisions as to wrong or right, and those having to do with the allocation and distribution of limited resources. Conflict arises from individual differences; personal, social, psychological, cultural, physical and even the gender-related biological differences within our specie. Human conflict has both micro and macro origins; generated between individuals, groups, institutions or larger society, races or cultures. The nature of conflict as it exists within our lives rests heavily on our knowledge of selves and others and in our ability to foster tolerance and adapt to change within all contexts effectively.

Cultural exchange is the most fervent perpetrator of change and conflict as we each encounter different ways of behaving, different social values, norms, mores, attitudes, reactions and ideas to human thoughts and actions. With the proliferation in cultural exchange resulting from globalization and increased travel and communications, change and conflict have become increasingly dominant in human personal and business affairs. There seems to be a silent cultural war wherein values and beliefs, social roles and behaviors clash to produce conflict in our daily interaction as leaders, managers, and followers. Change and conflict should be expected, especially today, given the differences between individuals and their social values and cultural training. The major issue therefore is the degree to which each individual embraces or refuses change and the reactionary stance such a person chooses. This is what produces conflicts among us. Within business organizations, individual values are not secondary to organizational culture, and this must be taken into consideration when dealing with change. Though organizations have their own unique culture the individual's social values and cultural training through more fundamental societal institutions, namely, the family and religion, will still have even more powerful bearing on their ability to adapt to change of any nature. We are social creatures and most of the change we experience takes place at the affective level where most of our experiences are translated into life-long meanings. Therefore, conflict should naturally be expected when changes arrive, whether they are planned or unplanned. Organizational leaders and managers must then act as effective supporters in the education and adaptation process when it comes to employees and followers accepting change and dealing with the conflicts which arise.

Leaders of the 21st century must practice being effective supporters in counseling their subordinates to deal with change and in managing conflicts. It is important that managers and leaders of the 21st century do not strive to be or exemplify themselves as propagators of radical or mass social and organizational changes, but rather as facilitators in the change process. This will better enable them to address resistance as well as to deal with conflict. Conflict and change management should be practiced alongside each other for the best result, since they are closely interrelated and change and conflict strive from and feed on each other. Managers and leaders of today's institutions and organizations must possess a wide knowledge base and familiarity with cultures and individuals' social values in order to effectively arrive at the heart of conflict and uniquely address issues and problems. Cultural diversity as an initiative of 21st century organizations has added much complexity to change and conflict as individuals from varied backgrounds and societies encounter each other in active working relationships.

Conflict like change cannot be avoided, it can only be dealt with, and managers and leaders must become aware of this fact. Our differences as individuals serve to perpetuate change and conflict. Knowing this fact, life then is best seen as a process of adapting to change and dealing with conflict, and the best way we can approach this is by effective change management and conflict management. The field of conflict resolution has not done much for us as a society, and this is immediately evident in the widespread social problems we experience today. One of the grave issues is the speed at which social change takes place; so rapid that it is best termed social revolution. Social revolution has perpetuated conflict throughout all corners of our society and this conflict is multiple in character. There are conflicts which are gender-based, generational-related, economic-based, racially-based, culturally-based, and the list goes on. The rate at which change is taking place at all levels of our society is alarming and as such evades our ability and comprehension to deal with it effectively. The rapid nature of change has affected our ability to address conflicts across the board as we struggle to deal with several issues at once. This puts a strain on individual knowledge and scope, as well as on the limited resources we have available including time to resolve many conflicts. Resulting from this is the need for effective stress management. Stress is a major factor of social and other related problems in individuals and organizations. In fact, it seems to be a major health issue in highly developed and industrialized nations.

The relationship existing between stress, change, and conflict is one which becomes quite obvious when we consider the fact that they usually arise simultaneously within social contexts or situations or proceed immediately out of each other's existence.

The relationship between change, conflict, and stress is a highly interrelated one in so much that one does not exist without the other. This has great implications for leaders and managers. Stress management, conflict management and change management must become an integrated task if success is to be achieved in any of these. Leaders and managers of 21st century institutions and organizations must effectively integrate stress, conflict, and change management into a comprehensive program in order to effectively address the issues and problems stemming from globalization, cultural change, and technological and social revolutions.

Change in today's society is alarmingly fast-paced and this is the major issue which most individuals seem to find difficult to confront. As human beings we like to feel comfortable in a safe zone where stability guarantees us certain psychological and social needs. Change can disrupt our lives and wreck our world into disaster, especially when change has the characteristic unpredictability it does in our technologically advanced society. The 21st century society has the highest degree of uncertainty that our civilization has witnessed throughout generations this far, and with individual knowledge of this fact, our resistance to change should come as no surprise. Change can be drastic and dramatic, devastating, devouring, disastrous, and destructive. Such change where culture, religion, way of life, survival, and life itself are crushed is the most fearful and problematic, causing severe cultural, social and psychological stress and damage. As shown in Figure 1.1, stress is created by change and change can cause conflict; at the same time, conflict can cause change and further stress. The variables of change, stress, and conflict have an interdependent relationship and they tend to impact one another; change in one can cause a positive or negative impact on the others.

Figure 1.1 - The Relationship between Change, Conflict and Stress

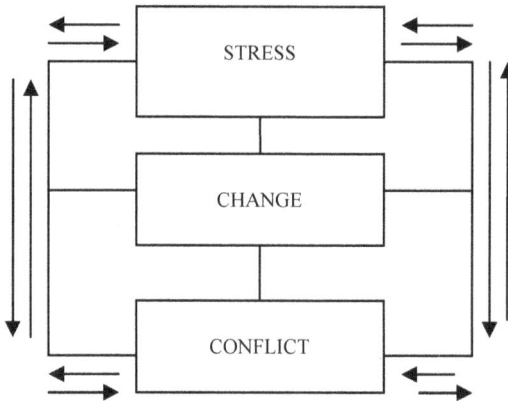

When change is natural it is a different issue than when it is a change resulting from willful enforcement such as the change experienced by the people of Iraq and Afghanistan with the interferences of outside forces. Forceful change does not allow for adaptation or negotiation; it imposes and penalizes and ridicules, and brings with it the most severe forms of stress and conflict. This is the type of change we fear; change that rocks our world and turns it upside down. Examples of such recent change have been experienced by victims of the Tsunami of Asia, earthquakes in Pakistan and China, and the hurricanes that have swept across the United States and the Caribbean over the past decade. Change appears to be best when it is planned, since it has a greater degree of flexibility and its lasting results are at best predictable.

Managers and leaders of 21st century institutions and organizations must not impose change without consensus, and when such change is introduced, implementation in an incremental manner is the best method or approach. Too much change too fast and in too little time can upset progress by affecting individual satisfaction, performance, concentration, skills, and ability to cope with tasks and responsibilities. Therefore, it is important to educate individuals about change and make them aware of the type of change and how it will affect them. This will reduce stress as well as conflict and the resistance to change.

As a civilization, we have perhaps individually and collectively experienced more of the devastating and negative side of change than the positive one. Dramatic change has shaped our entire progress, destiny and century. For example, World War I, World War II, the Vietnam War, The Gulf War, The Iraq Invasion, challenges in Afghanistan, etc. All these have been examples of change in its most devastating aspect witnessed by civilization, and which have affected peoples' lives in numerous ways. Change can be beautiful or ugly, and it is the ugly type of change that people fear. Furthermore, within social contexts change is not always welcome as it affects human interaction and relationships; our most fundamental needs. For example, change in a relationship often affects one partner's comfort or may be initiated or experienced at some cost. Therefore; it is the cost-benefit factor that makes change something that causes stress and conflict. Change can be very costly as we have witnessed from the earthquakes over the past decade which killed over 100,000 people in Pakistan, China, and Myanmar, and the hurricanes which have hit the city of New Orleans as well as its surrounding areas. When change is costly it displaces people mentally, physically, psychologically, socially, and emotionally.

Positive change is what we seek and require as individuals and when this fails to show itself we are confounded and stressed. When we plan change it often involves less stress and conflict. Managers and leaders of the 21st century must invest heavily in fostering and promoting positive change to motivate employees and deal with conflicts. Change can be the source of new growth or the precursor of failure and losses.

Coaching Others through Change and Stress

While management is a very useful tool, the value of managers coaching employees for maximum productivity amid major change and stress must be emphasized. Due to the changing demographics of the business world such as more competition and the introduction of new technologies, organizations are discovering that traditional tactics of management are no longer enough to remain competitive. As such, coaching is coming to be recognized and practiced as an effective tool to increase morale, performance and the bottom line through the success of each individual associate. For example, studies have shown that about 90% of employees who received coaching in their jobs say that it improved their job performance and professional success. In organizations where coaching is effectively practiced as a management style, the bottom-line performance is two to three times better than the traditional "command-and-control" type of organizations. Furthermore, it has been demonstrated that employee commitment increases when there is a strong, positive relationship between the manager and his/her employees. These types of relationships are developed best as a result of effective coaching. It is interesting to note that in ancient civilizations, apprenticeship and mentoring approaches were very much a part of improving skills, developing expertise, and gaining experience. The coaches and mentors provided "hands-on" know-how and were ready to challenge, motivate and support the apprentices.

Effective relationship-oriented coaching creates more knowledgeable and competent employees, reduces errors and rework, and it greatly assists in bringing new changes to the culture. Both effective and ineffective managers tend to know what makes a good coach. The difference lies in being able to transfer this knowledge into successful actions with employees to increase their performance and success. Effective coaching skills make a manager's job easier as it enables greater delegation leaving him/her time to take on bigger projects. It builds the manager's reputation as a developer of people while increasing productivity since everyone will know the expectations and the fact that what they do matters. It also can develop trust and a good relationship between managers and employees. Last but not least, good coaching skills can increase creativity, innovation, morale, and teamwork since everyone will feel safe working in an inclusive environment.

So what is coaching? *Coaching* is about developing a trusting relationship with employees so one can jointly clarify expectations and departmental goals thereby leading to specific action plans for their achievement. As such, there are many situations where coaching skills will be very effective and the following are some of them.

1. Reinforcing good performance.
2. Motivating employees to new heights and peak performance levels.
3. Orienting a new employee into the department or organization.
4. Providing new knowledge to individuals about changes and tactics.
5. Training a new skill for a new task that needs performing.
6. Following up on competencies passed on during a training session.
7. Explaining the current or new standards and how they can be achieved.
8. Setting priorities for effective time management with those employees who need it.
9. Inculcating someone into the cliques and groups which may exist within the political circles.
10. Clarifying expectations and correcting poor performance.
11. Increasing the self confidence of an employee about the task or new responsibilities and challenges.
12. Conducting a performance review.

Coaching is not an innate skill, but rather it is learned. It occurs through one's experience personally and professionally. Effective coaching is the process of letting people know that what they do matters to you and to the organization. Coaching also helps them build their self-confidence. Furthermore, it is about letting them know that you are there to help them be the best they can be as their success is important because it matters to you. It is also about being sincere, specific and to the point about both good and poor performance so they can take personal responsibility for their achievements. From this perspective, coaching is and it can be one of the most important functions managers perform because it communicates performance levels, expectations, importance of the tasks and responsibilities, and it communicates a caring attitude. The following list summarizes some of the main elements involved in coaching.

1. Before beginning the coaching session, be sure to plan exactly what you want to achieve, and the potential benefits for the other person.
2. Start on a positive note and establish a common ground by having a supportive environment.
3. Communicate clearly, listen effectively, show that you care, and do not "beat around the bush." Clearly and caringly state the challenge, opportunity, and/or expectations.
4. Be respectful of the other person's feelings, honor and dignity. Create a non-threatening environment for the interaction, dialogue and discussion.
5. Be culturally sensitive by getting to know the other person's background, values, and anticipate his/her reactions.
6. Avoid value judgments, stereotyping and labeling the behavior of others.
7. Use active and empathic listening skills to clarify your understanding and the other person's perspective.
8. Stay with the point and do not get side tracked with other issues. Restate the purpose of the session and ask what specific things can be done to increase or improve performance. You can offer assistance but avoid providing solutions –let the individual come up with the solutions. Your job is to lead them in the right direction.
9. Document and clarify the specific plan suggested by the employee, the expected level of performance and how the plan will improve performance. Seek agreement and summarize the conversation.
10. End on a positive note and thank the person for coming up with the specific plan.

Effective coaches encourage, inform, praise, raise awareness, collaborate, set clear expectations, serve as role models, empower, help, challenge, serve as vehicles for change, remove barriers, and enable others to reach their full potential. One should remember that coaching can be the single most important thing you do as a leader or manager. Also, managers and coaches should never let good or poor performance go unnoticed. When effective coaches and managers see good performance, they say it and praise it. One should not let poor performance go unnoticed; as such, when one sees poor performance one can privately communicate with the person while making the discussion positively geared toward future performance. For real personal issues and poor personal habits: first, prepare the teammate/associate, and second, be gentle and to the point in stating the problem that needs fixing.

Managers have gotten where they are because somebody guided and helped them toward the right direction and eventually trusted their judgment. So, as a global change agent, be there for your people and effectively coach them toward maximum productivity amid personal, professional, societal, and cultural changes. Coaches can also make sure that an effective and thorough change management process is used to deal with change initiatives to reduce stress and conflict in the workplace. Coaches should remember that the best option during an inevitable change is to proactively begin the adaptation process and thus reap the benefits.

Coaches know that change is inevitable and it is continuous for human beings from birth to death. Twenty-first century change agents must realize that change is constant, therefore it requires managing; change can be threatening and cumbersome;

change can create chaos and inefficiency; and change can cause people to respond quickly and reactively. Reactive responses are unplanned, situational, and may involve more time and cost; and proactive responses are based on values, planned, goal-oriented, more effective, and require a change management plan. Proactive leaders, managers, and all other change agents throughout the organization can strategically manage change by following the five steps included in the change management process, as demonstrated in Figure 1.2.

Figure 1.2- The Change Management Process

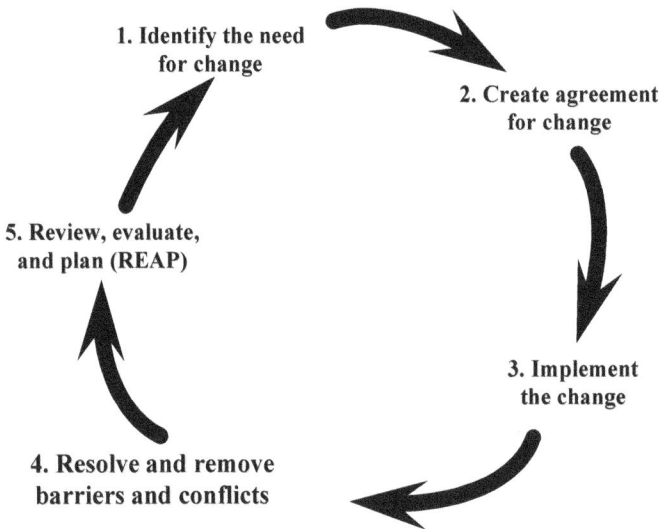

People grow like fruits, plants, and trees. Just as fruits are either green and growing or ripe and rotting, people can also be either growing or experiencing atrophy. Plants best flourish when they receive sufficient amounts of rain and sun. Too much of anything can kill them but the right balance will help them grow. If you want to become successful, you must align yourself with changes and situations that offer opportunities for the achievement of your goals.

According to John P. Kotter and Leonard A. Schlesinger's 1979 March/April article in *Harvard Business Review*, which was titled "*Choosing strategies for change,*" among people there are four common psychological reasons for resisting change and they are:

1. Potential loss of something valuable such as authority, control, loss of job or status, freedom in procedures, etc.
2. Misunderstanding of prospective change and lack of trust in those initiating or implementing change. The common phrase is that top echelons are trying to get more (usually in terms of profits) out of people without giving anything in return to their associates.

3. A belief that new change is not necessary and not needed which may be based on incomplete or wrong paradigms.
4. A belief that one may not be able to adapt to a new change and may lose face among peers.

While there might be many other reasons why people resist change, there are also many strategies for effectively handling resistance to change. It is the responsibility of change agents to find out what the reasons for resistance are and work on reducing it. The following are some of the suggestions that can be applied by change agents to understand and effectively handle stress, conflict, and resistance to change.

Listen. Become an active or an empathic listener by seeing people's emotions, hearing them from the heart, and acknowledging their resistance. Try to sincerely understand their point of view and once you fully understand them, they feel understood, and they have overcome their anger, then try to explain the reasons for change and their role in making this change successful. It is important that you listen to them at their pace and not rush them because most people become strongly attached to how they have been doing things and change is usually seen as the enemy. So, be patient, listen with empathy, and then help them understand the need for change and provide emotional support.

Involve people in the process. The greatest human need is probably involvement and recognition of one's contribution to worthwhile causes and services. Everybody wants to be involved and contribute to a greater cause or service; therefore involving people in the change process and asking for their cooperation from the outset would be the best way to expect successful implementation of change. Involvement and contribution creates "buy-in" which helps people become much more accepting of the change. Involving people from the outset helps them understand the need for change and consequently agree with the change. Involvement also increases trust and commitment on everyone's part thereby making them formal or informal change catalysts or agents. Some people fear that involving people in the process will create chaos and they might lose control; however, they do not realize that not involving them will create more hassles and chaos because people may remain resistant for a long time and may resort to shirking.

Educate and train people beforehand. Education is important because it provides knowledge about the change, and of-course a little knowledge is appreciated be everyone. Training is the key in transforming knowledge into production. People say that "knowledge is power," which is not really the case because it is the application of knowledge that creates result which may or may not create power, depending on other variables such as the need for the result, the availability of the results from other sources, and so on. So, when people are trained and educated about the change then they may be fully prepared to deal with change, and thus, change will not be a threat to them as much as before.

Reward and recognize. People are motivated internally by different needs and those needs may become fulfilled by different rewards, incentives or recognition programs. It is important that appropriate monetary and non-monetary rewards are linked with implementing the change successfully. In order for people to change their way of doing things, the change should be supported or aligned with appropriate recognition and reward programs. Keep in mind that according to the principles of behavior modification, behavior that is rewarded will get repeated and behavior that is ignored may disappear.

Celebrate the change publicly. When the change is made public and celebrated with happiness and joy then people may become more accepting of it because they realize that it is not another fad or a thing that will go away when another fad becomes popular. People are better able to see that the change has been committed into the culture and that they are not alone because it is affecting others who will be going through the same difficulty of adjusting to the new change. Henri Nouwen said:

> What we see, and like to see, is cure and change. But what we do see and do not want to see is care, the participation in the pain, solidarity in suffering, the sharing in the experience of brokenness. And still, cure without care is as dehumanizing as a gift given with a cold heart (as cited by in *The Magic of Conflict* by Crum, 1987).

Mentoring Others through Change and Stress

Senior leaders and managers can help those impacted by major change by becoming mentors to them. Mentoring is an art that can be used by top leaders, managers, employees, union members, government officials, customers, and suppliers to influence others toward positive change or direction. Mentoring is a continuous process of sharing relevant information with selected people that can maximize the success of an institution, while guiding and supporting each person toward individual and collective achievement opportunities. Similar to coaching, mentoring is a developmental, caring, sharing, and helping relationship where the mentor helps the mentee. Being an effective mentor or mentee can be learned and its skills can be developed.

Mentoring relationships lead to effective learning organizations and they also relieve stress within the organization. It has been observed that the best mentors are also the best mentees (protégés). Once an individual has had a successful relationship as a protégé, he or she is much more likely to be a successful mentor. Mentors and protégés, however, bring different expectations into the relationship. For women, a protégé's ability and potential are the most critical element in a mentor accepting a protégé, while for men a potential protégé's ability is not as important.

A mentor can be a person who offers knowledge, insight, perspective or wisdom that is helpful to another person in a relationship that goes beyond duty or obligation. A mentor creates opportunities for exposure, provides challenging and educational assignments, and serves as a role model and adviser to the mentee. Such relationships often evolve informally, but managers can encourage and formalize them. Effective mentoring requires listening, caring and other forms of involvement between mentors and mentees. According to experts, mentoring is often used to achieve the interests of special groups and populations, conserve and transfer special know-how, encourage mentee contributions, bring employees together in a new social environment, help people reach their full potential, enhance the competitive position of a person or department and develop better relationships around the globe.

Mentoring is a collaborative effort on the part of the mentor and the mentee. Effective mentoring is a relationship built on trust where the mentee confides personal information and characteristics to the mentor and the mentor guides the mentee toward growth and learning opportunities. A good mentoring program is usually focused on specific learning objectives where both the mentor and mentee receive training.

There are many deliverables originating from a mentoring program, including easier recruitment of the best talent; more rapid induction of new recruits; improved staff retention; improved opportunities, performance and diversity management; increased effectiveness of formal training; reinforcement of cultural change; improved networking and communication; and reinforcement of other learning initiatives. Successful organizations recognize the value of mentoring programs as an effective way to address diversity, manage organizational knowledge, retain stellar performers, and prepare for succession. There are many organizations that have found benefits in mentoring individuals from underrepresented groups, specifically women, Asians, Hispanics, Native Americans, and African Americans in the fields of business and education. According to experts, there are many roles that professional mentors play, including teacher or tutor, coach, friend, counselor, information source, nurturer, adviser, networker, advocate, and role model. Regardless of the mentoring location, highly effective mentors and leaders share some of the same characteristics. They:

- Are experienced and respected in the field.
- Have current knowledge
- Are trustworthy, confident and show high self-efficacy
- Use transformational leadership skills
- Willingly share their knowledge and guide others
- Remain approachable
- Have great passion for their work
- Know what to communicate, how to communicate, when to communicate, and how to help improve the mentee
- Connect well and challenge mentees to reach their full potential
- Get extraordinary results using a variety of skills to get their points across and to bring about the needed behavioral changes in their mentees

The goal of a mentoring program should be to help leaders, managers, coaches, and employees in a firm become highly skilled, self-aware, inclusive, energetic and creative, and to carry a zest for mentoring into the organization every day. Mentoring is not an easy task, but such is the obligation bestowed on the lucky ones. Highly effective mentors and leaders understand that developing others requires self-reflection, sensitivity, risk-taking, interdependency, and teamwork among all parties (mentors, mentees, managers, peers, and senior officers). They also understand that such a synergy requires forging a partnership, inspiring commitment, growing both the mentor and mentee's skills, promoting persistency, and shaping the environment so all parties can achieve their goals. At the minimum, both mentors and mentees should master the essential skills of change management, which are planning, communicating and following up, if they are to be effective change agents.

Summary

Stress, conflict and change have been a part of everyone's life since birth, and they are likely to be with everyone until death. One becomes what he or she is because of changes experienced thus far. These changes are not always likable or enjoyable as they can also be tragic; yet they shape one's life and actions thereby making them who they are at this moment of their life. Change is all around, and it impacts people in many ways. One way in which change impacts people is through high amounts of stress. Therefore, each person must come up with a coping mechanism to effectively deal with stress. Each person can remember the three-step process (otherwise known as the Triple-A Model) of awareness, action, and attitude to effectively cope with stress.

1. *Awareness.* Become aware of the stressors in your life. Determine why they are stressing you and how they can be best managed or balanced.
2. *Action.* Take appropriate actions to eliminate, reduce, or balance things (stressors) that are stressing you too much.
3. *Attitude.* Think positively and focus on the positive aspects of your achievements thus far. Consciously feed your mind positive input by taking about 30 minutes each day to think, exercise, and mentally refresh yourself with joyful thoughts or readings.

The Triple-A Model, or the "awareness, action, and attitude coping mechanism," can serve as a self-chosen process to deal with the stress of life and change. This chapter offered awareness of change, stress, and conflict as well as suggestions for dealing with them. Overall, the coming chapters expand on these thoughts and offer various approaches and strategies for individuals to productively deal with stress and conflict in their places of work, while successfully initiating, executing, managing, and leading change without much undue stress on people.

CHAPTER TWO

2 - CHANGE MANAGEMENT

There is no panacea or structured magical solutions to managing human behavior during change implementation which can cause complex human responses. The solution depends on the situation and the progressive and dynamic readiness levels of each individual going through the change. As such, understanding and effectively managing human behavior requires assessment, management, and leadership skills. Human behaviors toward change can be best influenced by gathering the right information, understanding the situation through a careful assessment, having a holistic perspective, and truthfully communicating with everyone who is impacted by the change. According to experts, after a careful analysis and assessment of the culture, managers and change agents can proactively develop an action plan to modify behaviors, or at least reduce the ones that can hinder the progress of change initiatives and the empowerment of employees.

According to Ian Mitroff (2005), for managers and employees who are responsible for seeing their businesses through crises, the question is not whether they will experience unexpected events, but rather when and how much of change will it be from the norm. Managing this change and effectively navigating through such unexpected events on a continuous basis will depend on the responses of today's leaders. Mitroff draws on years of experience in the field of crisis management to challenge change agents so they can meet unexpected crisis and challenging events head on. Mitroff suggests seven distinct competencies that change agents and twenty-first century's learning organizations must demonstrate to be successful in this changing environment. The seven competencies or intelligences are:

1. Accepting that crisis can occur,
2. Using creative thinking to consider types of crisis,
3. Understanding that businesses are affected by challenges that are universal in nature,
4. Seeing crisis and solutions as complex, but understanding that preparation can simplify the path to survival,
5. Using controlled paranoia to discover where a business is vulnerable,
6. Making crisis management central to all business activity, and
7. Understanding the connection between one's work and spirit.

According to Daryl Conner, the basic human reaction to change seems to be similar in everyone...managers and change agents "who successfully implement change, regardless of their location, display many of the same basic emotions, behaviors, and approaches" (Conner, 1992, p. 6). These change agents and managers demonstrate resiliency in their leadership style and change management; *resiliency* refers to their capacity to absorb high levels of change while displaying minimal dysfunctional behavior. Conner states that light travels through space at a constant speed of 186,281 miles each second as the laws of universe dictate this pace with no deviation. However, workers travel in their life and at work often without a fixed speed or velocity. People move at variable pace which fluctuates according to their capacity for assimilating new information and influences. How well human beings absorb new information and make good use of it determines how well they manage and re-direct change to their benefits or pre-determined goals. Life is more comfortable, effective, and efficient when it is moving at a speed that allows one to appropriately assimilate the change one faces. The appropriate speed is one at which one is able to effectively absorb change with a minimum of dysfunctional behavior. When one is no longer able to effectively deal with the actual and perceived change, one is likely to display dysfunctional behavior. Since the future is guaranteed to bring about more ambiguity, change and chaos than what is present today, learning to raise one's individual and team resiliency is an imperative for effective change management. As Conner states, people respond to change at different intellectual and emotional rates. As people adjust to organizational change, they often enter a pattern of observing that a change has occurred or is possible; developing their opinion toward the change; making a decision to support or resist the change; and taking action on that decision (Conner, 1992, p. 155).

What Is Change?

Change, in its simplest form, is the art of making things different. It is a modification to the way things are, or how things are done. In other words, change is a modification to the status quo. *Change* is the process of turning things from one state to another. *Change management,* then, is the art of effectively and efficiently making things different. Change is not something that only top executives or community leaders decide to bring about. Change is brought about often by outside forces that are beyond one's immediate control. It is driven by technological advancements, a better workforce, globalization, diversity, natural environmental forces, and other variables that one may not be able to fully control. Therefore, human beings are pressured into adapting with these changes and making the best of each change. There are at least three types of change which are "passive or natural," "mandated," and "self-generated" that affect individuals throughout their lives.

- *Passive or natural changes* are those changes that are not noticeable at the personal level but nonetheless do take place, i.e. growing, crawling, walking, etc.
- *Mandated changes* come from top down to the individual level in the form of laws, demands and/or policies.
- *Self-generated or proactive change* is usually initiated by an individual, a team or an organization. Its successful implementation needs

research, support, reliability, reasons, credibility, and/or strong leadership.

People learn or adapt to the passive or natural changes by osmosis and usually there are not many things one can do to prevent or stop these changes. For example, parents and care-takers usually attempt to help or encourage children to walk or crawl but these developments will take place regardless of outside forces or influences. This passive change can be very dangerous at the organizational level because often top executives are caught by surprise when they are not prepared for it. Mandated changes are usually decided upon by the top people of the society or an organization to prevent chaotic situations from taking place. For example, having traffic rules saves many lives while not having such general rules can be very costly. These are usually based on the Golden Rule principle which states that one should do unto others as he or she would have them do unto him or her. Finally, the self-generated changes are the best types and usually the most difficult to deal with in the initial states. It is the self-generated changes that create the planned results in the long-term. Self-generated changes are proactive and value-driven. Therefore, they can be goal-oriented and focused toward self-chosen ends and targets. This deals with Newton's principle of physics which states that a body in motion moving to a certain path tends to stay in motion in that path until acted upon by outside forces. So, if you generate purposeful changes toward certain goals then you are likely to get those results unless you are confronted by resistance which cannot be overcome.

One of the most stressful situations throughout the world, especially in the Untied States, is balancing work and family lives because while people may value being connected to their families they often may be away from them in order to work and produce the basic necessities of life in order to have a family. This is why many professionals plan to work and go to school at the same time to get a more advanced education. According to Pamela Babcock (September 2005), author of the article entitled "*A Calling for Change*," more and more company leaders are trying to make human resources a truly global function so the department's professionals can always be a strategic partner. Babcock advises HR professionals in charge of managing change to keep in mind that just because the senior manager is ready for a change does not mean all workers are ready to accept a transformation. Therefore, one must not assume that everyone wants change and welcomes it. As such, change agents must try to get others to "buy-in" to the new change before beginning the implementation process. It is also critical to remember that change can be time consuming, stressful, painful, and disruptive for anyone. Effective change management through the human resources personnel and change agents requires the right skill sets and an approach that balances speed with inclusiveness and collaboration since engaging everyone impacted by the change in the system is critical if the change is to be sustained. The attributes required to bring about effective change include integrity, a proven track record, leadership skills, the ability to capture the respect of other business leaders, and a vision for what the future can be. Other important traits that change agents need to possess are financial acumen and great presentation skills in one-on-one format and to large audiences (Babcock, 2005). Overall, change agents need to initially learn the organization's culture and assess its problems by getting the company's pulse and developing a good relationship with leaders and their staff.

Change is present all around twenty-first century workers; its momentum, volume, and complexity are increasing at speeds to which many workers show difficulty adjusting. Geller (1994) states that the driving forces for change can include, but are not limited to, a diverse workforce, technological advancements, faster communication, increased global competition, social and political pressures, and limited resources. So, what can be done to deal with so much change? Geller recommends that managers and leaders manage change and its corresponding resistance through proactive planning and anticipation of its consequences. Furthermore, twenty-first century employees need to learn to accept disruptions, while taking advantage of new opportunities that accompany it. Of course, the first step should be to understand the change, and assess both organizational and individual readiness for its acceptance.

Roles in the Change Process

Change can be positive or negative. It may affect one for the good or perhaps somewhat negatively, but that is not a good reason to view change as negative because one cannot be sure of the situation or its future results. Also, one should keep in mind what actually happens does not necessarily make or break a person but it is one's response to the situation that can make or break a person. So, there are changes that will affect one positively, and then there are changes that can affect one negatively. For example, getting married, promotions, moving to one's dream home, and finishing high school are considered to be positive changes. While deaths, accidents, demotions, getting laid-off from a good position, and other unexpected or traumatic changes are considered to be negative changes that require patience and a future-oriented focus in order to overcome their negative "side effects." Both positive as well as negative change can be very stressful and may cause an individual to respond negatively to it. Change, especially if it is unexpected, can be scary, difficult to deal with or accept, cumbersome, and at times very frustrating. Human beings are all expected to die sooner or later, but most people are not properly prepared to deal with such circumstances appropriately. Accidents, illness, violence, and mature age take the lives of many people every day. This can be difficult emotionally and financially, especially if relatives and family members are not prepared at all. According to the National Funeral Directors Association and based on personal experiences, the average cost of a funeral in the United States is running at about $6,000 to $15,000 these days. There are many companies that are using "reduction in force" strategies to become more competitive or because of survival which causes much frustration to many people both emotionally and financially. However, human beings have dealt with change from the beginning of time, and the only difference is that now it comes much faster than it has ever come. Therefore, people need to learn to adapt to change as quickly as possible in order to minimize or eliminate the negative impact of change. Generally, there are two responses to change from a company or individual perspective: reactive and proactive.

Reactive. Reactive responses are unplanned and their purpose is to catch-up with the industry or competition before the firm, or industry along with the people, are out of the "picture." Reactive responses are negative because they are often based on emotions, feelings, and circumstances without much consideration for or reflection on one's mission or purpose in life. Reactive companies and people are usually on the defensive and this can lead people to live lives that are based on urgency. In this situation, people are driven into many directions which creates a very stressful life because they cannot find time to plan.

Proactive. Proactive people and firms are opportunity-minded and they plan for the future as much as possible, and they plan for and expect change. Proactive people are visionaries and see things from a larger perspective. They see things from a bird's eye view as well as a worm's eye view. Proactive responses are anticipated, planned and aligned with the company or one's personal purpose and mission in life. Proactive people do not resist or meet change through a head-on collision. When proactive people encounter change, they move from having a point of view to a viewing point in order to see all the possibilities and perspectives of change. They use change to their advantage and thrive on it similar to martial artists who go along with change in the same direction and simultaneously gain more power and fluidity as they strike the target. Proactivity allows a person to turn a life of work into a work of art. Proactive people do what they love and consequently love what they do. Therefore, they never have to "go to work" because they choose to do things they love and things they want to accomplish for personal joy.

Some people enjoy change while others loathe it. Generally, responses to a major change can include the stages or feelings of immobilization, denial, anger, bargaining, depression, and testing before eventually accepting the change (Conner, 1993; Geller, 1994). Geller states that, on a psychological or attitudinal level, one may have strong emotional reactions to changes; the reaction can be so strong that one may become numb and unable to respond appropriately. Change agents, managers, and leaders must be aware of such diverse reactions and respond according to the needs of each person and situation in order to help him or her transition effectively. The following are the common definitions of roles involved in the change process: sponsors, agents, targets, and others.

Sponsors: These are individuals who want the change and legitimize it. Sponsors initiate the need for change, the change itself, and may or may not be involved in implementing the change. Sponsors can choose to be the change agents or they can delegate the implementation process to others. Sponsors can also be the targets as well.

Agents: These are individuals who are the driving force and are leading and guiding the process of change in the society or in the organization. Success as a change agent depends in large part on the capabilities and strengths of the human resources team and the department's leaders as well as their credibility with employees in the organization (Babcock, 2005).

Targets. Target includes the group, population, department, or individual that should, need to, or must actually change. Change agents may include systems, processes, and/or people or individual(s) in departments and organizations. The best way for the target to adapt to change would be to become change agents themselves.

Others. These are people who are indirectly affected by the change. These people may be advocates, adversaries, or neutral to the change. Sometimes, the people of the community could be the driving force or the restraining force for change. Their support or discontent could mean taking two distinct routes. For example, lobbyists are not change agents but they could be supporters of the change and that would make a big difference in the decision of the company or government. There could be many internal and external advocates or adversaries of change such as employees, stockholders, and customers.

Initiating and leading major organizational changes is not an easy task. However, making or bringing about major changes requires experience, skill, and integrity. One human resource professional states: "Quite frankly, as a profession we haven't done a good job of giving people enough opportunities to lead and sustain organizational change efforts." Change agents must remember not to underestimate the power of the culture they are about to change. Change agents and managers also must be clear, concise, and consistent in their roles as communicators of the new change and process. In their roles as change agents, workers and managers must "have a very strong ownership culture where all employees are involved and engaged" (Babcock, 2005).

Change Management Process and Steps

Change will have either a positive or a negative effect on the individual depending on how the individual responds or adapts to change. Change can affect a person's motivation, morale, desire, skills, attitude, level of control, commitment, as well as his or her level of performance. Changes in some of these areas will take more time than others and, similarly, some will be a little more difficult to change than others. Every individual goes through an intrinsic emotional change cycle when he or she is changing his or her usual method of doing things. This cycle can be described in terms of five gradual stages (DREAM).

1. **D**enial and anger.
2. **R**easons and justification.
3. **E**xploration of alternatives and benefits.
4. **A**cceptance of the change.
5. **M**otivation to be a catalyst in the change process.

Figure 2.1 – The Emotional Cycle of Change (DREAM)

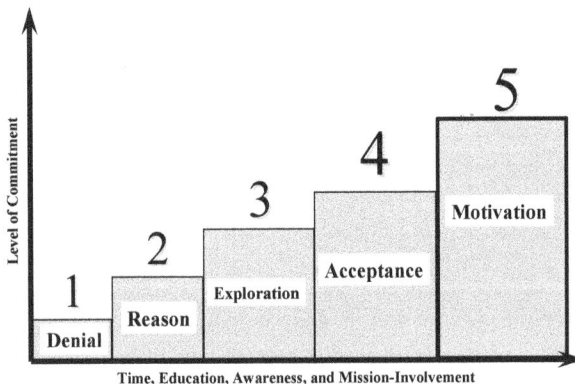

Level of Commitment

1 Denial
2 Reason
3 Exploration
4 Acceptance
5 Motivation

Time, Education, Awareness, and Mission-Involvement

20

People can choose to respond positively, negatively or be totally indifferent to change. However, most individuals will go through an emotional cycle which has positive and negative consequences. Flexible and successful people will attempt to shorten or minimize the gap between the first and the last stages in the process. Normally, an individual can go through five stages of emotional change and experience denial and anger, reasoning, exploration, acceptance, and finally motivation to make the change happen. Each individual may go through these stages at his or her own pace. Some people go through them faster than others and some people never seem to make it to higher stages. Let us discuss some of the characteristics of people in each stage.

Denial and Anger – People are usually shocked that the change is actually taking place. They cannot believe it is happening to them. They may be angry at the world or themselves for being put in such a position. Individuals at this stage may have a tendency to talk with others, complain, and seek affirmation of their thoughts and feelings about the new process or change. They may be resentful of the company and those who are implementing the change. They may even plan to work against the new change and sabotage the new plan or process that is affecting them.

Reason – At this stage, people usually attempt to justify their own reasons in order to reject the change in a logical fashion. They try to come up with all types of reasons which to them would logically support why the change will not work. This can have an aggregate effect on the individual because the more one sees the negative aspect of a situation, the more reasons he or she will be able to gather in order not to go along with the change. People may choose to blame the change on others and reason that the initiators of the change, sponsors and change agents do not really know everything about the change or the job. They only attempt to see why the change is wrong for them and for their jobs, tasks or departments. This would be a cause for staying longer in the first two stages of DREAM.

Exploration – At this stage, people realize that the options of denial, reasons, and negativity have not produced positive results; therefore they are not happy with them. By this time, people are usually more knowledgeable about the change and can see their role in the new process as important. They also may realize that change is inevitable if they want to feel better, work more productively, get along with the team, and support the upper echelon. Now, people are able to see different options and opportunities in the new process or change. At this stage the possibilities and benefits of change become much clearer to the individual and he or she may attempt to discover many ways of dealing with the change positively.

Acceptance. At this stage, the individual has already dealt with his or her emotions, anger, reasons, and frustration. The individual has concluded that he or she can accept and effectively deal with the new change and perhaps support it. At this point the individual is at peace and will want to be part of the team and support the team to simply implement the change.

Motivation. This is where the person totally understands the change, is aware of the consequences of the change, agrees with the change, wants the change, and is totally committed to make the change happen because his or her involvement is an integral part of the process. The individual sees himself or herself as having the sole responsibility for making things happen and he or she is proud to be a part of it. As can be seen in Figure 2.2, people at this stage have a higher level of good stress, also known as *eustress*.

Highly proactive and effective individuals are able to reach stage five of the change cycle in the shortest period of time and with minimum stress or loss of productivity. Change always causes some uncertainty to individuals and firms; however successful firms are able to bounce back to the top quicker than others because they are flexible, ready, and expect opportunities from change. Those individuals who are flexible, resilient, open-minded, and those who welcome change will be better able to complete the first stages of the "DREAM" cycle than those who fear or resist change. Individuals can experience "DREAM" because of a change in any part of the system. One level of change can affect other levels because in many cases they are interdependent. Change can take place at environmental, organizational, or interpersonal levels, and still affect the individual(s). The key is to effectively handle change at the individual level; thereby minimizing "distress" and increasing "eustress." At the organizational level, managers must also be aware of both intentional and unintentional distress as "Intentional infliction of emotional distress cases in the private employment context are frequently intertwined with claims for discrimination and harassment" (Cavico, 2003, p.153). Similarly, Professor Cavico continues to state that "Emotional distress can readily result from purposeful discrimination or harassment, which can be in the form of physical conduct or merely words" (p. 153). Managers not only must be aware of their own behaviors but they should also know how their employees treat each other in the department. As needed, inappropriate, disrespectful and discriminatory practices must be changed before too much emotional distress is caused on employees who may sue the company to bring about effective changes.

Figure 2.2 – The Emotional Cycle of Change and Stress

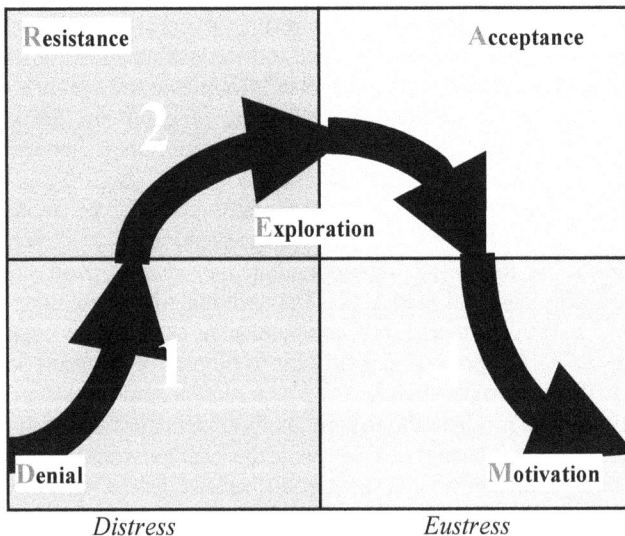

22

Change is equivocally ubiquitous and constant throughout our lives. At times, these changes will create stress which needs to be managed quickly, continuously, and at a personal level. That means that workers have to take personal responsibility for their own well-being and routinely attempt to manage and overcome stress in a positive manner. There are at least three steps that individuals should take to reduce stress in their lives. *First*, set specific times during the day and/or week to relax and enjoy doing things that bring joy into your life. This requires knowing or learning about your favorite reading topics, games, exercises, and perhaps meditation techniques. You need to continuously practice relaxation techniques both in and out of work environment. *Second*, find out what causes stress in one's life, why it causes stress, and work on reducing and/or eliminating the root causes of these stress-creators immediately. Be aware of situations that cause stress and proactively work to eliminate its root causes. *Third*, be a source of positive light and energy while maintaining an open mind and a positive attitude toward change, life, and new opportunities. When life gives you lemons, make lemonade and enjoy drinking it along with other friends and family members as if it is a sunny summer day.

Change with Others. When you are with others, try the following tension releasers: Active listening (good eye contact, listen to the words, clarify discussion), empathic listening (reflect the other persons feelings seeking first to understand), self-talk "remain calm," be open-minded and objective, remember that other factors could be contributing to the stressful situation, don't take it personally, keep emotions in control, find a conducive environment for discussion, eliminate any barriers to discussion (interruptions), respect the other person's feelings (even if you disagree), use appropriate body language and be relaxed, keep personal space between yourself and the other person, approach solutions to the conflict when possible, stop, think and select an appropriate response, count silently to yourself, take a deep breath, have a physical signal that reminds you to stay calm (such as index finger touching thumb or hands placed flatly together), know when to politely excuse yourself (situation getting out of hand—explosive), and refer the person to others when necessary or appropriate.

Change with Oneself. Take a break, remind yourself, "if it doesn't kill you, you'll be okay," take a stress walk, get some fresh air outside, give yourself time to calm down, step back to review the situation, consider your personal stress level conditions, go outside and scream, delegate duties when possible, do work that is physical—stocking, loading, stacking, gardening, cleaning and so on, eat foods that you like moderately, use positive self-talk, focus on what you can control, plan to do something fun (later that day or on weekend), talk with a friend, become quiet and meditate, pray, review your schedule, plan ways to gain control of your time, listen to calming music, and release energy by hitting a punching bag or by challenging yourself to doing one hundred pushups in one minute.

It is extremely important to manage change appropriately and consciously. Change management requires proactive planning and working the plan efficiently. People do not plan to fail; however, people do fail to plan. Planning can prepare individuals to deal with unexpected circumstances in a positive fashion. Human beings are very complex; however there are certain common patterns that are characteristics of all individuals. If one can predict these patterns of behavior then one can be prepared to eliminate its negative impacts through planning.

One must keep in mind that people often go through several stages before they can be productive with the new change. People often *hold on* to their old habits as long as they can before they *let go;* and, of course, they have to let go before they can *move on* to the new methods. According to the bulk of research, in a major change people may experience shock, denial, anger, bargaining, and/or depression- which are the first three stages of "DREAM"- before they can move to acceptance.

As an effective change agent, one can properly prepare and manage change proactively. As previously presented, there are five stages to the change management process and they are:
1. Identifying the need and strategy for the change,
2. Gaining consensus of the target,
3. Implementing the change,
4. Resolving and removing barriers to change, and
5. Following up and evaluating the implemented change.

1- Identifying the Need and Strategy for Change
The suggested change management model has five stages which will take managers and change agents from the beginning stage of a change to its conclusion and follow up process. During each stage, the sponsors and change agents may have different responsibilities unless the sponsors are also change agents. Originally, the sponsors should identify the need and strategy for the prospective change. This need should be determined according to the vision, mission, and purpose of the company or team. The sponsors should distinguish and state whether the change is mandated or self-generated because this may play a role in the strategy-making process. The sponsors should also clearly state why the change is needed as well as the results if the change is implemented successfully. They should further determine the timeline for accomplishing the change along with identifying the levels which will be affected by the prospective change. The individuals affected by the change should also be determined by the sponsors of the change. Overall, the sponsors should determine the following strategy for implementing the change:
1. Clearly state the need for change,
2. Determine the best strategy to implement the planned change,
3. Determine change agents,
4. Determine driving forces for change:
    *   Determine the available forces that would support the change,
    *   Every driving force can create an equally strong opposing force; therefore decreasing these opposing forces can be effective tools to drive the change forward,
5. Determine restraining forces for change. Determine possible forces that may prevent this change from being implemented successfully, and
6. Clarify and provide resources to support change.

2- Gaining Consensus for Change

The best way to make change happen successfully is to make sure everyone agrees with and supports the change before it is implemented. Change requires planning, preparation, education, skill, teamwork, and involvement from all stakeholders. Change agents can use the seven "RESPECT" steps to better prepare targets for agreeing and accepting the new change. Skills for gaining agreement to change are:

1. Recognize resistance and create a common vision,
2. Educate and train people beforehand,
3. Support people and provide them with resources to successfully deal with change,
4. Personalize rewards, training, and support for change,
5. Empower and involve people in the process,
6. Communicate the change along with its consequences clearly and listen empathically, and
7. Treasure and value people as well as teamwork.

The following thoughts are included in the "RESPECT" model, and need to be done in order to expect the target group to agree and support the change:

Recognize Resistance and Create a Common Vision – Resistance can provide new information that was not seen in the beginning. Resistance can also make the organization a little safer because people are not accepting the status quo but are taking a leadership role by asking why something needs to be done. Resistance can mobilize people to take action and responsibility for their jobs. It is important that everyone on the team is pushing or pulling in the same direction and not in opposite directions. The best way to create a buy-in for the mission is to involve them in the process of building it up from the ground floor. This mission should be clear, concise, and understood by everyone on the team. Make sure the mission statement is capable of energizing people to work in its direction regardless of failures. Because when you are going in the right direction, you will eventually get there through hard work and dedication regardless of failures. A journey of a thousand miles begins with the first step and eventually it can be completed as long as one is going in that direction. The principles of physics support this notion because a body in motion tends to stay in motion in the same direction unless acted upon by outside forces.

Educate and Train People Beforehand – Education is important because it provides knowledge about the change and of-course a little knowledge is appreciated by everyone. Training is the key to transforming knowledge into production. People say that "knowledge is power" which may not be totally true because knowledge that is not put into use is no better than not having it. A person who is able to read but does not read is no better than one who cannot read. So, it is the application of knowledge that creates results which may or may not create power depending on other variables such as the need for the result, the availability of the results from other sources, and so on. So, when people are trained and educated about the change then they may be fully prepared to deal with change, and change will not be a threat to them as much as before. Education helps people grow and growing is a biological imperative unless one wants to die. Most fruits are either green and growing or ripe and dying. People are the same as well: they are either green and growing or ripe and

25

rotting. The only way to prolong the growing part is through continuous learning. Education is the only way to keep growing continuously. Educating the team also helps everyone see their part in the overall scheme of things. For example, when a worker at the Houston space center during the mid-1960s was asked what do you do here? He responded by saying "I am helping put a man on the moon." This worker was a janitor and did his work with pride and commitment because he was part of a team that wanted to accomplish something worthwhile to everyone in the society. This person was aware of the long-term mission and had "bought" into it.

Support People and Provide Resources for all Associates – Any change involves some cost and it should be taken into consideration before implementing the change. If the "cost" is spent appropriately, it can eliminate crisis, chaos, and inefficiency throughout the implementation process. It is suggested that companies provide awareness programs about the new change, stress management workshops, time for people to work through their grief and frustration, as well as an on-going resource to support them climb the ladder of change.

Personalize Rewards, Training, and Support – People are motivated internally by different needs, and those needs may become fulfilled by different rewards, incentives, or recognition programs. It is important that people are rewarded at the right time, for the right reasons, and for the right values. One cannot water flower A, which is on the next block to flower B, and expect flower B to grow. Watering the right flower at the right times and using the right amount is very important and extremely crucial to its survival. It is important that appropriate monetary and non-monetary rewards are associated with implementing the change successfully. In order for people to change their way of doing things the change should be supported or aligned with recognition and reward programs that are of some value to the people.

Empower and Involve People in the Process – When you empower people to the fullest extent, they will give you maximum performance. One of the greatest human needs is involvement and recognition of one's contribution to worthwhile causes and services. Everybody wants to be involved and contribute to a greater cause or service; therefore involving people in the change process and asking for their cooperation from the outset would be the best way to expect successful implementation of change. Involvement and contribution creates "buy-in," which helps people become much more accepting of the change. Involving people from the outset helps them understand the need for change and consequently agree with the change. Once people see the obvious benefits of change, agree with the change and accept it, then they will not be tempted to go back to their old methods. For example, how many teenagers or adults do we see that would crawl instead of walk in order to get from one place to the next. Involvement also increases trust and commitment on everyone's part thereby making them formal or informal change catalysts or agents. Some people fear that involving people in the process will create chaos and they might lose control; however, they do not realize that not involving them will create more hassles and chaos because people may remain resistant for a long time and may resort to shirking.

Communicate the Change Along with its Consequences Clearly and Listen – Tell everyone about the prospective change as much in advance as possible. Have an open door policy so concerned associates can voice their opinion to appropriate authorities without fear of losing their jobs. Make sure everybody's input is sincerely appreciated and their feelings are acknowledged. Become an empathic listener by seeing people's emotions, hearing them from the heart, and acknowledging their resistance. Try to sincerely understand their point of view and once you fully understand them, they feel understood, and they have overcome their anger, then try to explain the reasons for change and their role in making this change successful. Another key element of listening is finding out the right time to communicate back to associates what they need to know. Feedback should be specific, meaningful, accurate, relevant, and timely (SMART) in order for it to be effective. Feedback to associates has been proven to be one of the most important factors in job satisfaction among employees. It has been said that feedback is the breakfast of champions and an effective strategy for change agents.

Treasure and Value People as well as Teamwork - Human beings are the most important asset for any organization or society. Henry Ford once said, "You can destroy my cars, you can destroy my buildings and my factories, but give me people and I will build them right back." Walt Disney and Oliver Wendell Holmes have been cited as saying that the greatest waste in the organization is not the waste of natural resources, although that could be a great waste, but the greatest waste is the waste of human resources. Change agents need to respect the opinions of others and value their contributions to the organization. This is the power of diversity and should be taken advantage of to create competitive advantage. The true power of teams lies within each individual and not in the team leader, although he or she may have a very important role in the process.

The success of any change is dependent on the targets' acceptance and implementation of the proposed change. So in order to gain their acceptance and agreement then they must be involved in the process as much as possible. They must also be educated and trained on the new process as well as the skills needed to be productive. Uncertainty about the future should be minimized as much as possible so people can feel safer and more in control as they are looking ahead. One should also keep in mind that the consequences of not changing successfully could mean loss of learning and/or advancement opportunities, loss of reputation and social image, bankruptcy or loss of competitive advantage, and the risk of survival or progress in the long-term. Change at each level may affect other levels because they are highly interdependent.

3- Implementing the Change

For the success of implementing change, it is absolutely necessary that people are well educated about the change before the implementation stage begins. This is especially important in cases where people's routine habits are affected. The implementation can change and vary according to the situation and feedback from the recipients or as more information becomes available from various sources. There are three tasks involved in the implementation process, and they are initiating the change, supporting the change, and coaching the target to deal positively with the change.

Initiating the change. Before the change is implemented, make sure that everyone is well aware of the change, their respective roles, their responsibilities, their rewards in making the change successful, and the importance of this change for them. Then roll out the change to targets and make a public statement about the change. Make sure people understand that this change is not a fad but a real solution or opportunity to the situation. It is important to be aware that some individuals will be playing multiple roles in this change process. Many well respected and influential individuals may be change agents and targets simultaneously and may need time and project management skills to juggle all their responsibilities. So, some just-in-time training may be necessary to help people manage different roles and projects successfully. People may need to use project management skills and planners to organize their activities in order of importance to use their time efficiently. This will help them to keep track of important dates, activities, responsibilities, things to delegate, and all other activities involved in the change process.

Supporting the change. Supporting the change means total commitment without any hesitation whatsoever. It means being an adamant advocate of the change consciously and subconsciously. It requires continuously talking about the change, celebrating the change, and reaffirming the change in a public way. In order to encourage the new behavior (change), change agents and managers may reward those who are successful at implementing the change or even those who are attempting to implement the change. So, the change needs to be supported economically, publicly, privately, and in terms of human talent and muscle.

Coaching the target(s). The change sponsors and change agents can serve as mentors, coaches, guides, and resources for the target group. Sometimes long-term change requires time, patience, and experimentation (heuristics) for trial and error purpose at the individual level. Therefore, having a resource and guide would be helpful. Coaching would require welcoming, appreciating, and integrating targets' feedback to the new process. Coaching also requires giving people emotional support and guidance so they can positively deal with change and overcome the change cycle quickly. Coaching the target means meeting people where they are and gradually taking them to the desired place at their pace, and not yours, otherwise the situation may become too stressful.

4- Recognizing and Resolving Barriers to Change

Implementing change can be very difficult because most often it involves people and new ways of doing things which can be somewhat cumbersome. However, it can be helpful to anticipate some of these obstacles beforehand and prepare everyone accordingly. One should keep in mind that change often takes longer than anticipated because it is virtually impossible to predict all the elements which may get in the way. Adults, in general, learn very slowly and have a tendency to forget easily, therefore more time and repetition may be required to reinforce desired habits and procedures. The key is to be consistent and stay with the plan. Vince Lombardi, a longtime coach of the Green Bay Packers, once said, "Mental toughness wins more games than great skill and fancy game plans." It is also important not to exaggerate too much result too quickly because if the success or results are not delivered on time, then people get disappointed. It may be best to under-promise or promise the least and deliver the most as quickly as possible. Some people also procrastinate starting new and cumbersome tasks, behaviors, or acts. Therefore, it might be wise to follow up with people regularly or break large tasks into small chunks that can be managed on an hourly or daily basis. James A. Belasco (1990) wrote if you want to get things moving in the organization, the first task for a leader is to create a fire that employees can see and smell, a fire that empowers people to create the desired change. It is important to keep this fire under control and not let it get out of hand. To achieve success in change implementation, Belasco (1990) suggested three things:

1- *Build a sense of urgency*. Make sure you are prepared to deal with change because change is constant, and so should be your response to it.

2- *Create a clear tomorrow*. The best way to get people's agreement and support is to show them a better tomorrow. Make sure they are clear about the "promised land" because it can be a pulling or driving force for the change.

3- *Show the way*. Create a clear mission or purpose for the people and the company with everyone's involvement. A sense of a worthwhile and worthy purpose can be a great motivator for change. Be the model which you would like to see your people become.

Anything that prevents the progressive realization of the expected change can be seen as a barrier or resistance. Barriers can come from people, systems, structures, environment, rules, policies, machines, and other indirect or direct variables. Most barriers would fall in the category of resistance or systems that do not support or are not aligned with the expected change. One way to make sure that change happens successfully is to make sure the rules, structures, compensation programs, and policies are totally aligned with the change. The other method would be to reduce or eliminate resistance. Resistance to change can be a source of opportunity because it can let the change agents know some of the things that may not work very well. People are different and each person has his or her own personality or individuality; therefore individuals may respond differently to change based on their paradigms. While some individuals are able to adapt to change easily, others may resist the change. *Resistance* serves as a guard and is the mobilization of energy during a perceived or real threat. Common reasons for resistance include the feeling of being controlled, loss of skill or span of control, lack of adequate information, not being able to meet the new requirement, stress of uncertainty, having difficulty learning, personal goals do not match organizational goals, informal processes may be rewarding production and not the new change or process, misalignment of goals between departments, too many things to do in a given period of time, etc. This resistance may come in many different forms, and some of the common forms of resisting change are passive, overt and covert.

1. *Passive resistance*: This is where people choose to remain quiet, not share their ideas with the group, and not follow the predetermined plan. People may also voluntarily choose not to use their new skills or tools on the job.

2. *Overt resistance*: This is where people refuse to change their way of doing things because they do not see the need for change. They may avoid a very important workshop because they are very busy with current customers or workload. They verbally oppose the change and express their anger and disagreement openly. They may also sabotage the company, department, new process, and/or even the change agents in a variety of ways.

3. *Covert resistance*: In this situation, people may not go along with the agreed changes even though they agreed with it. People may withhold information and reduce productivity as well as participation. They may attempt to keep busy to avoid important activities and delay the process. They may also either directly or indirectly advise others not to follow the new procedures. They are sabotaging the new change without appearing as though they are against it.

The most effective way of successfully implementing change would be to reduce restraining forces while increasing driving forces, which can further help reduce resistance to change. In physics, it is learned that for every action there is an equal and opposite reaction. Therefore, for every driving force, there will be an equal and opposite restraining force that will be attempting to stop the change. So, reducing restraining forces can be very helpful in implementing change successfully. The following are some of the methods to reduce restraining forces:
1. Create dissatisfaction with maintaining the status quo.
2. Eliminate the fear of losing control, status, or power.
3. Eliminate the fear of losing existing benefits and rewards.
4. Eliminate incentives for maintaining group norms if the current norms do not support change.
5. Eliminate target complacency with current methods.
6. Make use of current skill and experience in the future so people can feel fulfilled.
7. Diminish uncertainty about the future as much as possible.
8. Acknowledge, understand, and handle resistance positively.

It should be mentioned that if the "RESPECT" process has been implemented properly, then most of the target group should go through the "DREAM" stages somewhat quickly. One should find out what is prohibiting the change from proceeding before doing anything, because rewarding the wrong thing may prove to be chaotic and increase confusion. It also can be helpful to increase driving forces in order to successfully implement change. The following are some of the things that can be done to increase driving forces:
1. Increase "RESPECT."
2. Training for the use of new process, method, and/or technology can be helpful.
3. Innovation and technology can be great change drivers.
4. Increase the commitment level of management and key leaders.
5. Encourage advocates to share their thoughts, reasons, and benefits about the change.

5- Following Up and Evaluating the Implemented Change
It is very important to follow-up on implemented changes to make sure they were carried out as planned and have produced the expected results. The follow-up process is also important for documentation of the final processes, activities, and future planning. An Afghan proverb states that "Those who forget the past are likely to

repeat it, those who only live in the present are likely to be hedonistic, those who do not plan for the future are not likely to have a prosperous one. However, those who remember the past, plan for the future, and live in the present are likely to be happy and enjoy a prosperous life." So, planning with proper follow-up is very important in change management. There are four stages in the implementation process and they are evaluation of the results, reviewing and documenting the change, standardizing the implemented change, and planning for the future.

1. *Evaluate the results of the implemented change.* Find out if the initial change has been implemented and become part of the daily routine as originally planned. Find out any alterations, causes for those alterations, and the results. Finally, find out if the results of the change are positive and satisfactory to all stakeholders.

2. *Review and document the implemented change process.* If the process has changed from the original outline, then document the new process and its results. Document the time, cost, resources, skills, people, and other important elements that contributed to the success of the process. Can the process be duplicated in the future or other areas in the organization? In some cases, unique situations may require a unique solution which cannot be implemented in other places because of the contextual elements and variables involved.

3. *Standardize the implemented change.* Make sure the new process is documented and communicated as the new method of doing things. This needs to be clear so everyone including new associates can understand and follow them without any difficulties. The new process should also be integrated into training programs.

4. *Plan and prepare for future change.* Change is the only constant and experience can certainly be helpful to plan for future changes. Experience means nothing unless it is documented for future references and usage. People change in organizations, so it is important to document things for future changes and decisions. Make sure people understand that change is constant, that they should be flexible and appreciative of change. Document and plan toward prospective changes that may affect the environment, organization, interpersonal relationships, and/or the individuals in the near future.

Summary

Change has become a way of life and it comes in a variety of shapes, sizes, and forms. Change can be passive or inactive, mandated, and self-generated or proactive. Each type of change may have different affects on people because the variables and elements may be different. However, we know that successful implementation of organizational change entails both learning how people go through the "DREAM" stages of the change cycle and learning how to use "RESPECT" in order to get people excited about change and move them into a brighter future, perhaps a little quicker and with less stress in the process. The resilient individuals or change agents will have a better chance of moving from the denial and reasoning stages to the acceptance and motivation stages much more quickly and more successfully. Today's environment demands that each individual becomes a change agent and take responsibility for his or her own future by mentally creating it, and then working toward accomplishing it on a daily basis. Once the vision of the future is clear, then people can align the changing world to fit their goals and objectives. There is something valuable in each learning experience even if it is just experience.

Change is a reality of life and all human beings go through it personally, professionally, physically, mentally, socially, and spiritually. Change management is about making sure that one is able to see the positive side of the issue and, as a change agent, make sure that every person impacted by the transition goes through the change process effectively without much undue negative stress or conflict. Change and winning are not mutually exclusive; therefore, both can happen simultaneously and everyone can and should become winners.

Survey of Organizational Climate for Change

The Survey of Organizational Climate for Change is based on the research by Symmetrix, a Massachusetts consulting firm (Robbins, 2001). Answer each question in a Likert scale format on the continuum from strongly agreeing (5), agreeing (4), neutral (3), disagreeing (2), to strongly disagreeing (1) with each statement. Circle a number from 1-5 on the ratings column and then total the choices by adding them.

Survey of Organizational Climate for Change

Questions	Ratings
1. The sponsor of change is senior, powerful or influential enough to effectively deal with foreseeable change.	1 2 3 4 5
2. The leadership of the operation is supportive of the change and committed to it.	1 2 3 4 5
3. There is a strong sense of urgency from senior management about the need for change and it is shared by the rest of the organization.	1 2 3 4 5
4. Management has a clear vision of how the future will look different from the present.	1 2 3 4 5
5. There are objective measures in place to evaluate the change effort and reward systems are explicitly designed to reinforce them.	1 2 3 4 5
6. The specific change is consistent with other changes going on with the organization.	1 2 3 4 5
7. Functional managers are willing to sacrifice their personal interest for the good of the organization as a whole.	1 2 3 4 5
8. Management prides itself on closely monitoring changes and actions taken by competitors.	1 2 3 4 5
9. The importance of the customer and knowledge of customer needs are well accepted by everyone in the workforce.	1 2 3 4 5
10. Managers and employees are rewarded for taking risks, being innovative, and looking for new solutions.	1 2 3 4 5
11. The organizational structure is flexible.	1 2 3 4 5
12. Communication channels are open both downward and upward.	1 2 3 4 5
13. The organization's hierarchy is relatively flat.	1 2 3 4 5
14. The organization has successfully implemented major changes in recent past years.	1 2 3 4 5
15. Employee satisfaction and trust in management are high.	1 2 3 4 5
16. There is a high degree of cross-boundary interactions and cooperation between various units in the organizations.	1 2 3 4 5
17. Decisions are made quickly, taking into account a wide variety of suggestions.	1 2 3 4 5
Total Score =	

The higher the total score on the *Survey of Organizational Climate for Change*, the greater is the likelihood that the change initiatives and efforts will succeed in this organization. Questions that receive low ratings from a large number of employees in the organization are areas of opportunities for improvement in the reduction of resistance to change.

CHAPTER THREE

3 - CONFLICT MANAGEMENT

I n today's global economy, cooperation among diverse individuals and cultures is imperative for a company's success because people of different nations are now interdependently tied together by information. Technology has made communication and travel easier and has increased the amount and speed of global interaction. Therefore, technology has made the world a smaller place. Similar to the convergence of technology, there are useful global strategies for effective communication, negotiation, and conflict resolution that are common to global managers. The purposes of this chapter are to explain the significance of effective communication in the conflict resolution process and to provide recommendations for global managers to effectively manage and resolve conflicts. This chapter will focus on interpersonal conflict and a wide range of conflicts that people experience in organizations. We will also explore how conflicts can impact and are displayed in every aspect of a person's life.

Conflict is often assumed to be a contest and it is not. Conflict is part of nature; neither positive nor negative, it just is, said Thomas Crum (1987). People can choose whether to make conflict a contest, a game which requires that some players become winners and some losers. Winning and losing are generally the goals of games but not the goal of conflict management. Effective conflict management requires "thinking win-win" with the goals of jointly learning, growing, and cooperating. Thomas Crum states that conflict can be seen as the interference pattern of energies as seen in nature: "Nature uses conflict as its primary motivator for change, creating beautiful beaches, canyons, mountains, and pearls" (1987, p. 49). It is not whether one has a conflict in his or her life because everyone experiences it; but rather it is what one does with the conflict that makes a positive or negative difference. Crum states that in order for human beings to move beyond success, they need to strive for turning or making their life of work into a work of art. People need to naturally move into a "you and me" mentality where they see the world as abundant and supportive in all aspects of their lives, from their health to their financial well-being. Crum defines "*alchemy*" as one's ability to change the ordinary into the extraordinary. The ability to change the ordinary to the extraordinary in the middle-ages involved changing common metals into gold; but the alchemy of today involves changing ourselves.

Crum states that "It is the pressure of conflict, the interference patterns of energies caused by differences, that provides the motivation and opportunity to change" (p. 25). Nature sees conflict in a positive light and uses it as a primary motivator for bringing about lasting changes. For human beings, the strength, the will and the needed skills are available so long as they are willing to let go of tension, fear, stereotypes, biases, and boundaries.

Conflict: A Fact of Life

Conflict is a given human variable. From the time we were born our world has consisted of interacting with people and having to deal with conflict. In spite of the "commonality" of this variable, human beings have difficulty in effectively coping with conflict and if a manager or parent, supervisor, leader or anyone hopes to influence behavior positively, he or she should be able to effectively manage conflict towards "win- win" solutions which is a goal that one should hope to achieve. To imply that conflict is bad or should be avoided, only adds to the problem of allowing it to develop, sometimes in serious productivity difficulties, alienations, decision-making, problem-solving, and negative stress. The good news is that conflict if handled correctly could "clear the air," enhance creativity and diminish distress. It can be used as a powerful instrument for change.

Conflict can be defined as a process where an individual or group does not perceive a particular situation in the same manner. That is, there are differing views on a situation that stops a process from being completed, due to the lack of accord. We may find ourselves in conflict over simple personal things, for example, whether the kitchen should be painted blue or black. We may also find ourselves failing to follow a new office procedure, vigorously resisting change; or some individuals, like a Union leader for example may have people "stop work" or "go slow" because of conflict between them and management. Conflict, therefore, permeates every aspect of human interaction in our intimate, workplace and leisure environments.

Conflict poses a serious problem in organizations, creating difficulties that impact on relationships and productivity. The manner by which it is understood and managed will make significant differences as to whether the organization will grow, remain stagnant or cease to exist. It has been alleged that the two most crucial aspects in the processes of organizations as to its survival, is the efficiency of its problem-solving, decision-making and conflict resolution.

Types of Conflict

Some people assume that all conflict is bad and use this word synonymously with such terms as violence, destruction and irrational to reinforce its negative connotation. Conflict by this view and definition is harmful and should be avoided. However, there is another view to conflict and it should be explored.

The human relation's view which dominated conflict theory from the 1940's to the 1970's, argued that conflict is a natural occurrence in all groups and organizations. This acceptance of conflict gave indicators that some conflict was beneficial to the organization. The interactionist view actually encouraged minimal levels of conflict which were believed to "keep the group viable, self critical and creative" (Robbins, 2005).

36

Conflict, therefore, is inevitable in organizations and it can be both a positive and a negative force that can be easily determined by the organization. Functional conflict or positive conflict is an interaction between groups that may be confrontational and improve the performance of the organization. It "clears the air" and allows for constructive debate, decision-making and problem solving. It stimulates change strategies and provides positive growth for the organization.

Dysfunctional conflict or negative conflict has destructive implications on the organization, interpersonal relationships and productivity. Discontent, unresolved incidents, poor communication, infighting, sabotage can all result in the eventual demise of an organization. It affects the very core of the organizations' products and the achievement of organizational goals. Research strategies and methodologies over the years have developed tools that individuals and organizations can use to create an environment of functional conflict. This approach explores conflict management techniques that have been successful on a personal level as well as an organizational level to create positive outcomes.

Figure 3.1 - The Conflict Management Process

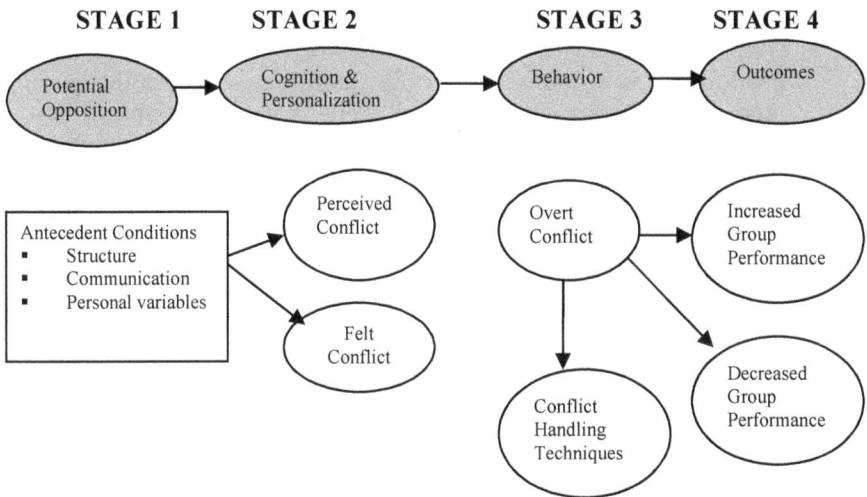

Conflict handling behaviors can include resolution, negotiation, and stimulation.

A. *RESOLUTION*:
- Problem-solving
- Super ordinate goals
- Expansion of resources
- Avoidance
- Smoothing
- Compromise

- Authoritative command
- Alter the human variable
- Alter the structural variable

B. *NEGOTIATIONS*:
- Pre-negotiation tasks
- Group situations
- Mediation
- Arbitration

C. *STIMULATION*:
- Communication
- Bringing outside individuals into group
- Altering the organizational structure
- Stimulating competition

General causes of conflict seem to fall in the categories of group interdependence, resource competition, difference in goals, and differences in perspective. As demonstrated in the Conflict Management Process model (Figure 3.1), there appears to be a four stage conflict processing:

1) Potential opposition emerges either between individuals or groups. With regard to organizational conflict on this stage, the conflict puts one group against the other and there is no compromise. The antagonists see only their side of the issue and are oblivious to the other sides' position.
2) Cognition takes place and personalization. Is when the conflict is personalized and people are attacked not due to the conflict per se but as individuals. Each side criticizes individuals rather than their behaviors.
3) Emergent behavior or acting out is manifested. Conflict can manifest any number of behaviors shouting, cursing, finger pointing, walking away, threatening etc.
4) The resultant outcomes of the conflict and acting out behavior. The outcomes are naturally negative which affects not only interpersonal relationships but productivity.

The conflict perspective (Drafke, 2006) implies looking at the conflict from the other side and writing down your position; then putting yourself in the other side's position and writing down how you see that side and what your position would now be. Then try a third view, that of a disinterested outsider (Fisher, Hopelman & Schneider, 1996). Once this has been accomplished try to understand your message as the other side would see it. They usually see your message in three ways.

1) *Conflict Demand*- which is what you are asking for.
2) *Conflict Threat*- what would happen if your conflict is not met.
3) *Conflict Offer*- what you have to give if your conflict demand is met.

Organizations have developed various strategies to deal with conflict. Research over the years has highlighted four major areas of organizational conflict:

1) *Group interdependence.* Within the organization, there are essentially three areas of intergroup interdependence in which conflict can be high, medium or low.

   - *Pooled-* Departments are relatively independent of each other but then goals contribute to the overall organization. The degree of dependence is low and conflict potential is low.
   - *Sequential-* The output of one department is an input for the next. The degree of dependence is medium and the conflict potential is high.
   - *Reciprocal-* The output of each department becomes the input for the others as well as for possibly still other groups. The degree of dependence is high and conflict potential is high.

2) *Resource Competition.* When there is a limited resource situation in an organization, there is a win-lose competition that can easily develop dysfunctional conflict when groups refuse to cooperate.

3) *Differences in Goals.* Even though every department in an organization works toward achieving organizational goals as these departments become specialized, they often develop dissimilar goals. As a result, different expectations, different customers, group decision participation, etc. can cause conflict when they interact.

4) *Differences in Perspectives (Perceptions).* Perceptions are real to groups, even though it is an evaluation or analysis of an event. The differing views and disagreements can lead to conflict. Usually there are differences in:

   - Time Horizons
   - Status Incongruency
   - Increased demand for specialists
   - Inaccurate perceptions

Researchers have spent much time analyzing how dysfunctional intergroup conflict affects those who experience it (Sherif & Sherif, 1953). They have found that groups placed in conflict situations tend to react in fairly predictable intragroup and intergroup behaviors as a result of dysfunctional conflict. As mentioned before, organizations use resolution, stimulation, and negotiation strategies to manage conflict.

Resolution

Each situation might have a diverse number of variables with different priority levels attached to each. Therefore, the situation determines how one may resolve a conflict. A review of literature demonstrates that conflict resolution strategies can include some of the following strategies.

1. *Problem-solving.* Face-to-face meetings of the feuding groups where conflicts are identified and they can openly debate them with the hope of resolving them.
2. *Super ordinate goals.* Developing a common set of goals and objects that cannot be achieved without the cooperation of the conflicting groups. These goals are for the overall good.
3. *Expansion of resources.* Trying to cater realistically to the needs of the conflicting groups with equity so as not to have them believe that one is not getting what the other has.
4. *Avoidance.* This approach is short term. It doesn't solve conflict but lead time may allow groups to "cool down" as it may be misinterpreted that everyone is in accord. The conflict must eventually be addressed.
5. *Smoothing.* This technique emphasizes the common interests of the conflicting groups and downplays their differences with the hope that common goals will be reached. If the conflict is very serious, smoothing may be a short-run solution like avoidance.
6. *Compromise.* This is the most common and traditional method. The goal is to create a win-win solution. Groups gain essential values and lose those that are not sufficiently important to continue the conflict. Sometimes a third party may be used to facilitate compromise.
7. *Authoritative command.* Management usually solves the conflict and communicates its solution to the conflicting groups. This approach focuses on the results and does not examine the causes of the conflict. Like avoidance and smoothing the resultants are short-run and conflicts may again occur.
8. *Altering the human variable.* The organization tries to change the groups' behavior as it focuses on the causes of the conflict, the attitudes of the people involved and the suggestions of alternate behaviors to resolve the conflict. The process is slow and costly and usually the resultants are long-run.
9. *Altering the structural variable.* The organizational structure is changed so that some members are transferred, exchanged or rotated with a coordinator/manager who keeps the conflicting groups communicating with each other.

Stimulation
Stimulation skills for conflict resolution can include the following strategies.
1. *Communication.* Managers can stimulate positive conflicts by intelligent use of communication channels. They can use rumors, threatening information, ambiguity or new ideas to get feedback, reduce apathy and collectively plan strategies.
2. *Using an outside consultant.* The organization hires or transfers individuals whose values, attitudes and background are different from those of the groups' present members. This stimulates other viewpoints, new perspectives and diversity to the organization. Also, oftentimes, when there are vacant positions in the organization's management instead of promoting from within will hire from outside.

3. *Altering the organizational structure.* This strategy has to be carefully planned because it can exacerbate conflict as well. The new structure should be of such to stimulate competition, fit the right person for the job, engender new responsibilities and develop a refreshing new attitude to getting the job done.

4. *Stimulating competition.* Incentives such as awards are successful techniques for stimulating competition to minimize conflict and or develop functional conflict. Incentives, recognitions and allowed creativity can be useful. It should be noted that if not carefully planned, competition, as a conflict diffuser can quickly become dysfunctional conflict.

Negotiation

The negotiation process can be very successful when conflict parties (groups) in good faith are prepared to have an "open mind" and through a five stage process agree to some resolution. The process consists of:

1. *Preparation and planning.* The specific conflicts must be clearly understood including the nature of the conflict, the protagonists and their perception of the conflict, and the desired expectations and goals.

2. *Definition of ground rules.* These are the procedures that will govern the negotiation groups, where it will take place, who will attend, what are the time constraints, who will do the negotiation, what issues are to be negotiated, time limits and what to do if the conflict persists and there is an impasse.

3. *Clarification and justification.* This is when issues are clarified and the reasons for such, and when each party explains, amplifies and justifies their original demands.

4. *Bargaining and problem-solving.* This is the core of the process. The expertise and professional language and behavior of the negotiators are very important. Cultural factors are important variables as well, as they impact the "amount and type of preparation for bargaining, the relative emphasis on task versus interpersonal relationships, and the tactics used and even where the negotiation should be conducted" (Robbins, 2005).

5. *Closure and implementation.* An agreement has been worked out (negotiated) and the necessary procedures for implementation and monitoring are defined. Many times, a formal contract is agreed upon and in some situations where the level of trust is high, just a handshake is sufficient. Due to the situation of the world today, and the different ethical issues that are apparent, it is best to demand a "legal" document in most cases.

In any situation , when there is an impasse and participants are unable to resolve their differences they may agree to consult or appoint a neutral third party to help them find a solution. There are basically four third party roles:

1. *Mediator*- A neutral third party who facilitates a negotiated solution by using their professional skills of conflict management expertise.

2. *Arbitrator-* A third party to a negotiation who has the legal authority to make a determination which is legally binding.
3. *Conciliator-* A respected third party with integrity who provides an informal "communication bridge" between the negotiations.
4. *Consultant-* An accepted third party professional, fairly experienced in conflict management processes and who has the ability to develop, through analysis communication and creative problem-solving. It should be noted that the consultant's role is not to settle the conflict, but to teach conflict management skills that will improve the relationships between the conflicting parties so that they on their own, may arrive at a resolution. This process is good for the overall future handling skills if there are future difficulties.

Individual Conflict Management Skills

There are many guidelines and methodologies suggested by authors, consultants, and professors in effectively managing conflict. We will generalize some suggestions and then share some thoughts about the art of dealing with conflict in the workplace that has been very successful in the authors' experience and which is shared with students, organizations and families in their quest for resolving conflicts. Some general guidelines and suggestions include the following:

1) Always maintain professionalism dealing with the conflict and not the person (s).
2) Concentrate on the conflict and be specific about the issues without including your own value judgments.
3) Avoid name calling and emotional outbursts and voice modulations that may imply anger and or irrational thinking.
4) Avoid generalities.
5) Focus on the aspects that can be realistically resolved with "win-win" goals in mind.
6) Do not attempt to confuse issues by trying to solve a myriad of conflicts.
7) Be prepared to compromise. Nobody may get all that he or she wants, but everyone gets something.
8) Aim for win-win solutions for all parties.

Lawrence D. Schwimmer and associates produced a training video in 1992 entitled *"The Art of Resolving Conflict in the Workplace,"* that has been used very successfully by trainers. The methodology is no panacea, but even though it only uses situations including two persons with conflict, its' application can be applied to any situation, be they groups, families or organizations. *The Art of Resolving Conflict in the Workplace* video suggests six techniques that are used which can be used singularly or in combination to deal with any situation that may arise. In part one, the techniques are discussed and role-played. In part two, there are examples used to illustrate conflicts caused by:

- Aggressive behavior,
- Role confusion,

- Stereotyping, and
- Manipulation.

The techniques emphasize that the process is not a science, but a structured process that can resolve any conflict situation with the underlying theory being a thorough knowledge of human behavior. The language and projected examples are decidedly American, but the basic techniques are cross-cultural, which makes it an excellent tool to use. The six techniques are:

1) *Using "I" versus "You" language.* When there is a conflict and people are confronted with "you did this", or "you did that", they become very defensive, would usually deny the accusations and use it as an "invitation to fight." When I, is used, the accuser takes full responsibility for the statement, expresses their concern regarding the conflict, diffuses denial and defensiveness and opens the way for positive dialogue.

Starting with, for example, "I am very concerned about the constant mistakes that you are making and I would like to make suggestions to alleviate them" is a much more powerful approach to them instead of saying "you are constantly making mistakes and "you must do something about it." The language that is used, a conciliatory and helpful tone of voice and a suggestion to help solve the problem can be very successful in resolving a conflict.

2) *Anticipation.* Many times in the workplace, people make mistakes, are not successful in achieving goals or they use techniques that did not accomplish specific tasks. These employees may have learned from their mistakes and would want to prove to the organization that they have now mastered the task. Their past 'track record' is still remembered by the organization and more than likely; they would not give the employee another chance. If the employee understands this, they can use the technique of anticipation to resolve this matter.

"I know that in the past I've made serious mistakes, but I've learned from them, worked out the difficulties and would like to be given another chance to complete this project." This approach is likely to get an approval when anticipation is used rather than asking without an explanation. The method is analyzing the situation, monitoring the past negative outcomes and positively suggesting that they should be given another chance.

3) *Self- Interest.* All human beings by their very nature have their self-interests at heart. "Out of all my mama's children, I love myself the best" is not only true but demonstrates how amenable a person can be when "what is in it for me" explains "what is in it for them." When the self interest of the conflicting person (or group) is taken into consideration and clearly articulated to them, they are more than likely to listen, negotiate and solve a conflict.

4) *Meta-Talk.* This technique uses a Greek word meaning "above and beyond." From a practical viewpoint it implies making assumptions about one's body language such as tone of voice, gestures, body stance, physical manifestations; (all within one's cultural framework) indicating positive, negative or indifference of the person whose "body language" is being read. A person can say anything and lie or use verbal convincing techniques, but ones' body language doesn't lie. When there is a confrontation, meeting or dispute, if one can engage in "meta talk" it can diffuse an

explosive situation or have clarified the concerns of the person. For example, the video example illustrated a person in the office engaged in work when a fellow employee comes into the office and asks "can I speak with you for a moment?" The other employee throws her pen down, turns to the person and in a sarcastic voice says "and what can I do for you?" The tone of voice is hostile and for someone who does not have conflict handling experience, would naturally take offense and probably "storm out" or perhaps say "who the hell do you think you're talking to" or something similar to it. Using the technique of meta- talk, the person focuses on the tone of voice, sarcastic language and 'hostile' body gestures. She replies "I'm sorry; it appears that you are very upset about something." This diffuses the situation; the other person explains why they are frustrated and apologizes to the person for the rude outburst. There is an understanding and they make a specific appointment to meet later that day. When people are upset or under a lot of pressure, it is best to focus on the body language, clarify the situation and professionally decide how to solve the problem, either immediately or later.

5) *Setting Limits.* Conflicts generally arise when there are mixed messages as to the responsibility of people who work together. When theses specific responsibilities are not clarified, it may cause confusion, a lack of strategic planning and many times, affect the efficiency of the person, department or organization. Setting limits is especially powerful in "superior- subordinate" relationships in the organization when the superior makes unrealistic demands on the subordinate and tasks are not completed. This may cause serious difficulties, loss of work and efficiency. The technique is to clarify and realistically determine the situation and have both parties set their limits and/or allow the superior to determine the priorities of the situation so that strategies that are mutually accepted may not point at blame or seriously affect the organization.

6) *Consequences.* When conflict management techniques have not been effective, then there is the utilization of ensuing consequences. Consequences indicate the result that will be implemented when there has been no change in behavior or there has developed defiance, non-reliance, stubbornness, insubordination, and rule breaking. Consequences should never be used as a threat and it is best to start with lesser consequences and increasing to the most severe, in most cases, of firing. One can use consequences with other techniques to improve positive results.

It is useful for the management of conflict skills to be effective in utilizing communication for problem-solving, where there are specific rules for learning how to accuse and how to react to accusations. Conflict managing skills can be even more effective if one can learn the technique of "communication for problem-solving." There are specific rules for learning how to accuse and how to react to accusations. These are discussed in the future chapters.

Determining Your Conflict Management Style

People come into a conflict situation with some experience and assumptions based upon their conflicting situations. Some employees and managers who face a conflict tend to "fight" it, while others might choose the "flight" approach. For example, would you choose the fight or flight approach if you were to have a conflict with your employee, your colleague, or your boss? Often times, people tend to fall somewhere in between the continuum of "fight" or "flight." Once one determines what his or her natural approach might be to a conflicting situation with others, then he or she can determine the advantages and disadvantages of this approach, his or her approach's probability of success in various conflicting situations, and the means of adapting different styles to be more successful. Most people tend to have one of the five conflict resolution approaches in the continuum of being assertive (meeting one's own needs) to being supportive (meeting others' needs): avoiding, accommodating, competing, compromising, and collaborating. To determine what your dominant style is, complete the conflict resolution survey (provided at the end of this chapter) and circle your dominant style(s). The conflict management styles, presented in Figure 3.2, are the commonly addressed approaches in literature and conflict management workshops.

Managers are likely to have one or two dominant style of resolving conflict. However, it is best to know one's natural tendencies and, if needed, improve upon them as desired. While in some cases "avoiding" might be an effective style for dealing with a conflict, other situations would require the use of collaborating or compromising in order to get things done with other team members. The situational variables should determine the best style. While situations do vary, a person should always keep his/her composure because objectivity and rational decision-making is critical for effective conflict resolution. Furthermore, effective conflict resolution process requires the use of excellent listening skills. While listening effectively, managers can use objective and open-ended questions to clarify further areas of interest for all parties involved.

Figure 3.2 – Conflict Management Styles

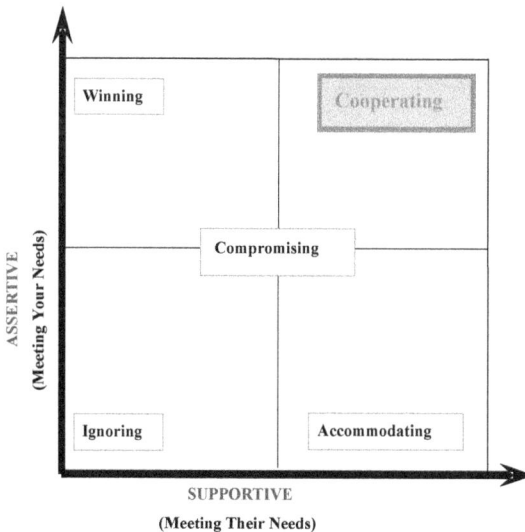

The essence of effective conflict resolution is to work together without offending anyone or being offended. Consequently, one should resolve all differences in a professional manner. It is also beneficial to remember that differences and disagreements can lead to better alternatives, better solutions, new ways of viewing each case, and opportunities for more quality communication. In each obstacle, there can be hidden opportunities. One needs to stay calm, stay "all together" in the face of disagreements, hear each other's differences and views, and then make sure one's views are heard by everyone on the team before agreeing on a final solution. In the case of performance-related conflict with employees, if the conflict resolution process does not resolve the situation, managers then can use the employee discipline and dismissal processes.

Culture and the 4-F Model
Culture and cultural differences can play an important role both in conflict creation and resolution. Authors Cliffor C. Clark and G. Douglas Lipp in 1998 introduced a seven-step process to help people eliminate conflicts due to misunderstanding of cultures. The seven-step process can help people from different cultures understand each other's intentions and perceptions so they can work together harmoniously based on real-world examples. The article *Conflict Resolutions for Contrasting Cultures* is divided in two parts: a case scenario, followed by the resolution of the case through the seven-step resolution model. The authors provide solutions to overcome cultural conflicts in any multinational organization with offshore subsidiaries, thus balancing the needs and objectives of the local workforce and customer base with those of the home country and headquarters. The seven-step conflict resolution model consists of (Clarke & Lipp, 1998):
1. Problem identification
2. Problem clarification
3. Cultural exploration
4. Organizational exploration
5. Conflict resolution
6. Impact assessment
7. Organizational integration

The model presented by Clark and Lipp advocates to managers the creation of harmony, instead of being content with being aware of cultural differences. One of the strongest points of the article is the suggestion of incorporating "harmony" in the corporate culture. This concept will help to create a sophisticated organizational culture where the values of employees are in sync with organizational values, and establish a value-driven organization where employees stick to the facts and future goals when resolving conflicts. Cultural differences can make conflict resolution more challenging and more time consuming. However, managers must work on resolving cultural conflicts as quickly as possible using as "simple" approaches as possible.

Quickly and effectively resolving conflicts can speed up the team's progress toward achieving its purpose. When dealing with day-to-day conflicts, misconducts, and disagreements, one can use the 4-F model by clarifying and emphasizing the facts, feelings, future expectations, and following up when appropriate.

> *Facts*. Stick with the facts and describe the behavior that is creating the problem or conflict. Avoid attacking the other person. Avoid using "you" statements.

> *Feelings*. State the impact of the problem or conflict, your feelings, the feelings of team members, and how the problem makes the team suffer. Avoid the use of "You" statements. Use "I" statements by mentioning how the above mentioned problem or fact impacts you or your employees and colleagues.

> *Future expectations*. Clearly describe future expectations, norms, and rules of conduct.

> *Following up*. Managers should follow up with the employee to make sure employees are meeting the expected standards as agreed. If they are, then the manager has an opportunity to reinforce this good behavior. Otherwise, the manager will have another opportunity to start the process again (or take drastic actions as appropriate).

The 4-F model provides the facts and expects a change in behavior or the discovery of a new method or process. According to Crum, discovery is one essential component of effective conflict management because *discovery* is a place that does not know, does not evaluate, and is willing to see what is; *discovery* sees beyond the fight to an open realm of possibilities; *discovery* enables people to let go of the filters of their past and the blinders of their expectations; *discovery* perceives not right and wrong, only inquiry and creativity; and *discovery* turns frustration into fascination and work into play (Crum, 1987, p. 129). Discovering the right response in each changing moment requires having an open mind as well as an open heart to see new opportunities and the way things are, and then the way they can be. The origin and evolution of every living species have been a lesson of change as various living species adapt to and evolve with their changing environments in order to flourish. The same means of adaptation applies to human beings since change in nature is not an ideological choice but rather one of survival. Change is a choice for learning, creativity, flexibility, and growth; and effective conflict management is the key to bringing about change in an efficient manner. Amid all the change, it is best to remember that flexibility allows one to stretch rather than shrink, and proactively welcoming and embracing change is about choosing a better or pre-determined future. Furthermore, choosing to be synergistic, while involving everyone in the change management process, can transform a "personal" vision into a "professional" vision for everyone in the department or the organization.

Summary

Conflict is neither good nor bad. Conflict is a reality of life and "Our lives are not dependent on whether or not we have conflict. It is what we do with conflict that makes the difference" (Crum, 1987, p. 21). Crum states that, during changing times and major conflicts, instead of seeing the rug being pulled out from under us, we must learn to dance on the shifting carpet. The key in managing conflict effectively is to learn how to convert frustration to fascination and disappointing and upsetting thoughts into growth. In all cases, handle conflicts with other individuals in a caring, dignified and respectful manner.

Conflict Resolution Survey

Conflict resolution styles. Effective leadership, management, and communication require an understanding of one's dominant conflict resolution style or one's natural tendencies. To understand your conflict resolution style, use the following scale to describe your typical behavior in conflict.

> 0 = I never behave this way
> 1 = I seldom behave this way
> 2 = I sometimes behave this way
> 3 = I often behave this way
> 4 = I very frequently behave this way

Review the following elements and give yourself a score of 0-5, as per the above scale, to determine your natural tendencies. Be honest and candid as you complete this survey.

___1. Insult the other person.
___2. Disregard the existence of a conflict.
___3. Passively comply with the other's demands.
___4. Seek a mutually beneficial solution.
___5. Seek a quick middle ground.
___6. Use threats to intimidate the other person.
___7. Postpone dealing with the issue.
___8. Sacrifice my own wishes for the sake of the other.
___9. Give information so the other can understand my feelings.
___10. Exchange concessions.
___11. Demand to have my way.
___12. Avoid communicating with the other person.
___13. Give in to the other person for the sake of harmony.
___14. Solicit information about the other's thoughts and feelings.
___15. Split the difference with the other person.
___16. Escalate the confrontation.
___17. Sidestep the area of disagreement.
___18. Protect my relationship with the other person rather than win the conflict.
___19. Explore alternative solutions to the problem.
___20. Bargain or trade with the other person.
___21. Punish the other person.
___22. Withdraw from the situation if it becomes threatening.
___23. Yield easily to the other's position.
___24. Attempt to negotiate so that neither person must compromise.
___25. Concede some points in order to win some other points.
___26. Lose my temper.
___27. Change the topic to avoid confrontation.
___28. Let the other person have his/her way.
___29. Cooperate to find areas of agreement.
___30. Compromise

Conflict response orientation survey calculation. To determine your conflict response orientation (CRO), calculate your conflict scores by adding the values marked for the question items in each column. The higher you score the greater your perceived tendency or orientation to utilize that specific communication style (Adapted from Tuttle, Waveland Press, 1985).

Competing	Avoiding	Accommodating	Collaborating	Compromising
1.	2.	3.	4.	5.
6.	7.	8.	9.	10.
11.	12.	13.	14.	15.
16.	17.	18.	19.	20.
21.	22.	23.	24.	25.
26.	27.	28.	29.	30.
Total =	Total =	Total =	Total =	Total =

> **CHAPTER FOUR**

4 - TIME MANAGEMENT AND PROBLEM SOLVING

E ffective time management skills are very important for stress management and productivity. Determining which actions are important and scheduling them into one's day, week, month, and year require time management skills. Regardless of how busy one's time may be or appear to be, at least at a personal level, one can manage it effectively while capitalizing on the opportunities that lie ahead.

One of the best time management concepts seems to be Stephen R. Covey's approach to leadership, life, value-based decision-making, and "putting first things first." Dr. Covey, author of the *Seven Habits of Highly Effective People* (1989), discusses "big rocks" and "small rocks" in his analogy for managing activities in the allotted times. The "big rocks" are a person's most important life roles and relationships. For example, one's job can be a big rock as can be one's status as a parent, son, daughter, mother, uncle, neighbor, or father. Each person must determine his/her important life goals and continuously do what is needed to nourish and develop the relevant relationships and competencies in each role.

Understanding Priorities

Many individuals spend a large percentage of their days and nights worrying about either the past or the future and achieve very little in the present. The past is gone but it can offer learning when one reflects upon it consciously for a limited amount of time. The future has not come but one can plan for it accordingly. However, actions must be taken in the present and these actions should be geared toward what is important in one's life. Stephen R. Covey (1989) presents the popular model of managing one's time based on priorities as demonstrated in the time management model, Figure 4.1.

In effective time management, activities can be categorized and understood as important, urgent, not important, and not urgent. The following definitions and concept are foundational in time management and effective decision-making.

◊   *Urgent* – Urgent is defined as activities that have the appearance of needing immediate attention.

◊ *Important* – Important is defined as all those activities that contribute to life's goals and mission.

Activities that are important will always produce better outcomes in the long-term. However, some activities are both important and urgent so they must be completed first. Activities that are neither important nor urgent can be left alone if they do not hinder your mission in life. The German philosopher, Johann Goethe, said "every man has only enough strength to complete those activities that he is fully convinced are important." So, discover your important activities in order not to waste time on the unimportant things. Some discipline is required when it comes to time management. When it comes to discipline Jim Rohn, motivational speaker and author, states "We must all suffer one of two things: the pain of discipline or the pain of regret or disappointment." Properly planning for doing what is important leaves no excuses for not achieving them. With regard to excuses Bob Burg, author and speaker, said "One trademark of successful people is that they don't let excuses deter them. They determine what it is they need to do - and then do it." So, focus on what is important by going in that direction one step at a time.

Figure 4.1 – Time Management Model

	Urgent	Not Urgent
Important	• Crises, emergencies • Must get done now tasks • Publish or perish projects	• Planning • Opportunities • Crisis prevention • Spending quality time with family • Relaxation exercises
Not Important	• Interruptions • Mail and reports • Some meetings • Certain phone calls, etc.	• Too much TV or exercise • Time wasters • Procrastination activities

Jackson W. Robinson, President of Winslow Management Company, said that "Defying conventional ideas can yield unconventional returns." Defying the status quo and creating new ideas takes energy, vision, hard work, and at times temporary setbacks. So, "Never allow your energy or enthusiasm to be dampened by the discouragements that must inevitably come" (James Whitcomb Riley, poet). Unfortunately, often people allow such temporary setbacks to impact their enthusiasm and sometimes even speak ill of others as a result. Will Durant, historian and author, summarized it well when he said "To speak ill of others is a dishonest way of praising ourselves." Consequently, one should be very cautious, and always think and speak based on one's values and what is important.

Focusing on the Important
It has been said that a person who does not make a choice actually makes a choice. Hopefully, choices are directed toward actions that lead one in the direction of what is important in one's life. Jawaharlal Nehru, Indian statesman, once said that "Action to be effective must be directed to clearly conceived ends." So, one must be focused toward end-results that are important. With regard to focusing Washington Gladden, writer and lecturer, said "It is better to say, 'This one thing I do' than to say, 'These forty things I dabble in.'" A mission statement can keep one focused on what is important and it provides the reasons for going toward a specific direction. Friedrich Nietzsche, philosopher, said "He who has a why can bear almost any how." A burning "why" will almost always find an efficient "how" in order to get to the predetermined destination. In the business perspective, the "why" deals with leadership while the "how" aspect deals with management tasks. One must know where and why before determining how to get there because going in the wrong direction will waste time, resources, and kill one's morale.

While focusing on the "big rocks" during one of his seminars, Dr. Covey, set up a bucket and asked a volunteer from the audience to take a smaller bucket of small rocks and several large rocks labeled things like self-improvement, big project at work, vacation time, family, etc. The small rocks represented the small fires or emergencies that we are hit with everyday at home and at work. The instructions for the volunteers are clear and simple - you must fit all of the large rocks and all of the small rocks in the large bucket. Several volunteers attempted the task, each time placing some small rocks in the bottom of the bucket and then carefully selecting the most important large rocks, cramming, shoving, and pushing, trying to fit all of the rocks. Most participants tend to miss the key concept of the exercise which is really the moral of the presentations: You will accomplish a lot more in your day, your week and your life if you start with the "big rocks" first and leave the remaining empty space for the "small rocks." And, as expected and planned, all of the rocks fit into the large bucket when you place the large ones in first and pour the small rocks into the gaps and holes between them.

The same exercise can be conducted a little differently using the same concept of "small rocks" and "big rocks." Imagine for a minute, if you will, that a professor stood before his "Change and Stress Management" class and had some items in front of him to demonstrate effective time management. When the class began, wordlessly, he picked up a very large and empty glass jar and proceeded to fill it with "*colorful golf balls.*" He then asked the students if the jar was full. They agreed that it was. So the professor then picked up a box of pebbles and poured them into the jar. He shook the jar lightly. The pebbles, of course, rolled into the open spaces between the colorful golf balls. He then asked the students again if the jar was full. They agreed it was. The professor picked up a box of sand and poured it into the jar. Of course, the sand filled up everything else. He then asked once more if the jar was full. The students agreed with a unanimous --yes! The professor then produced two bottles of water from under the table and proceeded to pour the entire contents into the jar effectively filling the empty space between the sand. The students laughed.

Now, the professor said, as the laughter subsided, I want you to recognize that this jar represents your life.

◊   The *colorful golf balls* are the important things -- your family, partner, health, children, friends, and your favorite passions such as your job/profession--things that if everything else was lost and only they remained, your life would still be full.

◊   The *pebbles* are the other things that matter like your hobbies, your house, and your car.

◊   The sand is everything else -- the small stuff! "If you put the sand into the jar first, then there is no room for the pebbles or the golf balls. The same goes for your life. If you spend all your time and energy on the small stuff, you will never have room for the things that are important to you. Pay attention to the things that are critical to your happiness. Play with your children. Take time to get medical checkups. Take your partner out dancing. Play another 18 holes of golf and a game of tennis or racquetball every now and then. There will always be time to work, clean the house, give a dinner party, and fix the disposal. Take care of the golf balls first -- the things that really matter. Set your priorities. The rest is just sand. One of the students raised her hand and inquired what the water represented. The professor smiled and said, I'm glad you asked.

◊   The *water* is a symbol and a reminder for enjoying, relaxing and taking time for you and for nourishing all of your roles in a balanced way. It just goes to show you that no matter how full your life may seem, there's always room for enjoying a couple glasses of cool water with your friends to satisfy your thirst and cleanse your system!

Water is the symbol of flexibility, and it makes a powerful statement as an ending to this quick demonstration of making sure that one's big rocks are clarified, planned and scheduled. Actually water is both flexible as well as adaptable to its surroundings as it can be fluid, solid ice, or it can become moisture and simply evaporate into thin air. All mission-oriented individuals need to remain flexible as well as adaptable in their daily activities by taking advantage of the wonderful opportunities life brings their way each and every day. With regard to important life moments, Susan B. Anthony, Women's Rights Advocate, states: "Sooner or later we all discover that the important moments in life are not the advertised ones, not the birthdays, the graduations, the weddings, not the great goals achieved. The real milestones are less prepossessing. They come to the door of memory unannounced, stray dogs that amble in, sniff around a bit and simply never leave. Our lives are measured by these." In other words, some unexpected events or opportunities that come your way may not be as attractive as others (that are stated in your goals), but they do make life fun, fulfilling and enjoyable if you can seize the opportunity and live in the moment.

Many time management experts use this philosophy when setting goals, writing an action plan, and prioritizing tasks. If needed, we should force ourselves to remember to work on the big rocks a little bit each day - otherwise we would become bogged down with small emergencies and never feel as though we have accomplished anything. Education is usually a "big rock" when we are trying to gain competency in our professions, and many competent professionals continue to hone their time management skills because they don't want important "small rocks" like some of the "big rocks" to get pushed aside from time to time. What is important is that you don't ignore "big rocks" for very long. Just like trees, "big rocks" such as your relationships need constant nourishment and development if they are to sustain and grow. As you know, after all is said and done, no matter how famous or important a person might be, the size of his/her funeral is going to depend a lot on the weather. Nonetheless, it is important that you focus on the "big rocks" well before inviting others to your funeral!

Conscious thinking, deep reflection, prioritizing according to one's mission, and planning improves time management skills which is bout managing the needed activities in the allotted time. Most of us have experienced the difficulties of balancing available time with the many commitments and opportunities we would like to fulfill. Each day, managers are bombarded by a multitude of tasks and demands in a setting of frequent interruptions, crisis and unexpected events. It can be easy to lose track of objectives and fall prey to what experts identify as "time wasters." For many of us, time is probably dominated by other people and/or by nonessential activities rather than our own "big rocks." Through personal benefits of improved focus, flexibility, coordination, control, and planning everyone can become better time managers. The following are quick tips on how to better manage scarce time.

◊ Do say "No" when others' requests will divert you from more important work toward your "big rocks" that you should be doing.
◊ Don't get bogged down in details and routines that should be left to others.
◊ Do establish a system for screening your telephone calls and unneeded office chit-chats.
◊ Don't let "drop in" or unannounced visitors use too much of your time.
◊ Do prioritize work tasks in order of their importance and urgency.
◊ Don't become "calendar bound" by losing control of your schedule or other important opportunities that surface. Adapt daily.
◊ Do work tasks in their order of priority by focusing on the most important first.
◊ Do take the time to laugh often with your friends and family members. Valerie Bell, author, says "Shared laughter is like family glue. It is the stuff of family well-being and all-is-well thoughts. It brings us together as few other things can."

Time management is important because more time for research on complex problems may equal better decisions. In some cases, having more time for proper research can prevent problems and disasters from taking place. Think of *Exxon Oil Valdez*, *The Chernobyl Disaster* in Russia, the *Space Shuttle Challenger*, and other examples where perhaps more time for research, reflection, and better decision-making may have led to different choices and results.

The organizational culture of most competitive firms tends to be fast paced and they usually require immediate solutions to problems. However, thinking of good ideas and creative solutions requires time. This is also true of our own lives. We need to take the time and see what makes sense for our purpose in life and how many hours we should devote to important tasks (big rocks) each week. Many of us might be wasting valuable time because we have a hard time determining what is important and eventually stop trying. Think, for a minute about meetings. How much time do professionals spend or waste in meetings? How many times have you thought to yourself after an hour-long meeting, we could have accomplished everything covered in a total of 15 minutes. The same is true for bureaucratic rules and regulations. How many hoops do we have to jump through in any given day? If these bureaucratic rules aren't followed to the letter, will it really make a difference? What happens sometimes is that we confuse what is important with what is urgent. Think about the busy lives of famous people who have accomplished great things. Did they have more time than other individuals or were they devoted to a cause that was important to them? If you are working toward a cause that is important, then it doesn't matter how many hours you work on it because it should be enjoyable to you!

Communicating Effectively

A book of this type would be remiss in not mentioning the process of communication as essential components of managing stress, conflict and change. The approach will not be to explore the mechanics of communication but to provide straightforward guidelines for effective communication and skill building exercises that will practically equip the person who wishes to become "communication-competent." Essentially, communication is the transfer of meaning from one person to another. If no information or ideas have been conveyed, communication hasn't taken place. Communication is obviously not limited to merely speaking words. Memo's, email, voice mail, bulletins, and visual aids (to name a few) constitute forms of communication. Understanding non-verbal communication is the key to effective communication. People's bodies usually tell the truth even when they verbalize differently. Types of non-verbal communications are: body orientation, posture, gestures, face and eyes, voice, touch, physical attractiveness, clothing, proxemics, territoriality, physical environment, and time. Also, understanding a person's culture, especially "cultural cues", are essential in communication. Essential skills to be practiced include: assertiveness, listening, questioning, influencing, understanding body language, recognizing defense mechanisms, giving feedback, constructive criticism, coaching techniques, handling conflict, and facilitating conversations. A visual communication model has been depicted according to the system presented in Figure 4.2.

Generally, with any communication, the sender encodes (selects words for a message) with gestures, tone of voice, etc. The encoded message is then sent via some media to the receiver. The receiver decodes (or translates) the message according to his or her feelings, moods, and circumstances. When there is two-way communication, the parties can confirm mutual understanding or clarification until both parties are satisfied. This all takes place in environments that are depicted as noise which can be anything (telephone ringing, hammering, radio playing, gestures etc.). An effective listening model has also been suggested where the receiver can listen, process and respond.

Figure 4.2 – The Communication System

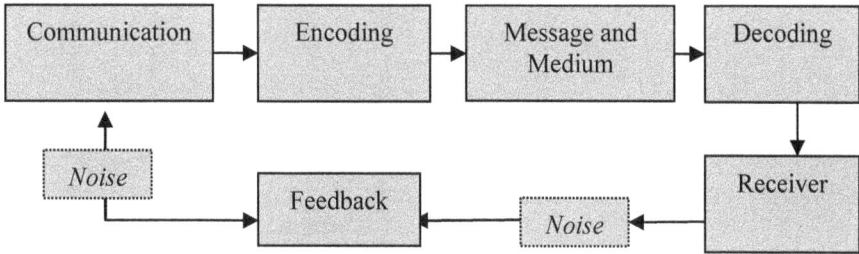

```
┌──────────────────┐     ┌──────────────┐     ┌──────────────┐     ┌──────────────┐
│  Communication   │ ──▶ │   Encoding   │ ──▶ │ Message and  │ ──▶ │   Decoding   │
│                  │     │              │     │   Medium     │     │              │
└──────────────────┘     └──────────────┘     └──────────────┘     └──────────────┘
         ▲                                                                 │
         │                                                                 ▼
┌────────────┐           ┌──────────────┐           ┌──────────┐   ┌──────────────┐
│   Noise    │           │   Feedback   │ ◀──────── │  Noise   │ ◀ │   Receiver   │
└────────────┘           └──────────────┘           └──────────┘   └──────────────┘
```

Overall, effective listening requires actively or emphatically processing what is being said and confirming understanding by appropriately responding as needed. From a practical viewpoint, creating an effective communication climate is the key to positive relationships. When this happens, you win, I win, and nobody loses. Confirming communication can include verbal or non-verbal recognition, acknowledgement, and endorsement. Similarly, discomforting communication can include verbal abuse, complaining, impervious responses, interrupting responses, irrelevant responses, tangential responses, impersonal responses, ambiguous responses, and incongruous responses. With globalization and diversity as givens for the modern organization, it is useful to realize that cross-cultural guidelines are important. Major barriers to communication in a cross-cultural work environment can include semantics, word connotation, tone differences, and different perceptions to name a few. In a cross-cultural work environment, it is best to adhere to the following guidelines:
1. Assume differences until similarity is proven.
2. Emphasize *description* rather than interpretation or evaluation
3. Practice *empathy*.
4. Treat your interpretation as a working hypothesis.

It is always best to remember that any idea, no matter how great, is useless until it is transmitted and understood by others. The meanings of words are *not* in the words, they are in *us*. Communication is an ongoing process and that requires attention and focus. One should also remember that men often have a tendency to use talk to emphasize status while women use it to create connection.

Managers, leaders, supervisors, and parents are all involved with departments, groups, etc. To be more effective in communication, one should:
1. Prepare a strategy for effective communication.
2. Ask questions and seek opinions.
3. Speak clearly.
4. Keep an open mind.
5. Listen.

6. Encourage cooperation.
7. Manage conflict.
8. Act ethically. And
9. Use an appropriate sense of humor.

Figure 4.3 – Listening Model and Process

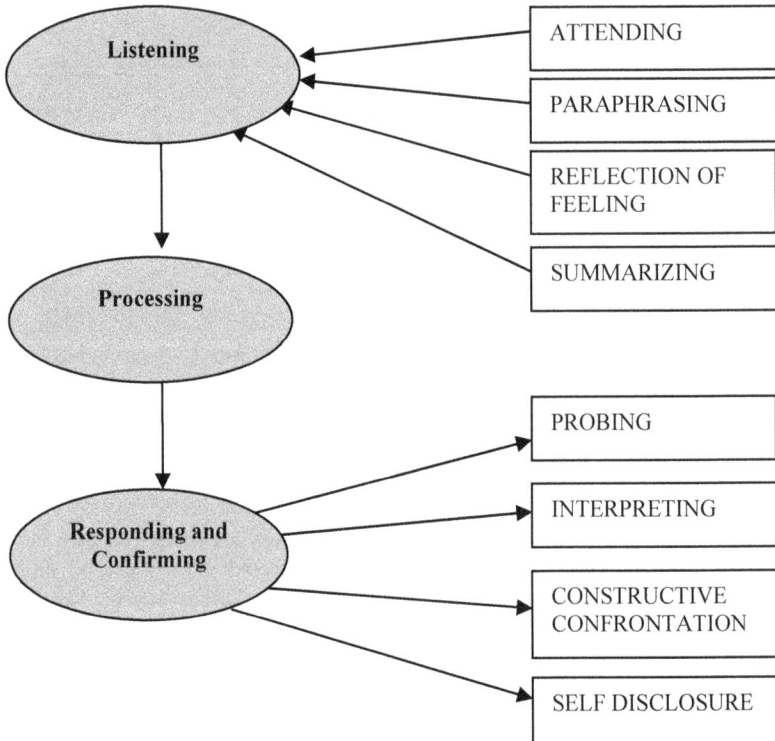

Dr. McCartney often mentions White's 1992 material on the "*ten commandments of poor communication*" which one must avoid at all times in order to be an effective communicator. The commandments of poor communication are:
1. Thou shalt disrespect me and what I say by your tone, body language and choice of words.
2. Thou shalt consistently interrupt or ignore me when I am expressing myself.
3. Thou shalt constantly finish my sentences as if you know my every thought.
4. Thou shalt look around when I speak.

5. Thou shalt make faces to let me know that my attempts to communicate bore you.
6. Thou shalt always attempt to teach me the real facts of the situation as I was ignorant of them all.
7. Thou shalt respond in such a way that I realize you had not listened to me but merely waited for me to finish so you could talk.
8. Thou shalt verbally or visually check with me to find out if we're hearing each other.
9. Thou shalt ignore my real ideas and meanings and argue about so-called facts, as you understand them.
10. Thou shalt never forgive past faults and constantly bring them up whenever we speak whether they are relevant or not (White, 1992 as mentioned by McCartney).

There are many skill building exercises that the authors have used over many years of practice and some of them have proved to be very useful. Skill building exercises are not a panacea, but for those who follow the directions and practice the process it can improve their communication and interpersonal relationships. The *"Communication for Problem Solving"* method was adopted from a tape on "communication" published by the psychological corporation in 1976 and adapted by McCartney (1978) to suit the needs of the environment in which he practiced at that time.

Communication for Problem-Solving

The method, when practiced, could enhance, clarify and significantly improve the communication process. All of us 'communicate' in some way since our styles and manners are cultural. The professional learns the language and technique of professionalism. For this technique to be used effectively, one must accept these basic assumptions:
1. People are generally well-meaning and don't want to hurt other people.
2. The difference between positive and negative communication is strategy.
3. Anger is a natural emotion. When it is 'managed' constructively, it 'clears the air' and promotes growth.
4. Usually, attempts to solve a problem are done by accusations. It is necessary to forget about blame! Who is wrong and who is right is not the problem.

The issue is to solve a problem for the benefits of all i.e., try a win-win situation. As long as we live, there will always be problems, so it is important that we master this skill. There are two principle factors to consider when there are problems; we must learn how to accuse effectively (i.e., how to make the proper statement about the problem) and how to react to accusations. Now, learn the rules and put them into practice!

Rules for the Accuser (i.e., how to accuse) are:
1. The purpose to the accusation is to solve a problem.
2. Accusations should be made one at a time.
3. Accusations should be specific and not vague.
4. Accusations should be accompanied by specific suggestions for change.

5. There should be no exaggerations.
6. Do not use any insults.
7. Watch the tone of your voice; it may carry insult.
8. Watch the frequency of the accusations. Nobody likes a nagger!

Rules for the Accusee (i.e., how to respond) are:
1. An accusation should never be denied.
2. Do not counter-accuse.
3. Do not interrupt the accuser.
4. Do not use the accusation as a pretext for initiating a destructive response, especially of past events.

There are some other general rules to remember for effective communication and skill-building and the following are some of them:
1. Avoid the invitation to fight.
2. Remember that people's memories are constantly distorting and their perceptions of events are real to them.
3. All human beings have faults and also strong opinions. There are faults that you will have to accept, but there are other faults that may have to be discussed. You must also agree to disagree!
4. Avoid unfair techniques, such as;
   - Blaming the person for something they can't help.
   - Silence,
   - Switching the subject,
   - Analyzing as if you were a 'shrink',
5. Don't make assumptions or try to 'read' the other person's mind. Always test your assumptions with the other person.
6. Be positive about long-range intentions and sincerity and respond positively.

You must develop a 'mind-set' of professionalism and learn from your mistakes. Communication for problem-solving is just one of the many techniques for effective communication, growth enrichment and maturity. The key is to practice effective communication at all times. Practice! Practice! Practice!

Communication is the key to success; whether it is individual, group, electronic, motivational or within a large organization. We all need to convey messages and receive information in order to function as human beings. We now know that to be successful and to lead people within teams, groups and organizations, effective communication is the key!

Problem-Solving Considerations
For the twenty-first century firm, the true sustainable advantages come from the success of each individual manager and employee within the organization. The business leader's goal should be to create managers and leaders with the requisite skills to compete effectively in national and global markets by focusing on what is important and by effectively managing priorities.

Educators and managers should provide relevant information about time management and problem solving skills for employees so they can learn, innovate, think critically, and to create value for their organizations and themselves. So, the first step towards empowerment and excellence through an empowered workforce is achieving the goal of appropriately educating the workforce to manage priorities based on importance. The second step is to empower employees to think for themselves so they can take advantage of every opportunity as they become better prepared to meet the competitive challenges of their day-to-day operations while balancing the most important activities. Having effective time management and problem solving skills are a good start toward independence and empowerment.

Understanding and Solving Problems

Peter Senge (1990), author of *"The Fifth Discipline,"* said that for most people real learning gets to the heart of what it means to be a human being. He further continued to stay that through real learning we recreate ourselves; through real learning we become able to do something we never were able to do; and through real learning we re-perceive the world and our relationship to it. After all, it is through learning that we extend our capacities to create, to be part of the generative process of life. Senge emphasized that there is within each person a deep hunger for real learning. We can continue and say that through learning we can become better problem-solvers for our organizations. The workplace has many challenges due to its fast-paced requirements and changing rules in order to remain competitive. Such complex changes require a competent workforce that can anticipate and proactively solve problems. Educated employees should be developed to think for themselves when it comes to tackling and solving problems to speed up the process in better serving the organization's relevant constituencies. The following are some relevant considerations for developing your problem-solving skills.

Do We Really Have Problems? You know that you have been in the corporate world too long if you think that you never have any problems in your life, just "issues" and "improvement opportunities." In reality, most issues and improvement opportunities are problems that need to be taken care of accurately, productively, and urgently in order to remain sane and competitive. Herman Melville once said that "a smooth sea never made a successful sailor" which means that through determination to constantly become better and make meaningful contributions we can overcome these issues and become better managers. Without these issues and opportunities, our lives would be very boring and repetitive. As a matter of fact, most managers spend close to eighty percent of their time solving problems. Yet, most of these managers were not taught how to solve management problems. They had to learn through *heuristics* - trial and error.

Defining the Problem and Its Owners: One can define a "problem" as the gap between the real and the ideal in goals while attempting to overcome challenging issues and improvement opportunities in the daily work environment. Furthermore, we can define problem owners as those who have unmet goals and objectives. Issues and improvement opportunities can be looked at as problems and problems can be seen as opportunities for improvement in order to maintain a positive attitude and outlook on life. Some problems are opportunities to simply improve while others are opportunities for turning wrongs into rights. Solving problems quickly and accurately is an art and a science that needs structure, practice, experience, intuition, and discipline. Solving management dilemmas and problems is no different than solving any other difficult problem. Often a problem exists when there is a discrepancy between what is actually happening and what should be happening. The first thing you need to do is determine exactly what the problem is and who owns it. A question that can guide one in determining who owns the problem is to ask, "Whose needs' are not being met."

Process or People Problems? Researchers have found that about eighty to eight five percent of problems are process or systems-related, and about five to ten percent are people-related. Only fifteen percent of associates' performance problems are due to lack of training; the other eighty five percent are due to lack of feedback, task interference, and negative consequences. So, find out the source of the problem and then plan for the appropriate solution since training people on communication or motivation may not be the solution to process-related challenges. Neither is empowering untrained people to resolve challenges that are beyond their abilities and/or level of comprehension.

Convergent and Divergent Approaches to Problem-Solving: The *convergent* approach is the structured, logical, purposeful and deliberate method of solving problems. Most scientific researchers use this method to analyze the problem and find solutions to them in a formal way. This way others can follow the same procedure and get the same results. The advantages are consistency and standardization while the disadvantages might be "red tape" and eliminating the human factor, which can be disastrous at times. The *divergent* approach is creative, innovative, customized, situational, and spontaneous method of solving problems. It states that no two situations are alike and each situation may require different ways of solving the problem. What works for one person may not necessarily work for another person under the same circumstances. According to experts, creativity diverges from the straight-and-narrow path that convergent thinking requires one to follow. Advantages of the divergent approach are the human factor and situational attention while the disadvantages can include cost, uncertainty, and lack of direction. The convergent approach integrates divergent thinking to problem solving in dealing with problems that take a significant chunk of a manager's time and effort. Regardless of which approach is used, a manager should:

a. *Focus on what is important:* It is critical to separate what is urgent and important from things that are urgent but not important. Pareto Law states that eighty percent of the results flow from twenty percent of activities. So, some activities have much more impact than others and one should focus on these high leverage activities. The Pareto principle tells us that eighty percent of problems are caused by twenty percent of subordinates. Obviously we do not want to spend eighty percent of our time with twenty percent of our associates that constantly keep causing problems. This will cause managers to keep putting out fires and there will be no time to plan for future important activities. Proactively focusing on what is important will reduce the need for putting out fires and increases your time to appropriately *plan* your strategies; *organize*, train, and prepare your people as well as resources to get the job done;

lead your people in the right direction, and *control* the unpredictable circumstances as they arise.

b. *Delegate appropriately*: Appropriate delegation means fully preparing people to the point where they can competently do the job without needing anyone's help. Most people cannot let go of things they feel comfortable doing and things that they enjoy doing. However, as a manager you cannot keep doing all the tasks by yourself and be successful. J. C. Penny once said, "the wisest decision I ever made was to let go when I realized that I couldn't do it all by myself anymore." Proper delegation requires mutual understanding between the manager and the associate with regards to the desired outcome, guidelines and boundaries of what to do and what not to do, resources available to accomplish the desired outcome, responsibility and accountability for the successful progress of the task, and the consequence of effectively performing the task. If the way a job is being done is too complex or time consuming and if you think there might be better ways of doing it, then delegate the job to the laziest person in your department and soon you will discover the easiest way of getting it done.

c. *Listen empathically*: There are four methods of communication which are reading, writing, speaking, and listening. According to most workshop participants, listening is the most important of all four methods. Ironically, it has also been the most neglected one in the education and training arena. Most people do not receive much training in listening and consequently need to improve their listening skills. It is a skill that almost everyone can improve upon to help eliminate misunderstandings. Are you a good listener or an excellent listener? To find out, complete the Listening Scale Survey (located at the end of this chapter) now before moving on. Listening carefully with the intent to understand what the speaker is saying is one of the highest forms of a complement you can pay to a person. Someone wrote, "We do not really listen to each other, at least not all the time; instead of a true dialogue we carry on two parallel monologues. I talk. My companion talks. But what we are really concentrating on is how to sound good, how to make our points stronger, and how to outshine the person with whom we are speaking." Managers should listen empathically with their eyes and heart for more than just words. According to Covey (1989), the highest level of listening is empathic listening, listening with the eyes and the heart for *feelings* and *emotions*. It is a way of seeing things from the other person's perspective, the way he or she is seeing it. Empathic listening requires you to avoid autobiographical responses while trying to understand the message. Autobiographical responses are based on your background and experiences which the listener may not want to hear when he or she does not feel understood. Autobiographical responses also discourage people to open up and tell you their feelings and thoughts.

d. *Do not take other people's monkeys.* Bill Oncken, in his article co-authored with Donald L. Wass and titled "*Management Time:*

Who's got the monkey?" published in *Harvard Business Review* in 1974, stated that a monkey is a problem or the next move a person needs to make when the dialogue breaks. Problems are like monkeys and taking too many monkeys can rob you of your valuable discretionary time. Often managers seem to run out of time while their subordinates seem to run out of work. This is because managers are taking their subordinates' monkeys for various reasons. Oncken and Wass suggest five rules with regard to taking care of monkeys. First, monkeys should be fed or shot; otherwise it wastes the manager's time and resources. Second, the monkey population should be kept below the maximum number that the manager can handle during a given period of time. Third, monkeys should be fed by appointment rather than having to hunt for them. Fourth, monkeys should be fed face-to-face or person-to-person over a telephone rather than email and documents. Fifth, every monkey should have a scheduled "next feeding time" and an assigned "degree of initiative." Effectively following these rules will reduce a manager's problems and allow him/her to spend more time focusing on what is important. According to Oncken, the best way to reduce procrastination and increase the urgency and importance of a project is to delegate it to subordinates.

e. *Avoid becoming an automatic answering machine.* Managers can and do face problems many times daily and they must provide answers to them accurately and quickly. The repetition of solving these problems and experiences can cause managers to automatically respond and solve the employee's problems without fully listening to his or her concerns. Consequently, this tendency can cause anger, resentment, feelings of not being heard, not being part of the team, and dissatisfaction on the employee's part. Some managers carry this tendency to their home lives as well and try to be problem-solvers. This tendency can ruin personal relationships and cause bad listening habits. There are many conscious and unconscious habits that can be very disturbing to the employees and becoming an automatic answering machine is one of them. Many of these habits are unconscious and stem from the natural tendency to solve problems quickly because of the mindset that "we are managers and it is our job to provide the answers." This mentality has been reinforced by the fast-paced work environment and the managers' expertise and experience. While managers may have total familiarity with most problem situations because of repetition and the nature of an employee's job, the employee does not know this and may think the manager does not care about his/her problem. While some of these habits are unconscious and routine, others are purposeful, some are trivial, some are therapeutic, and some are caused by the personality traits of the manager.

Using IDEAS to Solve Problems

The IDEAS model is a structured (convergent) problem-solving process for identifying and solving a problem. Instead of waiting for a solution to pop into your head from up above, the IDEAS model can help get you to the best solution one step at a time with available resources. IDEAS helps you think critically and creatively to investigate the problem, develop alternatives, examine and evaluate proposed alternatives, accept and administer the chosen alternative, and survey the results for success of current and future opportunities. Edward de Bono (1991), the guru of creative thinking in his book "*I Am Right You Are Wrong,*" said that the most effective critical thinking for each person is actually creative thinking, which is the ability of an individual to generate alternative and timely solutions. There is a need for attention to this type of thinking that is productive, constructive, generative, and creative. Reactive thinking and problem-solving, which are realities for most organizations, will not equip people to improve society. This is why a manager needs to proactively focus on planning and preparing others in order to avoid putting out fires and solving problems. The IDEAS model helps you solve significant problems and the following are the five steps of problem solving:

1. *Identify and Investigate the Problem.* Once a problem has been identified, the problem-solving process begins. It is important to make sure the right problem has been identified. So, the first and foremost important step is to *define the problem* statement accurately and clearly. Solution imagineering is the second step to identifying and investigating the problem. *Solution imagineering* involves mentally seeing the problem solved and its prospective results accomplished. The accomplished results can clarify the objectives of solving the problem. This can also be accomplished through brainstorming or "Six Hat Thinking" principles. The third step is to *investigate the real cause* of the problem. Often, the real cause of the problem is hidden underneath the surface. Just like an iceberg has its major parts under the water and its tip above the water, real causes of the problem can often be hidden under all the symptoms. A cause-and-effect diagram can be used to brainstorm and diagnose the real cause of the problem. Always measure twice and cut once because if you are solving the wrong problem, things will get worse. You cannot climb to the right place if your ladder is leaning against the wrong wall.

2. *Develop Alternatives.* Most people are able to form a solution to general problems based on their intuitive senses as soon as they come in contact with the problem. The truth of the matter is that most often solutions are based on past experiences and developed paradigms instead of facts surrounding the current issue or problem. While one may intuitively have the solution in mind, it is best to generate several other alternatives through brainstorming or "Six Hat Thinking" which is another form of brainstorming for creativity, formality and discipline. The main purpose of this step is to generate ideas, and the first rule of any brainstorming session is not to evaluate ideas as they are being generated.

3. *Evaluate and Examine Alternatives.* Upon successful generation of several workable alternatives, one must evaluate and examine them for cost and benefit analysis as it pertains to all stakeholders. One must analyze them, and then attempt to evaluate their benefits with regards to all stakeholders and check their alignment with one's personal and professional values. After summing the values and costs, one may determine whether to pursue an alternative or keep searching for better solutions. There are many roads that can lead you from here to your destination. However, the shortest road is the *"straight path"* which you should travel.

4. *Accept and Administer an Alternative.* The chosen alternative should solve the problem efficiently, productively, and with the least cost being imposed on the stakeholders. The alternative that respects everyone's rights and maximizes the benefits to everyone involved should be chosen and implemented. Implementation takes time, resources, planning, budgeting, and organizing all the related elements. The way a solution is implemented can make all the difference in the world because a solution is no better than the worst action taken to implement it. Implementation requires proper planning, organizing, control, and execution. Remember, implementation is an ***IMP***ortant ***LE***adership ele***MENT*** because knowledge by itself does not produce anything. It is properly applied or executed knowledge that produces results including power.

5. *Survey the Results and Suggest Improvements.* Once a decision is implemented, it is very important to follow through and examine the actual results. This can serve as an educational experience and as a confirmation tool to make sure the original root cause of the problem is eliminated. Upon close examination of the results one should take proper action and do what is necessary.

Always make a decision and proceed. It is through convergent and divergent problem-solving techniques that managers discover new opportunities, alternatives, and better methods. However, it is through determination, persistency, and decision-making abilities that managers get results and make things happen. We live in an imperfect world and our decisions need to be made in a timely manner with the available information. Because of deadlines, problem-solvers will inevitably need to make decisions through *"satisficing"* with the limited information in the allotted time, and they will need to become effective time managers. Overall, it well worth it for busy managers and professionals to proactively reflect upon their personal values and priorities on regular basis.

Summary
Effective time management and goal-setting are important for twenty-first century professionals and managers who often juggle many important issues simultaneously. The creation of a mission is a great start for one's management of time based on priorities. The priorities can then be linked with one's daily, weekly and monthly activities. One can focus on those "high leverage activities" or "big

rocks" in order to achieve one's life-long goals. Professional achievement of goals and sales or revenue targets can be planned since they fit into the category of big rocks. However, one must be clear about the importance of various roles, and thus should never allow high priority tasks to be at the mercy of tasks that add no value to one's purpose in life. The creation of a personal mission statement and value clarification can greatly assist in such a prioritization process.

Challenges and problems are common daily occurrences for today's workforce. Most large corporations provide the training needed to equip their associates for effectively dealing with such issues to efficiently solve these problems. The training sessions focus on a problem-solving process/model along with time management, stress management, project management, and effective communication topics since they are all relative to effective decision-making. As such, business leaders and managers must provide similar training and development opportunities in order to fully prepare their employees for effectively dealing with their day-to-day's operational challenges. Problem-solving and time management skills can help the workforce effectively manage stress and be competitive.

Listening Scale Survey

You can rate yourself on the listening behaviors using the Listening Scale Survey (LSS) and the following guidelines:

4= Almost always
3= Most of the time
2= Some of the time
1= Almost never

Place a check mark in the appropriate box. Multiply the rating number at the top of the columns by the number of check marks in that rating area and record the results in the sub-total columns. Add the sub-totals and place the results in the area marked "Total Overall."

	When listening I do the following:	4	3	2	1
1.	I pay attention, even though the subject may bore me				
2.	I refrain from finishing the other person's sentences				
3.	I wait for the speaker to finish before evaluating the message				
4.	I maintain eye contact				
5.	I listen for feelings as well as subject matter				
6.	I show nonverbal responses to demonstrate I'm listening: nodding, smiling, leaning forward				
7.	I give brief verbal responses: "Uh-hum, M-m-m, Oh"				
8.	I stop myself from interrupting the one speaking to me				
9.	I seek to reduce or eliminate distractions				
10.	I ask questions only to clarify something said				
11.	I demonstrate I have an open mind and do not respond negatively to the other's ideas or feelings				
12.	I often paraphrase what I hear to make sure I have heard it correctly				
13.	I work to make myself really want to listen				
14.	I listen carefully to understand the main message				
15.	I maintain emotional control, no matter what is said				
16.	*Sub-totals*				
17.	*Total Overall*				

Now that you have determined your overall total from the Listening Scale Survey (LSS), you can use the following ranges of numbers to determine your listening score area:

50-60	-Congratulations! You are an excellent listener.
40-49	-Good going! You are a good listener, and you could be even better.
30-39	-Keep working on it. Listening skills will help you solve problems. Practice the skills of active and empathic listening when you can.
15-29	-You really should get serious about learning to listen. Take classes and learn active listening skills. Try to consciously focus on hearing others and what they are trying to communicate both verbally and non-verbally. Once you have mastered active listening techniques, then, focus on using empathic listening skills when emotions are involved, when you don't understand the speaker, and when the other person does not feel understood.

CHAPTER FIVE

5 - STRESS MANAGEMENT

C hange can bring about an invisible pandemic known as stress. Major and continuous change can create a strong culture, where core values are intensely held and widely shared, where a high level of stress is the norm. Today's rate of change has been much greater than the past; yet, this is perhaps an initial start compared to the changes for tomorrow. Just look at the population growth which, for the first time ever in recorded history reached one billion in the 1860s. In the 1930s, the population doubled to two billion, and then it doubled again in 1975 to four billion people. As of 2007, there are over six and one-half billion individuals on earth which within a decade should pass seven billion, despite the fact that many couples in developing nations are having fewer children. In the early 1980s, people did not have personal computers; yet, many professionals today cannot effectively do their jobs without a computer and access to email or the internet. Pritchett and Pound, in their booklet entitled "*A Survival Guide to the Stress of Organizational Change,*" suggest that people should accommodate change, align their behaviors with it, and use it to their advantage instead of seeing it as an enemy. They suggest that in today's rate of change, sometimes one just has to "give up" or surrender to the change; another option would be to simply "toughen up" by developing higher levels of tolerance for adapting to change; and yet at other times, one has to "wise up" by not allowing self-induced stress to take over one's life.

Stress management is about being healthy and happy. With regards to happiness, Mahatma Gandhi states that "Happiness is when what you think, what you say, and what you do are in harmony." This relates to the consistency of what goes into one's heart, mind, and daily habits. Such a consistency can be best achieved when one's purpose and mission in life are clear. Dr. Viktor Frankl, a psychologist, states that each person has his/her own specific vision or mission in life; everyone must carry out a concrete goal that demands fulfillment. Therein he/she cannot be replaced, nor can his/her life be repeated, thus, everyone's task is unique as his/her specific opportunity to implement it.

For effective management of stress, one should work on building good rapport with one's colleagues and surroundings by adapting to changes that cannot be altered. Kevin Hogan, speaker and author, is reported to have said that "Building rapport begins with you. The entire process of building rapport is built on the foundation of concern, caring, compassion, interest, and a desire for the well-being of your customer." Besides having a good rapport with others, one must learn to "play." Brian Sutton, professor of education, states that "The opposite of play isn't work. It's depression. To play is to act out and be willful and committed as if one is assured of one's prospects." Good rapport with others and having fun at work can go a long way in creating happiness and success. It has been said by Orison Swett Marden, author, that, "The greatest thing a man can do in this world is to make the most possible out of the stuff that has been given him. This is success, and there is no other." It should be noted that success and happiness do not come from perfection but rather action. Ralph Marston, author, said "Hold yourself to a high standard, to be sure. But don't let that stop you. Though perfection is a worthy aim, there's plenty of good you can accomplish before you get there."Anne Frank, diarist, said "How wonderful it is that nobody need wait a single moment before starting to improve the world." One must remember that "It's not the load that breaks you down, it's the way you carry it," as stated by Lena Horne, singer and actress.

Dr. Randi Sims, professor of stress management at Nova Southeastern University mentions that since it is neither possible nor advantageous to prevent or avoid all stress from one's personal or professional life, control or management of stress becomes the key issue to one's success in day-to-day activities. Perhaps it is true that "the absence of stress is death." According to most experts, the first step in effectively managing stress is recognizing that there is excessive stress in one's personal or professional life, or both. The first step requires one to recognize the typical symptoms associated with stress, while linking the causes may be difficult at time to determine and associate with the consequences. In general, the typical symptoms of excessive stress can be physical, psychological, behavioral, or any combination of these or other such illnesses. The second step, after recognizing the symptoms, is to begin to look for the causes. Of course, the fact is that some stress cannot be avoided or controlled. As such, its awareness, proper planning, and balancing one's important goals can help in managing it. It is best to remember that stress can come from how one interprets an event or person, and not necessarily from that event or person directly. The effective management and control of stress is the final step or objective of an effective stress management program. Sims (2006) recommends that the individual differences between employees as well as their jobs and departments should be taken into consideration when planning a stress management program. Sims further states that the best way to know if a person will be comfortable with a stress management technique is to try it. While using a particular technique just one time will not always provide the maximum benefit possible, a person will be able to tell if he or she would be comfortable in giving the technique an opportunity for long-term stress management. According to Sims, once a specific technique has been used repeatedly for stress management, the individual begins to experience the benefits of it more quickly. Once a person comfortably practices a few stress management techniques, he or she will begin to feel relaxed just by getting ready to initiate the technique.

Stress Management

Modern life is fraught with pressures and frustrations. One only has to watch the news where there is 24 hour coverage of wars, terrorist attacks, earthquakes, tsunamis and hurricanes. Traffic jams, loss of electric power, downsizing, rising health costs, marital difficulties, drugs, alcohol, bankruptcies, corporation failures, and organizational confusion all add to those factors that not only the mind/body must adapt, but this 'wear and tear' may easily eventually result in physical or mental diseases (illness).

This mind/body adaptive mechanism due to change which is a constant factor has been labeled stress. The reactions to stress, however, are unique to each individual. Also when good interesting things happen to us- promotion on the job, increase in the quality of one's life, challenging work, new love, travel, good food and gatherings, spiritual peace; positive interpersonal relationships, good friends – cause adaptative reactions of this mind/body continuum as well. The remarkable factor is that whether good or bad, the body reacts the same physiologically.

In order to understand how to manage stress, one has to understand what stress is. We are fortunate that the development of theories, concepts and management techniques have evolved into a remarkable plethora of research results allowing anyone to not only understand the process but to be stress management specific! It is also important to become acquainted with other concepts of human behavior because as Hans Seyle stated in 1956, life without stress basically amounts to death. The methodology has to be holistic with approaches that understand mind-body connections. The concept of stress has its history in the early experiments and writings of Cannon, Seyle, Freidman and Rosenman, Wolff and Wolff, Benson, Holmes and Rae, Oixfeill, Eysenck, and Lazarus to name a few.

The earliest pioneers, Seyle and Cannon, provided the basic framework for the evolving understanding of the stress response as later researchers pursued their specialties. Hans Seyle was an endocrinologist who was able to study the body's reaction to various stimuli. Although he experimented with rats in the laboratory, he saw many patients in hospital in which he could not find a specific cause for their illness, virus, germs, etc. and determine a diagnosis and therefore labeled them as suffering from a "*syndrome of being sick.*" It is alleged that Seyle was having an after dinner drink at the home of a friend who was an engineer. His friend was working and calculating the stress and strain of certain metals as important information for the construction of bridges throughout Canada. Seyle likened this to the human body as it responds to the many stresses and strains of their internal and external environments. It is at this time, that the term stress was used to describe Seyle's idea of the human body as reacting to stress in a three phase process which he called the General Adaptation Syndrome (G.A.S.).

1. Phase I is the *alarm phase*: The body's first reaction to a stressor. This phase is comparable to Cannons' "fight or flight syndrome."
2. Phase II is the *reaction phase*: When the stressor is continuous the body reaches a "plateau" and resistance rises above normal.
3. Phase III is the *exhaustion phase*: When the stressor persists for a long time and the adaptation energy is exhausted; manifestations of physical and/or emotional illnesses and sometimes death appears.

Seyle (1974) also describes positive, energizing stress, as *eustress* and negative non-motivating stress as *distresss*. The interesting phenomenon is that both are experienced the same physiologically.

The first definitive research on stress was done by Walter B. Cannon, a well known physiologist from Harvard Medical School. He was the first to describe in detail the body's reaction to stress. Cannon experimented initially with cats and the kinds of manipulations he did to them would be condemned today by PETA (People for Ethical Treatment of Animals) or any local chapter or society for the prevention of cruelty to animals.

Cannon (1932) indicated that a reaction to stress could elicit either a confrontation (attack) on the stressor; running away from it or being in such a state of shock that one becomes immobilized. He proved that the body prepares itself by attempting to get as much energy as possible to the muscular-skeletal system in order to fight or run away. He called this reaction the "fight or flight syndrome." The body systems that are associated with strength and energy speed up their activity; those that are not involved slow down or shut down. There are also "surface reactions" like perspiration, pupil dilation and pilo-erection.

These two pioneering researchers paved the way for experiments in the U.S.A., England, Germany, Japan, and other parts of the world. Most have focused on other causes and reactions to stress; stressors, physiological and emotional responses, mind-body connections, stress, and disease. There have been explorations in finding effective methods to manage stress and the resurrection of ancient methods, such as prayer, yoga, meditation, and hypnosis as being useful.

A brief example of earlier experiments indicates some of the ground breaking research of the following experts:

(a) Friedman and Rosenman (1974) who identified the relations between stress and coronary disease. They developed a diagnostic questionnaire to determine one's susceptibility to coronary illness.

b) Desmond O'Neill (1960) a London psychiatrist wrote one of the first books on psychosomatic medicine.

c) Kasamatsu and Hirai (1966) studied meditation and noted changes in brain waves during the meditative state.

d) Hans Eysenck (1988) from London's Maudsley Clinic, researched a cancer-prone personality and a coronary heart disease prone personality.

e) Robert Adler of the University of Rochester, Ornestein and Sobel (1987) studied the chemical basis of communication between the mind and the body. They focused upon illness and healing effects the mind can have upon the body.

f) Dr. Candace Pert, a neuroscientist and the former section chief of brain biochemistry at the National Institute of Mental Health, investigated chemicals that send messages between cells to various parts of the brain and between the brain and other parts of the body.

Hundreds of these brain message transmitters (called neuropeptides) have been found that are produced by the brain itself. Pert believes some of these neuropathies are also produced in small amounts by the macrophages- white blood cells that ingest and destroy bacteria and viruses (Squires 1987). In addition, "the macrophages are attracted to neuropathies produced by the brain to fight off invasion of bacteria. For instance, macrophages will also travel to help combat the invasion. Since relaxation and some forms of visualization result in the production of neuropathies (for example, beta-endorphins) it may be possible to purposefully cause the brain to produce more of these substances, hereby making the immunological system more effective. The result may be less disease" (Greenberg, 1993).

At present, it appears that stress in all of its aspects, is widely researched throughout the world. The International Congress on Stress which had their first congress in 1988 was formed to assemble leading authorities worldwide to present cutting-edge research advances.

What is Stress?

Stress has many meanings to different people. It also depends on what aspects of stress that researchers are organizing under their focus. Simply, anything to which the body has to react or adapt to can be termed stress. Seyle's description of stress is still valid in that eustress describes the good or positive things that happen. *Eustress* is motivating and can initiate creativity and positive mental attitudes. *Distress* describes negative de-motivating stress that can oftentimes place an individual in a situation of inactivity or inertia. There are, inevitably hundreds of definitions that can be found in the literature. The most common may be that it is defined as a response or as a stimulus. It would appear that the most popular accepted concept of stress is that there is a stressor (which can be anything) that triggers off or has a response to (stress) either Eustress or Distress.

Research over the years has established this fact: The body and mind are consistently adjusting to balance and equilibration. 'Homeostasis,' the term used for physiological "balance," and 'equilibration,' or emotional balance, must be maintained. Any change or threat to equilibrium can be either eustress or distress. This concept may best be illustrated visually as demonstrated in Figure 5.1. In general:

1. The mind/body is in a state of homeostasis and equilibration.
2. There is a stressor or stressors.
3. The evaluative thoughts of the mind cause emotional responses which (emotions) are transduced into actual physiological responses that can be measured.

This is a psychosomatic response reaction. Some examples of this would be, learning of the accidental death of a spouse; being fired from a job; and being diagnosed with cancer. The term originates from the Greek word "psyche" meaning (mind/soul) and 'soma' meaning body. On the other hand:

1. The body / mind are in states of homeostasis and equilibration.
2. There is a stressor (s) trauma to the body which destabilizes mind and body.
3. The effect of the destabilization, if continued, causes mental/emotional states. That is, the body's adaptative processes, affect one's mental state.

This is a somato-psychic reaction and must be understood in the context that the physiological state of the body triggers off, through the evaluative processes of the mind, emotional states that are either eustress or distress. One example is having a mastectomy for breast cancer. The depression caused by having cancer, the self-esteem concept after a mastectomy and the constant worry as to whether cancer would come back, can trigger off a distress response.

Figure 5.1 – Mind and Body Homeostasis

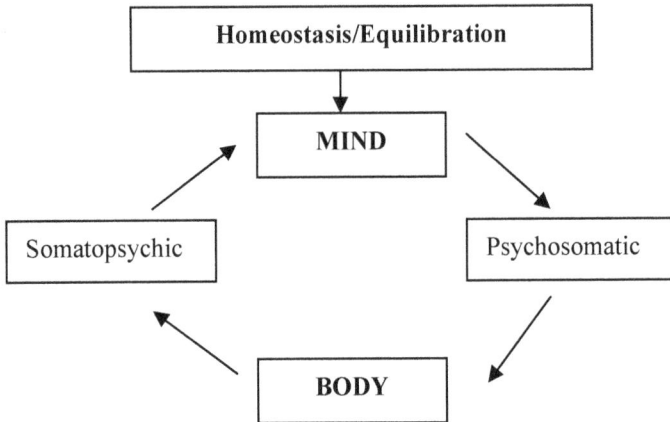

```
        ┌─────────────────────────────────────┐
        │     Homeostasis/Equilibration        │
        └─────────────────────────────────────┘
                        │
                        ▼
              ┌──────────────────┐
              │       MIND        │
              └──────────────────┘
           ↗                        ↘
┌──────────────────┐          ┌──────────────────┐
│  Somatopsychic   │          │  Psychosomatic   │
└──────────────────┘          └──────────────────┘
           ↖                        ↙
              ┌──────────────────┐
              │       BODY        │
              └──────────────────┘
```

It should be noted that these are real body/mind states. They are not imaginations or delusions. When an individual experiences for no known reason, illnesses, and is constantly imagining a disease, taking lots of medication, and complaining all of the time about one's health, this may be described as a hypochondrical reaction. The person is usually labeled as a hypochondriac. This reaction over a period of time could develop into a psychosomatic illness.

Stress, therefore, develops when the pressures and demands in one's life exceed one's ability to cope (distress). When the individual is motivated, creative, and finds balance in the three major environments in which they function, the stress becomes eustress.

Stress has been around from the inception of the beginning of life and even though stressors change with every year and stage of human development, much more is known about this process. More than 200 million Americans take medication for stress-related illnesses and symptoms. American organizations are losing more than $200 billion each year in workplace accidents, absenteeism, drug abuse, violence, medical insurance, and productivity (Edstronm, 1993). In England, the government sponsored a survey in the spring of 2004 to examine psychosocial working conditions in the British workplace prior to the launch of the Management Standards for Stress. Areas such as work, alcohol consumption and ill health, best practices in rehabilitating employees, reducing psycho-social risks, etc. were studied with recommendations.

Dr. Ester Sternberg, director of the Integration Neural Immune Program at the NIH's Maternal Institute of Mental Health (NIMH) has been rediscovering the links between the brain and the immune system. According to Dr. Steinberg, "if you're chronically stressed, the part of the brain that controls the stress response is going to be constantly pumping out a lot of stress hormones. The immune cells are being bathed in molecules which are essentially telling them to stop fighting. And so in situations of chronic stress your immune cells are less able to respond to an invader like a bacteria or a virus (Wein & Harrison 2000). One should not get the idea that all this is bad because as previously mentioned, eustress is good for you. Dr. Steinberg further comments (Wein & Harrison, 2000) that the objective here should not be to get rid of stress completely because this is impossible; stress is part of life and part of life is stress. We need to be able to use stress response optimally in stressful situations.

To summarize what we now know about stress (eustress and distress), the following should be noted:

1. Stress is a neuro-endocrine process that affects the metabolism of the body and has an input on every system of the body via the Nervous system, Immune System, Cardiovascular System, Digestive System, the Skin and the Muscular-Skeletal System.
2. A stressor is a stimulus that 'triggers off' the "fight or flight" response which is comparable to Seyle's Alarm state. Stressors can be physiological, biological, psycho-social, external and/or internal.
3. Psycho-somatic disease is real. It is not just "in the mind" (which is a hypochondrical reaction). It involves the mind and the body.
4. Stress related diseases include migraine headaches, backaches, asthma attacks, some cancers, allergies, stroke, coronary heart disease, hypertensions, tension headaches, and neck and shoulder pains.
5. Distress, especially chronic distress, tends to make your immune system more susceptible to colds, infections, inflammations, lupus, some cancers, and allergic reactions.
6. Stress begins with life situations that become very difficult to understand and which overwhelms individuals in any of the three environments in which humans primarily function (intimate, workplace and leisure).
7. After years of research and the understanding of mind/body processes, stress management techniques are "management-specific."
8. Work related stressors and those internal and external factors that impact employer and employees in organizations have been identified. Stress management techniques can restore health and improve productivity.
9. Knowledge, techniques and practice allows for the proper control and well being of the individual as distress can be transformed into eustress.

Job and Workplace Stress (Holistically)

We have defined and described stress as being an adaptative reaction to a stimulus which holistically effects the individual at emotional, mental, neurological, biochemical, and physical levels at any given instant of time. Job and workplace stress have their own peculiarities. The individual reacts to workplace stressors in a manner by which his/her individual characteristics (e.g. personality traits, anxiety levels, behavior patterns) deal with organizational and extra organized sources of stress (stressors).

We have also examined the expensive "fall out" of job and workplace stress in absenteeism, drug and alcohol abuse, poor decision making, hospitalizations, rising health benefit costs, violence, burnout, negative interpersonal relationships, and decreased productivity. We will try to provide managers and supervisors with information that can be useful in prevention, intervention and employee assistance advice.

Researchers state that stress prevention and management strategies can include: making person-environment fit; organizational programs such as employee assistance and wellness; and individual approaches such as cognitive techniques, relaxation training, meditation, and feedback. Gibson, Ivancevich, Donnelly and Konopaske (2005) suggested a model of stressors, stress and outcomes which are self-explanatory (see Figure 5.2).

Job-related stress is of particular concern to the study of change and stress management. Some jobs are more stress-producing than others. For instance, air traffic controllers, who face the daily pressures of protecting the lives of thousands of people, have an occupation that is considered highly stressful. Although this is one example, every job has potential stressors. Some of the most common stressors for the 21st century's global employees and managers are as follows:

1. *Information load.* Whether individuals are overloaded or under-loaded, they are likely to experience stress. The under-loaded individual is apathetic and bored from being cut off from necessary communication, whereas the overloaded employee feels harried and frantic. In either case absenteeism and turnover increase, and productivity decreases.
2. *Role ambiguity.* Whenever employees are not sure what their job is or the way it relates to other jobs in the organization, role ambiguity occurs. This in turn leads to confusion, lack of focus, and stress.
3. *Role conflict.* Stress occurs when various people seem to be expecting different things from a person. Supervisors are particularly susceptible to role conflict because both management and their subordinates often look to them as their representative. As they try to satisfy everyone's expectations, they often experience considerable personal stress.
4. *Occupational change.* Whenever the work environment changes, stress is inevitable. All change brings some uncertainty with it, and uncertainty interferes with one's mental and physical homeostasis.
5. *Stress carriers.* Employees are often brought into contact with Type A persons, who force stress upon them. The grumpy boss, the forgetful secretary, and the complaining major customer are stress carriers.
6. *Physical environment.* Noise, lighting, uncomfortable furniture, and temperature are examples of physical surroundings that can produce stress.

Figure 5.2 – Stress and Stressors (Gibson *et al.*, 2005)

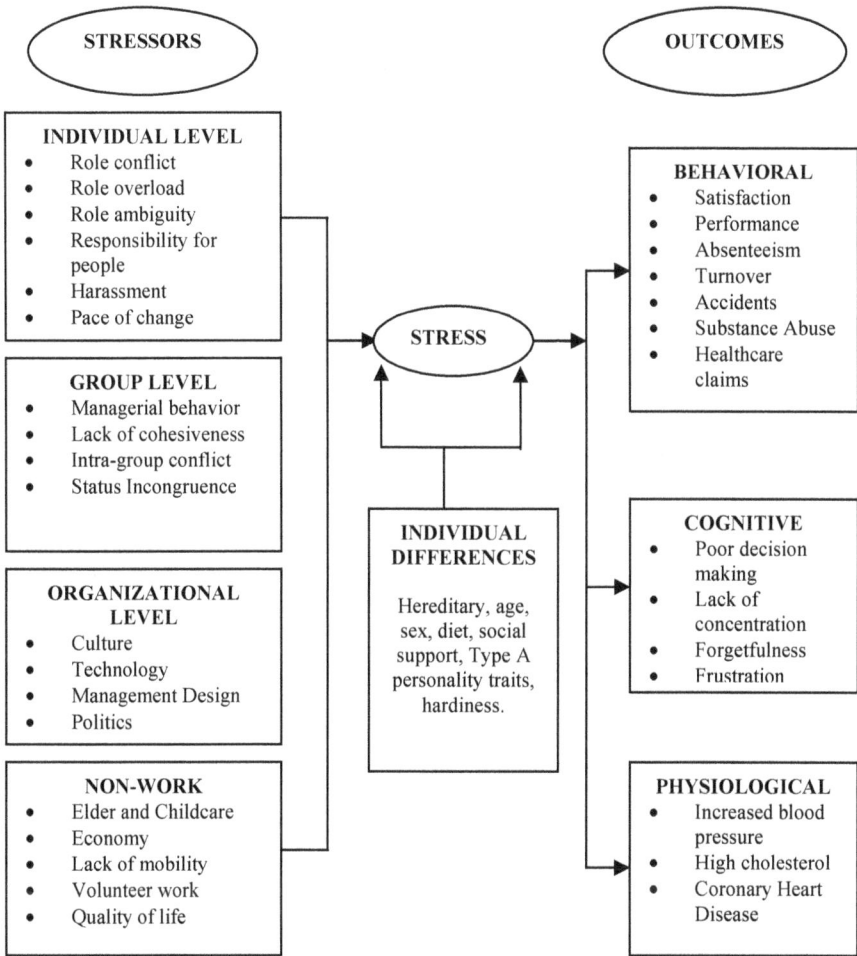

STRESSORS		OUTCOMES

INDIVIDUAL LEVEL
- Role conflict
- Role overload
- Role ambiguity
- Responsibility for people
- Harassment
- Pace of change

GROUP LEVEL
- Managerial behavior
- Lack of cohesiveness
- Intra-group conflict
- Status Incongruence

ORGANIZATIONAL LEVEL
- Culture
- Technology
- Management Design
- Politics

NON-WORK
- Elder and Childcare
- Economy
- Lack of mobility
- Volunteer work
- Quality of life

STRESS

INDIVIDUAL DIFFERENCES

Hereditary, age, sex, diet, social support, Type A personality traits, hardiness.

BEHAVIORAL
- Satisfaction
- Performance
- Absenteeism
- Turnover
- Accidents
- Substance Abuse
- Healthcare claims

COGNITIVE
- Poor decision making
- Lack of concentration
- Forgetfulness
- Frustration

PHYSIOLOGICAL
- Increased blood pressure
- High cholesterol
- Coronary Heart Disease

Pritchett and Pound, in the booklet entitled "*A Survival Guide to the Stress of Organizational Change,*" highlight many of the destructive behaviors that people must abandon if they are to manage change without being too stressed. Pritchett and Pound mention fifteen common mistakes and assumptions people make and they are as follows:

1. Expect someone else to reduce one's stress.
2. Decide not to change.
3. Act like a victim.
4. Try to play a new game by the old rules.
5. Shoot for a low-stress work setting.
6. Try to control the uncontrollable.
7. Choose your own pace of change.

8. Fail to abandon the expendable.
9. Slow down.
10. Be afraid of the future.
11. Pick the wrong battles.
12. Psychologically unplug from the job.
13. Avoid new assignments.
14. Try to eliminate uncertainty and instability.
15. Assume that "caring management' would or should keep employees comfortable.

Of course, the above assumptions are common mistakes that professionals in the twenty-first century environment should avoid if they are to reduce the level of stress and change with the times. As mentioned by experts, there are numerous forces driving major changes that impact people's day to day activities; and the major forces seem to be people, technology, information, innovation, and globalization. Instead of making the wrong assumptions in this new economy, it is perhaps more productive to surrender to upcoming changes by aligning one's behavior and expectations with it, while using the changes to one's advantage. A manager or worker should not expect others to come along and relieve his/her stress. Instead, today's professionals should put themselves in charge of managing the dynamic pressure since they are probably the best persons in their lives who will be able to do much to lighten their psychological load. When you seem to be going against the tides or against the whole world, just think of what Robert Orben said: "Sometimes I get the feeling that the whole world is against me, but deep down I know that is not true as some of the smaller countries are neutral."

Verspeji (1989) researched several American organizations to determine the kinds of stressors that impact organizations' personnel, externally as well as internally. Verspeji found the following as the frequent causes of stress.

1. High technology helpers. The rapid change of computer/information technology initially initiate the stressor of change and doubts as to whether one would be able to functionally operate the technology computer breakdown, jammed fax machines, new systems, etc. all contribute to this factor.
2. Supervisory problems dealing with alcohol or drug abuse by employees. The "bizarre" behaviors and rapid mood changes of drug abusers pose managerial understanding and control difficulties in the workplace.
3. Supervisory malfunction. It is common in these modern times for supervisors to have undergraduate and/or graduate degrees. Yet, many supervisors have no insight into their proper behavior and have difficulty in supervising, causing frustration, sabotage, de-motivation, and job change.
4. Quotas, deadlines and reduced staff levels to complete job. Downsizing appears to have had more negative affects on organizations especially in job insecurity, non-loyalty and morale.
5. Work environment. Social diversity issues, temperature, obsolete equipment, noise, toxic chemicals, etc.

6. Limited workplace privacy. The lack of adequate personal space gives rise to claustrophobia, monitoring of phone calls, contents of letters, and confidentiality.
7. Job insecurity. Increasing mergers and takeovers; acquisitions; downsizing
8. Corporate policies on smoking, AIDS, drug testing. All of the above are prominent stressors
9. Overload. Lots of work and not enough time to do it. The fears of not keeping up, having to take work home are stressor factors
10. "Two Places at Once" syndrome. The ability of trying to balance work and family appears to affect women more than men. It is reasonable to assume that many frustrations are displaced in either of these two environments (intimate and workplace) and can also negatively affect one's leisure environment as well, especially with alcohol or drug abuse as compensatory factors.

According to experts, the main distinction between work and non-work is blurred, overlaps, and is significant in a decision's analysis of stress (Gibson et al., 2005).

Job and work stress have widespread implications as well as having to pinpoint the specific stressors and analyze individual characteristics. The work environment itself, may pose difficulties with toxic chemicals, dust, social density issues temperature variations, dangerous tasks, high noise levels, poor lighting, and unpleasant odors. All of these can lead to emotional as well as physical difficulties. Group and organizational stressors may include organizational politics, organizational culture, and intra- and inter-group relationships, downsizing, lack of performance feedback, sexual harassment, promotion challenges, and inadequate career development difficulties. Non-Job stressors are those caused by factors outside of the organization that have impact on the individuals' performance and productivity. Some practical observations and advice for managers and supervisors are as follows:

1. Realize that what is a stressor for one employee may not be a stressor for another.
2. Be on the lookout for *burnout*. Employees who are over-zealous, workaholic and are always helping others as part of their job may exhibit signs of frequent depressive bouts, constant self-denigration, being emotionally exhausted, frequent visits to doctors, and perfectionist behavior.
3. When "out of character" employees are having interpersonal problems with fellow employees, customers, clients and management may be increasing levels of distress.
4. Management should have in place employee assistance programs that are readily available with the highest standards of confidentiality.
5. The organizations' physical plant should be as "stressor free" as possible with areas for relaxation, adequate temperature control, quick reaction-time to technological/physical problems, and attention to noise levels.
6. Individuals should try to be consistently positive in the three environments in which they function. A good balance between intimate, workplace and leisure environments cause less negative displacement consistency and equilibrium.
7. Practice effective interpersonal skills especially communication and problem-solving.

8. Learn how to set limits which prevents overload. Also learn how to say "No"!
9. Watch your emotional pressure points.
10. Don't waste time feeling guilty about what doesn't get done.
11. Try to enjoy whatever you are doing.
12. Ask yourself if your reaction of situations will help that is:
    a. Improve my productivity
    b. Relationship with others
    c. Is it worth putting pressure on my piece of mind and self confidence
    d. Improve my overall health
13. Don't sweat the small stuff. Change the way you evaluate situations. Remember it is how we analyze, evaluate or perceive situations that initiate our emotional responses.
14. Work smarter rather than harder.
15. Don't get involved in routine detail that should be delegated.
16. Attempt to "clean up your act." Avoid a general lack of self-discipline, personal disorganization, cluttered environments (desk, rooms, etc.).
17. Practice being an optimist and build on successes.
18. Do what is right and you will sleep better. *Ethics* is about doing what is right, regardless of whether anyone is watching on not. Be ethical and live according to universal principles, while standing for good, fair and just causes for all.

Research results on stress, psycho-remedial approaches, religious and spiritual cures and sometimes just reverting to ancient cultural practices have created literally hundreds of techniques for managing stress. The influxes of Eastern philosophical and religious belief systems have had an impact on the Western world and have stimulated other groups to find their cultural healing.

Exploring these methods has given valuable and practical guidelines as to what stress really is and the techniques are more than aiming to "hit the bulls eye" in a reasonably short time frame, restore the individual to a level of homeostasis and equilibrium. This approach suggests three basic areas that managers and supervisors can explore in order to understand these processes and to implement a program for effective stress management. The fact is that the stress response (neuro-endocrine) is one of the most damaging and comprehensive physiological reactions that alters the activity of body's only two regulatory systems. No organ system can avoid being affected in some way by the experience of stress. Most of the stress one experiences originates in the mind (psychogenic). To recap our knowledge of stress psychophysiology there are three linked facets:
1. The functional organization of the human brain.
2. The physiological workings of the mind-body links.
3. The physiological pathways and somatic effects of stress (Greenberg, 1993). The better you understand how your body and mind operates the greater will be your capacity to gain control over your own health. To this goal, therefore, three approaches will be explored in order to focus

on those factors that are essential in helping one understand and manage stress. These are:

a. Analyzing the three environments in which we operate/function: intimate, workplace, and leisure.
b. Understanding basic concepts of human behavior
c. Exploring the psycho-somatic stress pathway so as to apply a stress-specific management technique.

According to Greenberg (1993), the goal is to reduce the amount of distress and to change it into eustress. An optimal amount of stress is healthy and growth promoting. Adaptation to the changing circumstances and a healthy level of stress are essential for life and growth. Table 5.1 demonstrates how all encompassing the stress response is to the physical, cognitive, emotional, and behavioral aspects of human behavior.

Table 5.1 – Stress Responses

Physical	Cognitive	Emotional	Behavioral
Fatigue	blaming someone	Anxiety	changes in activity
Nausea	confusion	guilt	changes in speech
appetite change	poor attention span	denial	patterns
Twitches	poor decisions	severe panic (rare)	withdrawal
Insomnia	heightened or lowered	emotional shock	emotional outbursts
weight change	alertness	fear	suspiciousness
Colds	poor concentration	uncertainty	change in usual
chest pain or	memory problems	loss of emotional	communication
tightness	forgetfulness	control	loss or increase of
Difficulty breathing	Hyper vigilance	depression	appetite
elevated BP	difficulty identifying	inappropriate	increased alcohol
rapid heart rate	familiar objects or	emotional response	use, drug and
heart palpitation	people	apprehension	tobacco use
speech difficulty	increased or decreased	feeling overwhelmed	inability to rest
Thirst	awareness of	intense anger	antisocial acts
headaches	surroundings	agitation	nonspecific bodily
visual difficulties	distractibility	dread	complaints
vomiting	inattention	frustration	hyperactive to
grinding of teeth	poor problem-solving	the "blues"	environment
feelings of weakness	poor abstract	bad temper	increased startle
dizziness	thinking	nightmares	reflex
shock symptoms	loss of time, place or	crying spells	pacing
"freezing" or "going	person orientation	irritability	erratic movements
blanket"	disturbed thinking	"no one cares"	change in sexual
fainting	nightmares	nervous laugh	functioning
sweating	intrusive images	easily discouraged	low productivity
hot or cold sensations	negative attitude	little joy	isolation
dry mouth	whirling mind	worrying	intolerance of others
shallow breathing	lethargy	resentfulness	lashing out
stomach or intestinal	no new ideas	loneliness	hiding
distress	boredom	distrust of others	clamming up
muscle tightness	spacing out	emptiness	lowered sex drive
muscle aches	negative self-talk	loss of meaning	nagging
accident prone in	looking for magic	unforgiving	lack of intimacy
coordination	loss of direction	apathy	using people
foot-tapping		cynicism	

The Three Environments in which we Function!

This methodology allows individuals to evaluate the environments in which they function, specify areas of difficulties (stressors) and to plan strategies for coping and/or change. The process accomplishes this by extracting from existing theories, methodologies or technologies that can be practically applied and that can effectuate or modify change. The individual can develop a change structure (stress management technique) by dealing with the self, others (or groups/intra and interpersonal conditions) and the workplace (organizations). There are three environments in which people function and they are intimate, workplace and leisure (see Figure 5.3).

Figure 5.3 – Three Functioning Environments

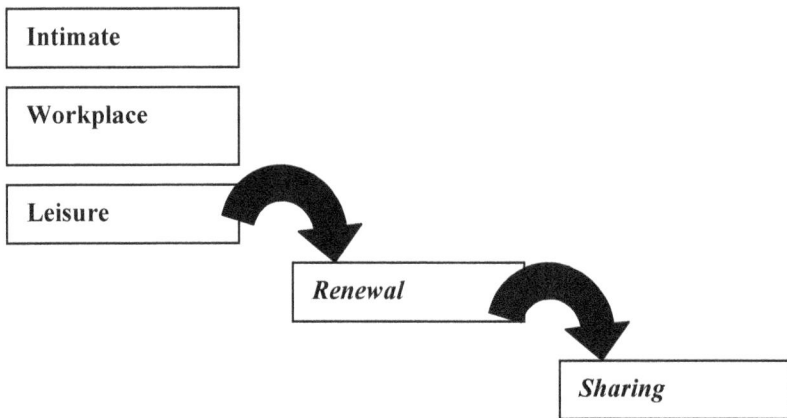

Intimate. In the intimate environment, people generally share intimacies with family; usually have the highest value priority; and this environment is important for roots, affinity, status, security, and intimacy.

Workplace. The workplace environment includes career development and actualization of educational preparation. This is usually the major income-producing environment. In this environment, there is a huge need for accepting change. This environment also requires the continual development of people skills and technological skills.

Leisure. The leisure environment includes the quality time spent on self, friends and community. This is usually the "glue" that maintains balance in the other two environments. Furthermore, leisure leads to renewal, uniquely for the self, and sharing oneself with one's community.

We know that when a person is consistent with understanding and finding "sync" across the three environments they tend to be more balanced, more productive and more physically and mentally healthy.

Basic Concepts of Human Behavior

The literature is full of ways in which to understand behavior and many books have attempted to describe the approaches to understand personality, which is the sum total of all that we are. Most textbooks mention three approaches: Trait theories; humanistic theories and psychodynamic theories. One can learn from these approaches but they appear not to be complete in fully understanding those approaches that affect our belief systems, values, perceptions and emotions. A more contemporary approach is as follows:

1. *Religious/Cultic Approaches.* Briefly, one cannot ignore a person's religious, cultic or spiritual beliefs. These may or may not be a part of our early programming but they still continue to influence our behaviors into adulthood. The conditions expected by these many belief systems can indeed become powerful stressors leading to serious Distress conditions.

2. *Psycho-analytic and Neo-analytical Approaches.* There is no denying that the impact of Sigmund Freud's philosophy/psychology psychoanalysis has/had (still does) a tremendous effect on how professionals attempt to understand human behavior. The exploration of the psyche (i.e. id, ego, superego) stages of development, ego defense mechanisms, the conscious, pre-conscious and unconscious functioning have "jump-started" powerful schools of theories, methodologies and technologies. Neo-analytic schools of thought have developed approaches that have caused a better understanding of human behavior.

3. *Humanistic/Existential Approaches.* Humanistic/Existential approaches initiated a totally different manner in which human beings were evaluated. The research and writings of Carl Rogers, Abraham Maslow, Rollo May, Jean Paul Sartre, Timothy Leary, to name a few, triggered off a "frenzy" of research and movements that impacted views on war, music, drugs, student riots fueled by world events like the Vietnam war and sensitivity to minority deprivation. The reason to be, "doing one's own thing," allowing the situation to determine one's reaction to situations devoid of any religious, moral or societal values are still cause for individual and collective stressors.

4. *Neuro-physio-bio-chemical Explorations.* Neuro-physio-bio-chemical approaches are more contemporary and the research and findings of Neuro sciences are the bedrock of understanding stress and its management. The explosion of gyms, nutrition concerns, wellness programs, preventative medicine, have all been for the better understanding of the Mind-Body continuum and the development of stress management-- specific approaches.

5. *Behavioral Approaches.* Behavioral approaches are more focused toward "doing something"– finding approaches to enhance, change or modify behavior. There are merits in each of the conditioning theories/methodologies but cognitive –affective techniques have become more holistic as we understand how emotional response (brain/mind) is transduced into actual physiological responses that can be measured. Behavioral approaches can be inclusive of:

6. There are many forms of conditioning that impact people and some of them are as follows:

a. Classical conditioning,
b. Operant conditioning,
c. Observational learning, and
d. Cognitive-affective learning.

Most textbooks supply the formula for behavior as being the interaction of an individual in an environment, i.e; (b=f (i) (e)) as Kurt Lewin originally proposed in the early 1930s. If we were to expand this concept to organizational behavior we can assume that organizational behavior is a function of individual and groups interacting in an organizational environment (workplace; culture). In order to simplify these concepts, attempts will be made to understand human behavior under these headings:

1. *Determinants of Personality* (or what are those factors that make persons who and what they are): These are important for determining one's natural tendencies for being impacted by stress.
2. *Human Functioning*: Important for understanding the stress response and for effective stress management
3. *Feelings*: These are the factors that perhaps have the greatest influence on our behavior.

Determinants of Personality

Most textbooks suggest that there are essentially two factors that determine one's personality: Hereditary (or Genetic) and environmental. McCartney and Neville (1998) suggest that there are three factors that determine one's personality: hereditary, environmental, and choice.

Hereditary (genetic factors). These are traits received from parents at conception. It is true that other forms of developing life (e.g. cloning) are now being experimented with, but for the present, our predispositions are made up of paternal and maternal genes and the entire historical development of same. The individual without any effort on their part is "saddled" with genetic inheritance of individual strengths and weaknesses. It is important for the person engaging in stress management techniques to explore their "roots" since we know that there are illnesses and behaviors and conditions that run in our families e.g. hypertension, diabetes, schizophrenia, depression, and alcoholism.

Environmental factors. Everything that has happened to us after being born, has very important influences on how we adjust to situations and react to stressors. Our lifestyle and manner of reacting to stimuli are all part of these environmental factors, which is, in essence, our culture. All human beings belong to some culture and our preferences in life – food, dress, worship, funerals, weddings, work styles, values are due to cultural programming. Children are socialized by their culture and the attitudes towards young and old people are determined by culture. A known fact is that the only differences that human beings have, are due to culture. That is, all humans have basic physical, social and psychological needs. How we satisfy and or adjust to those needs are only cultural; for example, human beings must eat. The kinds of food that we eat depend on our culture. Even the manner in which food is put into the mouth – chopsticks, hands, knives and forks, spoons, etc. are cultural. Since one's culture therefore ascribes values, beliefs, adjustment factors and various behaviors, stressors are very much a part of cultural programming. The literature usually describes only these two factors (hereditary and environmental) as being major determinants of personality. The authors believe that there is another crucial factor, especially from adolescence up to the day we die! Even earlier states from birth to adolescence allow us to have choices.

Choices. Choices are decisions that we make on an ongoing basis about our lives. All choices have consequences, and it is through these consequences that we either learn to change, modify or ignore the resultants of our choices. Most behaviors, except for instinctual ones, are learned. If we learn something we can modify or change them. The process of choices involves effective problem-solving and decision making. Choices are extremely important because if, on examining the other two factors that make us who and what we are, allows for modification or change. For example, if a person does not like certain aspects of their bodies (hair, nose, ears, mouth) through choice, there is the expertise to selectively modify or change it. If a person was born in a low socio-economic level, through choices- (education, hard work, perseverance) one doesn't have to stay poor. If one is culturally Hispanic and speaks Spanish, then one can learn to speak English or any other language for that matter. Choice, to some extent, can over-ride hereditary as well as environmental (cultural) factors.

Human Functioning

The ideas about the levels of human functioning come from the theories of Sigmund Freud. Modern research has explained in more detail Freud's original ideas and with the emergence of Neuroscience, has been more precise about the workings of the mind-body connection. There are three levels of human functioning: conscious, pre-conscious, and sub-conscious levels.

1- *Conscious level*:
- Immediate Awareness made possible by our brain and sense organ systems.
- The "here and now"; our-knowledge of what is happening; being involved with immediate events.

2- *Pre-conscious level*:
- Remembered (recalled) events that continue to affect how we think, feel and act. The "once bitten twice shy" concept, that is essential for learning.

3- *Sub-conscious level*:
- The repository level where everything that has happened to a person deposited.
- Events from conception are stored at this level.
- Can't remember, but humans are still affected in terms of how they 'feel' and 'act'.

Scientists used to believe that to change or modify behavior, it was necessary to explore the subconscious. Many methods such as free association, dream analysis and hypnosis were used to "tap-into" the subconscious. This was not only time consuming and expensive but if assumptions were made as to the cause of behavior it was still necessary to go through a re-educative process to change or modify those behaviors.

We now know, that most behaviors are learned and we can find ways to unlearn (modify or change) at the conscious level. This process takes time. It attempts to specify stressors which help to evaluate and initiate more effectively stress-management interventions. Another factor is that anyone (managers, supervisors, employees) can engage in their own behavior and emotional modifications. The last concept that will be explored is that of feelings.

Feelings

Feelings are part of our human response and they can range from mad and sad to excited and glad. There are essentially two types of feelings: physical and emotional.

Physical feelings. These are Stimulus-Response reactions made possible by the brain and sense organ systems. In spite of this, through the workings of will power and discipline, we have some measure of control! How individual's react to physical stimuli are part of hereditary, environmental and personal choice factors.

Emotional feelings. Emotional responses are the resultant of personal evaluations (analysis, perceptions) of events and happenings in our lives.

For many years, scientists were not able to describe/find the center of people's emotional responses. The evolution of neurology and neuroscience and other/biochemical studies have now been able to pinpoint our emotions to be in the limbic system, where hormonal systems, triggered off by the person's evaluation ability (as carried in the neo-cortex system) are transduced into physiological arousal and responses that can be measured.

The manner by which stressors are evaluated, analyzed and perceived gives a person his or her emotional responses. Individuals, often times, are surprised by the fact that their depression, anger, motivation, frustration, etc. are all caused by themselves. While it is true that others may try to influence one's feelings and behavior, persons will feel and react either how they have been programmed to react or after going through an evaluative or analytical process, make a choice. In considering how this process works, it is important to remember that:

1. *Thoughts come before feelings* (emotions). We can think (fantasize) anything!
2. *We alone, control our thoughts.* When we lose control of our thoughts we become psychotic and are in need of supervision
3. *Therefore, we alone control our feelings (emotions).* For further expansion of this important concept, it is suggested that the writings of Albert Ellis (1979), Biblio (1984) and Maxie Maultsby (1976) are read.

The manner, in which we perceive, analyze or evaluate the events or happenings in our lives, triggers off our emotional responses.

There is also the concept of cognitive dissonance or mixed feelings. These have been described as "watching your enemy drive over a cliff in your new Mercedes-Benz!" Dissonance is a major cause of distress. Rational thinking, over a period of time, can eliminate dissonance.

In any given situation, one should always remember that there is never just one way to think, feel or act. There are always alternatives that the individual can choose from. Overall, it is best to remember that:

1. We can, through *choices*, modify and/or change factors that determine our personality.
2. We acknowledge the importance of the sub-conscious, but we can adequately modify and/or change behaviors at the *conscious (awareness)* level of human functioning. Hard working professionals

have neither time nor inclination to probe beneath the surface. They want quick, reliable alternatives, and there are processes to achieve these and to maintain balance.

3. We have some measure of control over our physical feelings and almost *total control of our emotional responses.*

4. By rationally examining the three environments in which we function, a person can make rational decision/choices with regards to these environments.

5. Professional behavior, especially in "people skills" should be consistently, appropriately, and positively used in ALL of the environments in which one functions.

6. Coping skills at any transitional stage of development, if followed by applying the methodology of the "Professional Development Process" can cause less trauma, irrational behavior, and disruption of family and/or work. A vibrant spirituality, respect for human kind, and positive mental attitudes often eliminate the boredom/humdrum of life. Awareness of the many stages that we go through, understanding these concepts, and applying these skills, can provide the tools that help people actualize their proper potential, and find an all encompassing, growth enriching life.

The Psychosomatic Stress Pathway

It has been suggested by Greenberg (1993) that to effectively manage stress that is, to quantitatively reduce the amount of distress and qualitatively change it into eustress, the psychosomatic stress pathway should be understood in order to choose the most effective stress management method.

Recent research in the psychobiology of the stress response makes this approach more specifically stress management oriented. Stages of the pathway implies techniques that have, over a period of time, provided to be not only useful in minimizing distress but initiates lifestyle changes that work well for the individual. It is also useful to reiterate that the brain is the center of all activity and all feelings, physical and emotional. It is the seat of one's intelligence, beliefs, values, self awareness, and creativity. Furthermore, most of the stress we experience is psychogenic; that is, it originates in the mind. Regardless of the origin, workers and managers can develop effective skills to handle stress in their lives and workplaces. Effective skills can be inclusive of understanding various techniques related to social engineering, cognitive reappraisal, relaxation, diet and nutrition, and physical activity.

Social Engineering

This is just another term for developing effective people skills. It is the manner by which we deal with or control the stressor (which can be anything). We can do this through avoidance, time management, and effective people skills.

Avoidance. This is not a good technique because it does not address the stressor. We can get temporary relief from the stressor which may provide the energy to confront it.

Time management. Time management is very important for minimizing distress. Meetings, interactions, telephone calls, responding to male and female employees as well as constantly sharing their woes, take up time and build distress. There are many seminars/workshop to teach people "time management" skills since being able to prioritize one's work and maintain focus within adequate time frames helps to minimize distress.

Effective people skills. Learning how to communicate and listen effectively, understanding body language and ego defense mechanisms, minimizes distress. Problem-solving, decision making and conflict management are effective stressor blasters. Conflict management techniques strive for win-win situations. There are many techniques, also seminar/workshops that have been especially developed to more efficiently address conflict. Organizations have put systems into place to deal with conflict. Negotiation techniques are also used, so that parties may not have to go into arbitration.

Cognitive Reappraisal

The cognitive reappraisal process teaches individuals how to re-think potential psychogenic stressors. Maxie Maultsby's (1994) "rational behavior" approach has proved to be very effective. He postulates that our evaluative thoughts "trigger off" emotional responses. He has developed a self-help system by which individuals can deal with stressors. He posits that when a person *thinks* rationally he or she feels rational. The criteria of rational thinking may be in self-talk, according to Maultsby (1984), by asking oneself five rational questions:

1. Is my thinking here factual?
2. Will my thinking here best help me protect my life and health?
3. Will my thinking here best help me achieve my short term and long term goals?
4. Will my thinking here best help me avoid my most undesirable conflicts with others?
5. Will my thinking here best help me feel the emotions I want to feel?

Three honest "no" answers reveal unhealthy, irrational thinking that must be changed before unhealthy emotional feelings will change without drugs or elective shock, or brain damage (Maultsby, 1976, 1984). Therefore, examining emotions; engaging in self-talk (making a "camera check"); asking the five rational questions and practicing the new feelings and behavior, will over a period of time, change distress into eustress.

Physical Activity

This is the body's natural mechanism for reducing psycho-genic physiological arousal. It is important to get advice from one's physician as to the kinds of physical activity that the person can safely practice. There are three main goals:

1. To detoxify the stress related hormones quickly.
2. To strengthen the internal organ systems to make them more resistant to psychosomatic disease.
    ⇒ To improve cardio-vascular efficiency.
    ⇒ To improve muscle tone.
    ⇒ To improve energy levels.

3. To help displace negative cognitive states by focusing on the activity taking place. Physical exercise should be vigorous, sustained and regular.

Sexual activity triggers the release of beta-endorphins (the body's natural painkillers) and also relieves tension. So, with a loved one and when the time is right, be involved in this activity as often as your desires, thoughts, abilities, and opportunities allow. However, the authors recommend that you finish reading this chapter first!

Systematic Relaxation

This is a hybrid technique that can be used at any step of the psycho-somatic stress response. Systematic relaxation is designed to reduce psycho-physiological arousal, e.g. it lowers arterial blood pressure and blood sugar levels. Some of the more common relaxation techniques are:

⇒ Meditation
⇒ Hypnosis
⇒ Progressive neuro-muscular relaxation
⇒ Yoga
⇒ Sensory Awareness (touch; smell), and
⇒ Visual Imagery.

Systematic relaxation is enhanced by music, biofeedback, massage, acupuncture, acupressure, refloxogy, hydrotherapy, and other such activities.

Diet and Nutrition

According nutritionists (such as Anissa Qadir, personal communication on July 09, 2009), a very important adjunct to stress management techniques can be effective diet and nutrition. The following are some general guidelines for diet and nutrition:

1. Eat moderately a balanced of all healthy foods you enjoy.
2. Eat whole foods rather than processed foods.
3. Stock up on carbohydrates: cut down on fats: eat lots of fruit and vegetables.
4. Use salt, alcohol and sugar sparingly.
5. Eat smaller more frequent meals.
6. When hungry between meals use cushion foods (e.g. bananas, raw vegetables, etc.).
7. Eat more fiber (yams, oatmeal, cereals, etc.).
8. Use vitamins and minerals as supplements as advised by your doctor.

Summary

In this chapter, we have attempted to indicate the seriousness of stress, especially in the workplace, since it costs American business more than $200 billion a year. News from the European community as well, has labeled stress the second-biggest occupational health problem facing employers in Europe (Lewis, 2002). The pressure issues and quick changes of the twenty-first century and demands that individuals both on and off the job experience, create a huge need for managers and employees to understand stress and its management.

Perhaps the most effective way to think about stress is what has been emphasized in this book and the fact that the individual must make it his/her own responsibility to assume control as to how best to deal with stressors and distress. The statement, which should become one's personal mantra is that in any given situation, there is never just one way to think, feel or act allows for stress management strategies:

(1) Developing a low-stress attitude
- Building self confidence
- Examining the "rational thinking" questions
- Specifying your stressors
- Ability to evaluate, analyze and change the manner and/or environment in which stressors have developed.

(2) Practicing a low-stress lifestyle
- Setting one's priorities
- Creating a friendly workplace environment
- Find positive balance in the three environments in which we exist
- Evaluating one's strengths and weaknesses
- Accommodate change

(3) Creating low-stress relationships
- Practicing effective people skills
- Setting limits (boundaries)
- Delegating tasks
- Learning from mistakes
- Showing appreciation
- Smiling

(4) Using your resources
- Your employee assistance program
- Personal development; books, seminars, workshops
- Co-workers
- Workplace
- Family and friends
- Medical personnel, human resource managers, physicians, dentists, etc.

Studies show that if you "learn to feel that you are in control or actually take control of certain aspects of the situation that you are in, you can reduce your stress response" (NIIT World on Health, 2000). Therefore, you can help yourself cope not only with your distress (or illness) but help the illness (distress) itself.

Managing stress means managing one's food intake and having a regular exercise program. One should exercise regularly for about one hour or so at least three to four times each week. Do some exercises that you enjoy and something that stretches your abilities both mentally and physically. Professionals and busy managers should know that good nutrition and regular exercise helps them stay healthy and effectively manage stress. Regardless of your stress level, good nutrition also affects how one feels physically and emotionally. Good nutrition means eating variety of foods in moderation. Of course, one must remember that staying healthy through regular physical exercises can boost self-confidence by improving strength, stamina, flexibility, appearance, and sense of control which are needed by busy employees. So, eat healthy foods and exercise each week three to four times for durations of about one hour. If you don't make the time for exercise, will you really have time to stay sick in bed or in a hospital?

The Stress Management Handbook (1995) and stress management experts suggest a proactive approach. Wellness programs and healthy lifestyles help one to reflect on the positive aspects of one's job and contributions. To relay these thoughts in everyday language, the Stress Management Handbook offers the following commandments for stress management:

1. Don't let minor aggravations get to you.
2. Don't succumb to guilt.
3. Develop adaptation and coping strategies for new tasks and changes.
4. Learn to accept and adapt to change in new circumstances.
5. Change the way you look at stress by looking at it from several angles.
6. Develop a support system and social clique where trustworthy individuals can act as a sounding board to your concerns.
7. Separate things that are under your control from those that you can't control.
8. Learn to accept the things you can't change.
9. Focus on what is important as per your professional mission and purpose in life.
10. Develop a personal anti-stress regimen.
11. Don't take it personally, stay objective and focused on resolving the issue at hand.
12. Believe in yourself. Have enough self-confidence to find the necessary means of handling life's challenges and convert them to opportunities for yourself, your family members, and your colleagues.

Jeff Davidson (1997), author and stress management expert, states that most of what transpires in your life is the result of your personal choices with occasional interferences from the "left field." Overall, you make the choices that impact your life either positively or negatively. Davidson states that "being true to yourself means having inner directedness" in life. Understanding social changes helps one prepare for them while reducing some of the stress that is caused by the rapid change. So, pace yourself in a balanced way by focusing on all of your major goals (not just the professional ones). Being true to yourself, as well as honestly communicating your needs and desires both to yourself and others can help in keeping the level of stress in control.

The work environment of the twenty-first century should not have change agents and managers that are focused only on exceeding the weekly, monthly, or quarterly financial goals of the department or organization. These types of management approaches can lead to disastrous results, such as unethical decisions, and undue stress on employees. Unfortunately, many of today's managers are usually busy focusing on meeting the quarterly and weekly goals rather than taking the time to relax and focus on the big picture with their employees. They don't seem to have sufficient time to sit back and reflect on their purpose, mission, where they have been, what they have accomplished, and what is truly important in their personal and professional lives. Many managers seem to move from one problem to the next, being focused on urgent challenges which are not necessarily always important. If they were to proactively work on important goals, rather than only those that appear urgent, then they would have less "urgent" issues to deal with in their daily operations. Overall, there seems to be little to no time for reflection and relaxation in the life of today's managers in the United States. Of course, this type of a hectic lifestyle can be stressful for managers, their family members, and their employees. Since one cannot be totally stress-free, managers, change agents and workers should focus on effectively managing their level of stress.

Overall, one can say that the only persons without any real stress are probably those who have "departed" this world or a person who has a mental illness or disability. Otherwise, everyone seems to have some type of stress in his/her life. Change can bring and cause both good and bad stress. *Eustress* is good stress and *distress* is bad stress. Major and continuous change can create a strong culture, where a high level of stress is the norm. Today's rate of change has been much greater than the past; yet, this is perhaps an initial start compared to the changes for tomorrow. In order to effectively deal with stress that is caused by major changes, experts suggest that in today's rate of change, sometimes one just has to "give up" or surrender to the change; another option would be to simply "toughen up" by developing higher levels of tolerance for adapting to change; and yet at other times, one has to "wise up" by not allowing self-induced stress to take over one's life. The future promises greater rates of change with higher levels of complexity which can bring about more stress, when not managed properly. In many cases, the rate of change cannot be changed but one's behavior can be managed appropriately to effectively deal with unforeseen events, thereby reducing stress. Stress, the invisible pandemic, is neither good nor bad by itself when balanced. There is good stress, such as the tension caused by marriage or graduation; and there is bad stress, such as those that are brought upon one by organizational politics, inconsistent or unrealistic demands, and the abuse of one's power or status. Too much stress can make one unproductive or sick, at best, and it can cause death at worst. So, be the master of your domain by effectively balancing and managing your level of stress.

Thomas-Kilman Conflict Mode Instrument

The Thomas-Kilman Conflict Mode Instrument is created and made available online by Kenneth L. Thomas and Ralph H. Kilman. This conflict assessment has been in practice since the 1970's and is mainly utilized by consultants, trainers, human resource departments, and management. This instrument is designed to measure a person's behavior in various situations that involved personal or professional conflicts. Conflict situations are those where the concerns of two people appear incompatible due to differing views, politics, and/or limited resources. In such situations, one can describe an individual's behavior along two basic dimensions: (1) assertiveness, the extent to which the person attempts to satisfy his own concerns, and (2) cooperativeness, the extent to which the person attempts to satisfy the other person's concerns (Thomas-Killman Website, 2009).

Think of various situations in which you find your desires and wishes differing from those of another person in your team, department or organization. How do you usually respond to such situations where the conflict is apparent? This is where knowing your conflict management style and that of the other person's becomes important. On the Thomas-Kilman Conflict Mode Instrument are several pairs of statements describing possible behavioral responses. For each pair, please circle the "A" or "B" statement which is most characteristic of your own behavior. In many cases, neither the "A" nor the "B" statement may be very typical of your behavior, but you should select the response which you would be more likely to use.

Thomas-Kilman Conflict Mode Instrument:
Circle the answer that best describes you.

1.	A.	There are times when I let others take responsibility for solving the problem.	
	B.	Rather than negotiate the things on which we disagree, I try to stress those things on which we both agree.	
2.	A.	I try to find a compromise solution	
	B.	I attempt to deal with all of his/her and my concerns.	
3.	A.	I am usually firm in pursuing my goals	
	B.	I might try to smooth the other's feelings and preserve our relationship	
4.	A.	I try to find a compromise solution	
	B.	I sometimes sacrifice my own wishes for the wishes of the other person	
5.	A.	I consistently seek the other's help in working out a solution	
	B.	I try to do what is necessary to avoid useless tensions.	
6.	A.	I try to avoid creating unpleasantness for myself	
	B.	I try to win my position	
7.	A.	I try to postpone the issue until I have had some time to think it over.	
	B.	I give up some points for exchange of others	
8.	A.	I am usually firm in pursuing my goals	
	B.	I attempt to get all concerns and issues immediately out in the open	
9.	A. I feel that differences are not always worth worrying about		
	B. I make some effort to get my way		
10.	A. I am firm in pursuing my goals		
	B. I try to find a compromise solution		
11.	A. I attempt to get all concerns and issues immediately out in the open		
	B. I might try to smooth the other's feelings and preserve our relationship		
12.	A. I sometimes avoid taking positions that would create controversy		
	B. I will let other person have some of his/her positions if he/she lets me have some of mine.		

13.	A. I propose a middle ground	
	B. I press to get my points made	
14.	A. I tell the other person mu ideas and ask for his/hers	
	B. I try to show the other person the logic and benefits of my position	
15.	A. I might try to smooth the other's feelings and preserve our relationship	
	B. I try to do what is necessary to avoid tensions.	
16.	A. I try not to hurt the others persons feelings	
	B. I try to convince other person of the merits of my position	
17.	A. I am usually firm in pursuing my goals	
	B. I try to do what is necessary to avoid useless tensions	
18.	A. If it makes the other people happy, I might let them maintain their views	
	B. I will let other person have some of his/her positions if he/she lets me have some of mine.	
19.	A. I attempt to get all concerns and issues immediately out in the open	
	B. I try to postpone the issue until I have had some time to think it over.	
20.	A. I attempt to immediately work through our differences	
	B. I try to find a fair combination of gains and losses for both of us.	
21.	A. In approaching negotiations, I try to be considerate of the other person's wishes.	
	B. I always lean towards a direct discussion of the problem	
22.	A. I try to find a position that it is intermediate between his/hers and mine.	
	B. I assert my wishes	
23.	A. I am very often concern with satisfying your wishes	
	B. There are times when I let others take responsibility for solving the problem	
24.	A. If the other's position seems very important to him/her, I would try to meet his/her wishes.	
	B. I try to get the other person to settle for a compromise.	
25.	A. I try to show the other person the logic and benefits of my position	
	B. In approaching negotiations, I try to be considerate of other person's wishes.	
26.	A. I propose a middle ground	
	B. I am nearly always concerned with satisfying all your needs.	
27.	A. I sometimes avoid taking positions that would create controversy	
	B. If it makes the other people happy, I might let them maintain their views	
28.	A. I am usually firm in pursuing my goals	
	B. I usually seek the other's help in working out a solution	
29.	A. I propose a middle ground	
	B. I feel that differences are not always worth worrying about	
30.	A. I try not to hurt the other's feelings	
	B. I always share the problem with the other person so that we can work it out.	

Now, circle the letters below which correspond to the letter you circled on each item of the questionnaire and then total the number of items circled in each column. Your profile of scores indicates the repertoire of conflict handling skills which you, as an individual, use in the kinds of conflict situations you face.

Thomas-Kilman Conflict Styles Chart

	Competing (forcing)	Collaborating (problem solving)	Compromising (sharing)	Avoiding (withdrawal)	Accommodating (soothing)
1.	-	-	-	A	B
2.	-	B	A	-	-
3.	A	-	-	-	B
4.	-	-	A	-	B
5.	-	A	-	B	-
6.	B	-	-	A	-
7.	-	-	B	A	-
8.	A	B	-	-	-
9.	B	-	-	A	-
10.	A	-	B	-	-
11.	-	A	-	-	B
12.	-	-	B	A	-
13.	B	-	A	-	-
14.	B	A	-	-	-
15.	-	-	-	B	A
16.	B	-	-	-	A
17.	A	-	-	B	-
18.	-	-	B	-	A
19.	-	A	-	B	-
20.	-	A	B	-	-
21.	-	B	-	-	A
22.	B	-	A	B	-
23.	-	A	-	B	-
24.	-	-	B	-	A
25.	A	-	-	-	B
26.	-	B	A	-	-
27.	-	-	-	A	B
28.	A	B	-	-	-
29.	-	-	A	B	-
30.	-	B	-	-	A

Competing	Collaborating	Compromising	Avoiding	Accommodating
___	___	___	___	___

Glazer-Stress Control Life Style Survey

The Glazer test was designed by Dr. Howard L. Glazer and it is provided in the *Executive Stress* by Philip Goldberg and many stress management workshops. Each scale, in the set of twenty items, is composed of a pair of adjectives or phrases separated by a series of horizontal lines. Each pair has been chosen to represent two kinds of contrasting behaviors. Each person belongs somewhere along the line between the two extremes. Put a circle where you think you belong between the two extremes.

1.	Doesn't mind leaving things temporarily unfinished.	1 2 3 4 5 6 7	Must get things finished once started.
2.	Calm and unhurried about appointments.	1 2 3 4 5 6 7	Never late for appointments.
3.	Not competitive.	1 2 3 4 5 6 7	Highly competitive.
4.	Listens well, lets other finish talking.	1 2 3 4 5 6 7	Anticipates others in conversation (nods, interrupts, finishes sentences for others).
5.	Never in a hurry, even when pressured.	1 2 3 4 5 6 7	Always in a hurry.
6.	Able to wait calmly.	1 2 3 4 5 6 7	Uneasy when waiting.
7.	Easygoing.	1 2 3 4 5 6 7	Always going full speed ahead.
8.	Takes one thing at a time.	1 2 3 4 5 6 7	Tries to do more than one thing at a time, thinks about what to do next.
9.	Slow and deliberate.	1 2 3 4 5 6 7	Vigorous and forceful in speech (uses a lot of gestures).
10.	Concerned with satisfying himself, not others.	1 2 3 4 5 6 7	Wants recognition by others for a job well done.
11.	Slow doing things.	1 2 3 4 5 6 7	Fast doing things (eating, walking, etc.).
12.	Easygoing.	1 2 3 4 5 6 7	Hard driving.
13.	Expresses feelings openly.	1 2 3 4 5 6 7	Holds feelings in.
14.	Has large number of interests.	1 2 3 4 5 6 7	Few interests outside or work.
15.	Satisfied with job.	1 2 3 4 5 6 7	Ambitious, wants quick advancement on job.
16.	Never sets own deadlines.	1 2 3 4 5 6 7	Often sets own deadlines.
17.	Feels limited responsibility.	1 2 3 4 5 6 7	Always feels responsible.
18.	Never judges things in terms of numbers.	1 2 3 4 5 6 7	Often judges performance in terms of numbers (how many, how much).
19.	Casual about work.	1 2 3 4 5 6 7	Takes work very seriously (works weekends, brings work home).
20.	Not very precise.	1 2 3 4 5 6 7	Very precise (careful about detail).
	Subtotals	_ _ _ _ _ _ _	
	Total Score		

Now, add the scores for each area to get the subtotals and then total them up to get a total score. This test can give you some idea of where you stand in the discussion of Type A behavior. The higher your score, the more cardiac prone you tend to be. Remember, though, even Type B persons occasionally slip into Type A behavior, and any of these patterns can change over time. The following are some general classification and analysis of the Glazer-Stress Control Life Style Questionnaire.

Glazer-Stress Control Life Style Survey Scoring Guide

Total score = 110 – 140	Type A1	If you are in this category, and especially if you are over 40 and smoke, you are likely to have a high risk of developing cardiac illness.
Total score = 80 – 109	Type A2	You are in the direction of being cardiac prone, but your risk is not as high as the A1. You should, nevertheless, pay careful attention to the advice given to all Type As.
Total score = 60 – 79	Type AB	You are admixture of A and B patterns. This is a healthier pattern than either A1 or A2, but you have the potential for slipping into A behavior and you should recognize this.
Total score = 30 - 59	Type B2	Your behavior is on the less-cardiac-prone end of the spectrum. You are generally relaxed and cope adequately with stress.
Total score = 0 – 29	Type B	You tend to the extreme of non-cardiac traits. Your behavior expresses few of the reactions associated with cardiac disease.

CHAPTER SIX

6 – Stress, Personality and Behaviors

S tress is increasingly a concern for all working adults in a slowing economy. Despite the layoffs and the recession, only a moderate level of stress is found among the American respondents studied by the authors. However, older respondents and men tend to report higher stress scores. Since stress is a part of everyone's life and causes problems that many do not know how to manage, this chapter provides a comprehensive overview of stress and how it affects people's life. The suggestions can help in exploring stress in the workplace as well as on a personal level. This section explores both the benefits and challenges that many face in effectively managing stress, and lists ways to manage stress to the best of one's ability in any given time.

Stress, Personality, and Overload[1]

Stress can often be caused by taking on too many projects or tasks at work or at home. Sometimes people take on more projects than they can handle on a voluntarily basis and, at other times, it is delegated by one's superiors or colleagues. In either case, one should be very careful and understand that consistently overloading oneself can be problematic. According to Hyde and Allen (2006), stress overload can be qualitative or quantitative.

1. *Qualitative overload* is when a person is given tasks and responsibilities beyond his or her existing abilities without adequate training or skill building to get it done effectively. If a great basketball player is asked to have a boxing match with a skilled boxer, then he or she is likely to experience qualitative overload.

2. *Quantitative overload* is when you are asked to take on additional responsibilities, but you do not have enough time to get them done in the way you prefer. Having many assignments and excess workload with school and a fulltime job and family responsibilities is an example of overload which in return can cause stress and tension.

---

[1] This chapter is coauthored with Alejandrina Lara, Catherine King, Valencia Johnson, and Teri Mahanna, Nova Southeastern University.

Hyde and Allen (2006, p. 27) state that overload stressors can produce psychological, physiological and behavioral changes. Quantitative overload can cause elevation in blood cholesterol level which is associated with such disorders as atherosclerosis and coronary heart disease (Hyde and Allen, p. 27). Overload can decrease motivation toward learning / work performance. To manage stress better, know your optimal work load, for most people this is very hard to do because they want to be successful by doing more work. Try to manage your time by scheduling, planning and organizing your time in a balanced manner for family, school, and work. Set priorities, and determine what is important and what your limitations are, and know when to say no!

Life events can raise or lower a person's stress levels. The more things we have going on in our lives that all need to be done now and we can't get them all done quickly, the more stressful our lives can be. Certain life events can generate more stress than others; for example the death of a close family member versus a quarrel or squabble with the next door neighbor. The death of a close family member causes more stress than does a quarrel or squabble with a neighbor. Since stress can lower the body's immune system it has a great potential to increase our susceptibility to illness. The more life events which occur yield more stress which in turn lowers the body's immune system and increases potential for illness.

There are many factors that contribute to the positive or negative aspects of one's health. Such factors can be genetic make-up, specific behaviors, the environment, and/or one's personality. For example, one important factor contributing to one's health is their genetic make-up. Genetic make-up consists of the physiological aspects that help us adjust to stress such as heart rate and blood pressure. An example would be when a person gets upset and their blood pressure rises. Those that rise at a higher average rate could be said to have high blood pressure as their heart rate increases. This is why we hear at times when someone gets upset "Please, calm down, you have high blood pressure." Specific behaviors also contribute, either positively or negatively, to one's health such as regular exercise and healthy diet or smoking and drinking alcoholic beverages. The environment also has an effect on one's health like the location where one works. A person's personality also has a significant impact on personal health since self-esteem and emotional stability impact how one feels physiologically which can have an affect physically.

Personality: Advantages and Disadvantages of Type A and Type B!

Understanding personality is also linked to a person's locus of control. Understanding locus of control helps to better understand personality and stress. A person with internal locus of control tends to believe that he/she is largely in control of things such as job position, financial status, and quality of life. These individuals tend to believe that a deliberate effort and hard work can lead to desired goals. External locus of control individuals tend to believe that outside forces such as luck and fate, and other things are controlling events and outcomes.

The disadvantages of a Type A personality often include characteristics such as being overly aggressive, impatient, inconsiderate, and arrogant. These are not characteristics that most people would want to be associated with. It has also been shown that Type A personalities are more prone to psychosomatic diseases such as cardiovascular disease. The advantages of a Type A personality are that they tend to be more steady and laid back without being lazy (Hyde and Allen, 2006). Type A personalities also tend to be hardworking and tend to perform better than Type B personalities in some situations. Of course, the reality is that a capitalistic society often encourages behaviors that are closely linked to Type A personalities. Many of us experience this on a daily basis working within our organizations which are driven by deadlines, rewards, incentives, and, at times, backbiting politics. Employees who are aggressive, demonstrate a sense of time urgency, and people who are competitive tend to be rewarded better than those who get their work done in calmer manner. Those who fit into the Type B personality are viewed as less successful since they do not demonstrate characteristics that are expected in a competitive type of work environment. The disadvantages of Type B personalities are characteristics such as becoming angry, irritated, aggressive and upset, even though it may not be to the same extent as a Type A. Of course, one cannot see too many other characteristics of a Type B personality which can be considered a disadvantage. Then again, it is all relative; one could say that a disadvantage of a Type B is that they are slower moving than a Type A. This could illustrate that they are less productive...this may or may not be true. Type B personalities tend to be slower moving, but often choose quality over quantity. Others would say that the advantages of Type B personality include, showing much more patience than a Type A personality, not being so time sensitive, choosing quality over quantity, and appropriate speech patterns for the situation. The biggest advantage of a Type B personality is that they are not prone to psychosomatic diseases. It seems that Type B personalities do not display characteristics that appear to lead to additional stress like a Type A personality does. Type Bs are not constantly pushing to get things done when they have plenty of time. Type Bs are also not trying to juggle a hundred tasks at a time which could lead to additional stress.

Stress Response, Exercise and Time Management!

The response patterns to stress can consist of general, random, and rigid responder categories. The *general responder* shows some type of physiological response during a stressful situation. For instance, he/she may have a heart rate go up, muscles tense, or intestines slow down. A *random responder* displays different symptoms during different situations. Finally, *rigid responders* usually react to stress no matter what situation they are under.

The foods we eat can influence us physiologically, psychologically, and behaviorally. More specifically, the various components of our diets affects us a minimum of three ways. First, some of our food contains substances capable of stimulating the sympathetic nervous system and are referred to as "sympathomimetic agents." The most common sympathomimetic agent is caffeine, found in varying amounts in beverages, snacks and medicines. Second, certain dietary practices can contribute to low blood sugar (i.e. hypoglycemia) which can contribute to feelings of fatigue. When we get tired we often become grouchy and irritable. Finally, some of our dietary practices work in connection with the effects of stress in the etiology of certain psychosomatic disorders.

So what can be done to interrupt stresses of our lives? According to the Hyde and Allen (1996), there are at least three ways to interrupt the stress pathway: modifying the external environment, altering the way we appreciate a stressor, and retaining the body respond in a positive and controlled manner. Also, there are many ways of interrupting or reducing stress through effective time management. Experts state that "Time management can diminish the stress associated with the feelings of being under pressure. Events become planned and scheduled and deadlines are less apt to sneak up on you" (Hyde & Allen, p.140). An example of this could be something as simple as a spreadsheet outlining the schedule of assignments and due dates for classes. You could create this every few months and utilize it in your time management. It can be used to incorporate assignments and studying into your daily and weekly plan and reduce deadlines that sneak up on you, therefore reducing stress. Hyde and Allen state that "Time management provides a structure or framework in which you can get things done. You can plan to do specific things at specific times; times that are more convenient for you" (1996, p. 140). Hyde and Allen also state that "Time management enhances your sense of being in control. Being more organized enables us to feel more in control of things; more in charge of our lives" (1996, p. 140).

Selective Awareness and Self-Esteem!

As human beings, we all have a selective awareness of things....perhaps many things as we go through life. The *selective awareness* concept states that humans have a limited scope of awareness. We are designed to pay attention to environmental changes and are prone to tuning into painful, adverse, or threatening stimuli, and that ultimately we have the choice over where we focus our attention. Hyde and Allen state that we have trained our awareness to seek out stressors (1996, p. 84).

We all have the power to ultimately lower our stress levels by focusing our attention on positive rather than negative stressors. One example could be being stuck in traffic. You could let your natural awareness attract you to negative factors such as the noise outside, the congestion on the road, or simply wasting time. On the other hand, you could train yourself to focus your attention on things that lower or alleviate stress rather than increase it. You could put up the windows and focus on listening to a song you really enjoy on the radio, or having an opportunity to catch up on news by listening to the local radio station. You could take in what a beautiful sunset or sunrise there is outside depending on what time of the day it is. If it is raining instead of focusing on how it could negatively affect your day, focus on not having to water your garden that week and how you can spend that extra few minutes of free time, or enjoy the nice smell of the rain. If we could all teach ourselves to focus our attention on more positives we could lower the natural stressors in our lives.

One can consciously focus on building his/her self-esteem by internalizing positive internal self-talk. Some of self-supporting statements that we can use to build self-esteem when faced with stressful situations can include the following:

1. I am bigger and better than any mistake that I have made.
2. I am human and make mistakes from time to time but they are not indicative of my self-worth.
3. I am not perfect, but daily I am being perfected and practice self-acceptance in the good and bad times.
4. I can do all things through my Creator that strengthens me.
5. What does not kill me makes me stronger.

6. Strength does not come from winning. Your struggles develop your strength. When you go through hardship and decide not to surrender, that is strength.

Cognitive Appraisal, Social Engineering and Social Support!

A cognitive appraisal is an event or situation that we interpret a stressor. "Rarely, is any event in life inherently stressful. We become aroused, or stressed, because of the way we label or interpret the events and situations in our lives. This process is referred to as cognitive appraisal" (Hyde & Allen, 1996, p. 119). Everyone interprets events and situations differently. An example, of cognitive appraisal could be starting a new job. One person may see this as an exciting, happy event. Another person in the same situation may view this as a stressor, since he/she needs to learn new processes, learn how to perform new duties, and get to know new people.

What is the difference between social engineering and cognitive reappraisal? *Social engineering* is a process where daily behaviors are restructured so as to minimize frequency of encounter with stressors, without altering one's lifestyle or sacrificing desired goals. It involves identifying and analyzing common stressors and goals, and then restructuring-your goal-directed behavior so that the objectives are still met, but the amount of stress that was required to get there is reduced. *Cognitive reappraisal* is an effective strategy for coping with life's stressful situations and the wide variety of challenging moments it presents to us. It is also a way to control unwanted stress. The difference between cognitive reappraisal and social engineering is that social engineering deals with the stressor and cognitive reappraisal deals with the interpretation of events. Social engineering also prescribes a behavior change to avoid or reduce the experience of the stressful event, whereas cognitive reappraisal restructures the interpretation of a potential stressor that has already occurred, to avoid any further maladaptive mental or physical arousal.

The four types of social support mentioned by Hyde and Allen (1996) are emotional support, appraisal support, instrumental support, and informational support. Using the four different types of social support, one might be more important to you than the others at a given time. For example, the most important for one can be emotional support. It has been said that:

> Emotional support involves demonstrations of caring and concern. This might include letting a person know that you care about them. Attempts to make that person feel better and to bolster self-confidence would be important. As the provider of emotional support you are serving as a confidant, being accepting and understanding of their predicament. For example, someone who has just ended a relationship that at one time was very important to them may need emotional support. They may need someone to just listen in a non-judgmental, caring way (Hyde & Allen, 1996, p. 168).

What are some important aspects of social and emotional support? First of all, social support can be influenced by behavior. People with good social support that have friends who care about them are more likely to take good care of themselves. They are more likely to maintain healthy promoting behaviors and avoid bad habits. For example, if you really want to lose weight then go on a diet with a friend and jointly measure your progress. The same applies for starting to play basketball, volleyball, or other team sports to stay healthy. If you want to stop smoking, then start the program with a friend or colleague who is trying to do the same. Second, social support enables us to mobilize psychological resources from within ourselves, and minimizing or "buffering" the effect of stress. The point is that social and emotional support involves caring and concerns…by letting other persons know that you care about them. Making the person feel better will boost their self-confidence. As a provider of emotional support you will be a confidant, being accepting and understanding of their predicament. For example someone who ends a relationship that was once important to them will need someone to be supportive and listen in a non judgmental, caring way. Sometimes life challenges become too much for one to bear, and emotional support is normally the key to survival amongst other things. It is good to know that through it all someone is there for you as a pillar of strength and you can be a supporter for someone else. Once emotional support is present one would seem to embrace challenges with optimism, knowing that they are not alone. Interestingly, emotional support, both as a supporter or one seeking support, can boost one's self-esteem and reduce stress.

Communication Styles and Stress Management

Ineffective communication can cause much stress. So, you may ask what does the inability to effectively communicate thoughts and desires produce? The inability to effectively communicate thoughts and desires can produce a variety of negative feelings that include anger and depression, which can thereby lower ones' self esteem. Imagine trying to tell your spouse that you are feeling insecure with the fact that he/she is spending an excessive amount of time at work, and you are brushed off due to your inability to effectively communicate to your spouse. This can lead to feelings of thinking that "perhaps there is another person in his/her life" or that you have lost the qualities that used to keep him/her interested in you. A situation like this can be an emotional disaster, and a loss of self-esteem. If you come across as being overbearing, the coworker or your spouse can be left feeling insecure in your presence as a result. An example like this on the job can also lead to low productivity.

There are four categories of communication styles according to Hyde and Allen (1996) that you may see in the workplace…which are aggressive, passive-aggressive, non-assertive, and assertive.

Aggressive behavior or "The Intimidators": This behavior is an attempt to dominate others through intimidation. Angry and insulting threats, and demands and or comments that demean, humiliate and ridicule are some basic forms of this behavior. Other characteristics of aggressive behavior are glaring and hostile eyes, inappropriately loud and angry voice, finger pointing, and displays of impatience-hands on hips.

Passive-Aggressive Behavior -"The Manipulators: Passive-aggressive behavior is an inability to express honest feelings, thoughts, and desires coupled with behaviors that are "indirectly hostile." Passive-Aggressive can be identified because they often pout and sulk when they do not get their way, give others the "silent treatment", and they try to make others feel guilty.

Non-Assertive Behavior - "The Pleasers": Non-assertive people are usually unable to express honest thoughts, feelings and desires. They find it extremely difficult to make or refuse requests, and consistently sacrifice their own needs and desires to accommodate others. Non-assertive behavior includes: poor eye contact, usually looking down or away; conversation voice that is weak, timid or whining; always appearing to be nervous, uncomfortable, or meek; and posture that is slouching. People with non assertive behavior usually use the "follow the leader" mentality.

Assertive Behavior - "The Seekers of Respect": Assertive behavior can be thought of as the ability of self-expression. In includes the ability to stand up for your own rights, and to express your thoughts, beliefs, and feelings in an honest, direct, and socially acceptable manner without violating the rights of others. Assertive behavior includes appropriate eye contact, making clear and concise statements, speaking with a firm voice that is steady and strong, and good posture that conveys a sense of self-confidence. So, communicate assertively in every opportunity you get!

Benefits and Challenges of Managing Stress

Everyone experiences stress from time to time, so it is perfectly normal. Stress is brought on by the pressures in one's life. Pressure is what is happening to you, but stress is how you react to those pressures. Stress can be defined as a condition or feelings experienced when a person perceives that demands exceed the personal and social resources the individual is able to mobilize (Mindtools, 1995-2008). Because there can be so many stressors that we handle on a daily basis, learning to manage them could be the key to a successful and healthy life. Stress may be hard to avoid, but the ways in which one can manage it are within one's control.

Stress and its Leading Causes

Stress is a normal part of life and it pushes people to learn and grow. At the same time, too much of it can cause significant problems. Stress can be interpreted as known and unknown forces from the outside environment impinging on a person at a given time (Definition of Stress, 2002). Stress releases powerful neurochemicals and hormones that prepare one for action to fight or flee. The most damaging types of stress are prolonged, uninterrupted, unexpected, and unmanageable stress. If one does not take the necessary action to manage these kinds of stress, then it can lead to health problems.

Stress is experienced in two forms: eustress and distress. Eustress is a helpful kind of stress that is experienced with respect to things that are positive in nature. It is short-term stress that motivates and focuses energy, is perceived as within one's coping ability, feels exciting, and improves performance (Mills, 2008). It prepares your mind and body with the strength needed to handle specific tasks and life events. People often experience eustress. When professionals are facing project deadlines, eustress is what helps them focus and find the energy needed to complete the project to the best of their ability. Overall, eustress is the type of stress that gives one the strength to fight for what one needs to succeed in almost anything he/she does.

Distress is a negative stress that can cause an individual to feel anxiety or concern, feel unpleasant, decrease performance, be perceived as outside of one's coping abilities, be short-term or long-term, and can lead to mental and physical problems (Mills, 2008). Distress is caused by many different stressors at home, work, or anywhere else. Examples of work and employment concerns that can cause distress are excessive job demands, job insecurity, conflicts with teammates and supervisors, and inadequate authority necessary to carry out tasks.

In the early 1900's, researcher Hans Selye studied the science of stress and determined that stress occurs in three stages: alarm, resistance and exhaustion. Alarm, the first stage, describes the point at which the threat or stressor is recognized by the body. At this stage adrenaline is produced and the fight-or-flight response kicks in. Resistance, the second stage, is when the body attempts to cope with the stressor. The body realizes that it can't keep up with the changes and begins to slowly deplete its resources. Exhaustion, the third stage, is when the body has depleted its resources and acute side affects begin to occur. If this stage is extended, then the body can experience chronic physical and emotional affects.

Stress is a physical and emotional experience that the human body is exposed to daily. Stressors at work, at home, within society, and within the environment are several examples that exposes one to the consequences involved in dealing with stress. The three kinds of stress are acute stress, episodic acute stress, and chronic stress (Miller, 2004). Acute stress is the most common form of stress. It comes from demands and pressures of the recent past and anticipated demands and pressures of the near future. It is thrilling and exciting in small doses, but too much is exhausting. Miller (2004) says, "Overdoing on short-term stress can lead to psychological distress, tension headaches, upset stomach, and other symptoms (para. 2)." Acute stress is short term in nature and coincides with specific physical side effects, such as clammy hands, rapid heartbeat, dry mouth, etc. Situations that may lead to acute stress are everyday situations such as a job interview, deadline for school or work, an exam, being pulled over by a police officer, or a conflict with someone you love. Acute stress can become a part of anyone's life and is highly treatable and easily managed.

Episodic acute stress is when one suffers from acute stress frequently, and is always in a rush, but always late. If something can go wrong, it does. The cardiac prone or 'Type A' personality is similar to an extreme case of episodic acute stress. Type A people have an excessive competitive drive, aggressiveness and time urgency. Symptoms of those who suffer from episodic acute stress are symptoms of extended over arousal: persistent tension headaches, migraines, hypertension, chest pain, and heart disease. Episodic acute stress is difficult to manage because sufferers can be extremely resistant to change.

Chronic stress is stress due to prolonged experiences. It comes when someone never sees a way out of a miserable situation. There are many physical side effects that go along with chronic stress such as heart disease, high blood pressure, loss of appetite, depressions, sleeplessness, ulcers, etc. Chronic stress can stem from traumatic, early childhood experiences that become internalized and remain painful. Other examples of chronic stress could be a long term workplace problem, prolonged internal issues, a broken relationship, and financial worries. Chronic stress is difficult to treat because it can kill one through suicide, violence, heart attack, stroke, and, perhaps, even cancer (Miller, 2004). People suffering from it wear down to a final, fatal breakdown.

In 1967, Thomas H. Holmes and Richard H. Rahe, conducted a study on the leading causes of stress (Hart, 2007). In their research, they determined there were 43 main causes of stress, and by 2006 that number increased to 55 – a very telling story to the increased stressors people have experienced over time (Hart, 2007). The two researchers also developed the *Social Readjustment Rating Scale*. This written exercise/tool was designed to measure the amount of stress in an individual's life. The tool provides one with a quantitative assessment of where the main stressors are in one's life so he/she can focus on implementing behavioral life changes to combat them.

In her article, *7 Leading Causes of Stress*, Anna Hart (2007) listed what most studies believe are the leading causes of stress in today's society. The following is a list of the causes: finances, work, family, personal concerns, personal health and safety, personal relationships, and death. Finance has become a leading cause of stress in many people's lives now that the economy is in a state of recession. In an online poll conducted in 2005 by LifeCare, Inc., 23% of respondents named finances as their leading cause of stress for them (Hart, 2007). Major purchases, such as a car or home, can be one of the most stressful financial problems one can experience. Loss of income and retirement income has also become a major cause of financial stress, especially since the national economic downturn in the United States.

Stress at work is another leading cause of stress because one's job is important for one's income. People worry about getting and keeping adequate employment, new types of responsibilities, work conditions, and promotions. A common concern people have today is being laid off; people are in a constant state of worry due to the changing economic conditions. Another type of stress within one's workplace can occur when troubles between co-workers exist. According Marilyn Elias (2009), Americans have become increasingly more stressed and experience worsened mental health due to the economic downturn. Elias based her conclusions on the landmark Gallup-Healthways poll which came out during the second week of March 2009. Gallup-Healthways survey of 355,334 people is the largest, longest and most thorough poll showing how emotional well-being may shift with economic changes. Gallup-Healthways' research provides an Emotional Health Index (EHI) measure that weighs negatives attitudes such as depression, worry and stress and compares it with the positive feelings respondents experienced before the survey. The overall conclusions were as follows (Elias, 2009):

- Stress increased in 2008 due to the financial and economic crisis.
- Emotional well-being decreased due to the declines in mental health, especially for the poorest people.
- Experts agree that depression often increases smoking and excessive drinking among those who are impacted by it and it discourages regular exercise which eventually results in higher risks for heart disease.
- In regard to age, those between the ages of 30 to 55 years old might be suffering most from the economic and financial depression.
- There are some racial differences, and Hispanics demonstrated the worst emotional health for the entire 2008 year.

The fact that Hispanics demonstrated a low emotional health index may be rooted in cultural factors related to taking pride in family wellbeing as well as in economic roles. While women overall have higher depression rates than men in the United States, Hispanic women tend to show the highest rates of depression. Hispanic women might carry the economic burden more on their shoulders since they associate

their family's happiness with their work and achievements. Of course, taking blame for the economic crises is not linked to any specific gender or racial group, but people worry nonetheless. It appears that Hispanics, especially females, tend to stress themselves more as they might be taking the nose-diving of economy a bit more personally than everyone else. Since males tend to work in construction and farming industries in larger numbers than women, they are also being laid off at a higher ratio than females. Therefore, Hispanic women are perhaps financially supporting entire families by themselves as their male counterparts are losing jobs. The economic recession has caused many layoffs throughout the United States, as well as in South Florida where a large percentage of the population are Hispanics.

Family, for as much happiness as they bring one, can also play a major role in the cause of stress. Arguments, divorce, or an aging parent all contribute to the stress people experience on a daily basis. Fighting, as well as the flow of family life in general, causes stress upon all family members. Family health, such as a sick family member, pregnancy, miscarriage, or abortion, is also a leading cause of stress within a family (Hart, 2007). Family is a wonderful part of most people's life, but they can also cause a lot of stress because they are such an important part of people's identity.

Personal concerns can also lead to stress. The struggles one faces within oneself can become an overwhelming and powerful thing. Trying to overcome a bad habit, losing self-control, creating pressure on ones success, and personal change can negatively affect an individual (Hart, 2007). Losing self-control can be one of the most difficult things a person can experience because humans have a deep desire to always be in control of his or her own life.

Personal health and safety is an inducer of stress symptoms. From a health perspective, the stress to lose weight, overcome an addiction or deal with an injury or illness becomes an overwhelming stressor that can result in chronic stress. Personal health affects people of all ages, where as personal safety is a stress experienced more often by adults and parents than those who are young and childless.

The emotional attachment and disappointments involved in personal relationships can also cause a significant amount of stress. The emotional demands of personal relationships whether it is a divorce, a friendship or just being in the dating scene can be a source of ongoing stress because of the love one has for those causing the stress.

Death, a leading cause of stress, is probably the most wrenching cause (Hart, 2007). The stress associated with the death of a loved one or close friend can certainly become overwhelming and be a major source for acute stress. Even the death of a pet can be stressful. Death is a natural stress that one cannot avoid, which makes it even harder to deal with. Stress is something everyone experiences, but how one handles the stress involved with the death is what makes one stronger and able to cope.

Stress affects people of all ages and all races. According to the U.S. Department of Health and Human Services, 75% of the general population experience at least "some stress" every two weeks; half of those experience moderate or high levels of stress during the same two-week period (Stress facts, 1996-2000). Millions of Americans suffer from unhealthy levels of stress at work. A study several years ago estimated the number to be eleven million--given events since that time, this number has certainly more than tripled--studies in Sweden, Canada, and other Westernized countries show similar trends (Stress facts, 1996-2000).

The U.S. Public Health Service made reducing stress one of its major health promotion goals because stress contributes to heart disease, high blood pressure, strokes, and it affects the immune system, which protects us from many serious diseases (Stress facts, 1996-2000). Stress also contributes to alcoholism, obesity, suicide, drug addiction, cigarette addiction, and other harmful behaviors (Stress facts, 1996-2000). Stress management is especially important for men as they often tend to be victims of alcoholism, obesity, or cigarette addiction, and die earlier than their female counterparts (Stress facts, 1996-2000).

Undoubtedly, stress can affect every aspect of one's life. Moreover, it can present challenges both personally and professionally. One of the main sources of stress is one's ability to maintain a balance with relation to workplace responsibilities and the responsibilities to one's family. To gain further insight into possible tools that can be used to examine stress management, several surveys that are widely available have been reviewed and presented.

Personal and Work Life Stressors' Self Assessment

The *Personal and Work Life Stressors Self Assessment Questionnaire* is an online survey based on the premise that awareness of the levels of stress in one's life is paramount and necessary for the effective management of stress (Olmstead, 2006). The survey was designed for this reason and not only is it recommended to be completed by all employees in a company, but it is also recommended for periodic use as a personal assessment tool. The survey is designed to inform respondents about how they deal with stress in the following areas: personal time, money, health, family, and work. These different areas allow one to examine specific aspects of one's life and evaluate the levels of stress that they experience in relation to one another.

The survey consists of 56 statements and is preceded by detailed instructions asking the respondent to rate him or her on a scale ranging from 1 to 5 for each statement. The following scale is provided: 1 – Never; 2 – Seldom; 3 – Sometimes; 4 – Most of the time; 5 – Always. While completing the survey, the subject is instructed to take notes and make suggestions as to the areas in which adjustments or improvements can be made to the stress in his/her life. At the end of the survey is a chart titled "Action Plan." This chart has the following four column headings: "No" (the number of the statement), "Action Item Description" (the title of the area in question, for example, personal time, family and so on), "Responsibility" (what the subject can do to make changes), and "Deadline" (Olmstead, 2006). The goal of this chart is to encourage accountability for one's actions. After the chart is completed, the subject is to implement it and, as a means to ensuring success, designate someone as a motivator and coach.

Upon completion of the survey, the average score is calculated. No interpretation of the results is provided; however, the goal and intent of the survey is not to place emphasis on the score. The survey is for an individual to create an action plan and become more aware of the stressors that exist in various areas of his or her life and then devise strategies to better manage them.

Glazer-Stress Control Life Style Survey.

The Glazer-Stress Control Life Style Survey, as mention previously in this book, was designed by Dr. Howard L. Glazer. In this survey, the respondents' scores will determine whether or not they are likely to experience cardiac problems. The survey uses varying descriptors and classifications to determine personality types and behaviours within a scale of 20 sets of items. Each pair of descriptors represents two contrasting behaviors, putting the respondent between two extremes. One extreme lies to the left of the numbers from one to seven and the other extreme lies to the right. The subject is expected to choose one of these numbers, which will illustrate where he/she belongs between the two extremes.

All of the scores in the extremes to the left are then added to give a sub-total, followed by the extremes to the right. These subtotals are added together to find the total score. A total score ranging from 110 to 140 signifies that the subject exhibits Type A1 behavior, which signifies that he or she is likely to have great potential in developing maladies related to the heart. A score ranging from 80 to 109 constitutes a Type A2 behavior, which is similar to Type A1. Furthermore, a total score of 60 to 79 describes Type AB behavior and is a combination of A and B, which is considered healthier than A1 and A2. A score between 30 and 59 means the respondent has a Type B2 behaviour, which is less prone to illness. Lastly, Type B behavior ranges between 0 and 29. These people are relatively low-key and exhibit no likely traits relative to cardiac illness.

How Vulnerable Are You To Stress?

The "How Vulnerable Are You to Stress" survey is one that posits that although stress is a part of life, there are certain habits that would make one more prone or vulnerable to stress. The survey is very simple to complete. It is divided into five sections: rest and exercise, finances and time management, leisure and lifestyle, communicating, diet, and health and fitness (Health Library, 2009). Each section has three statements to which the respondent answers – always, occasionally, or never. Upon completion, the survey prompts the respondent to click on the caption "Analyze." The respondent then receives his/her evaluation of the survey. Respondents should take this assessment regularly to maintain a good level of stress management.

The Overload Stress Inventory

The Overload Stress Inventory, adapted from Hyde and Allen's conceptual analysis of overload (1996, pp. 29-30), can be used to assess the stress perception of respondents. This inventory has 10 statements, and, for each statement, the respondent indicates the degree to which he or she engages in the stated behavior. A rating of 1 means "Never" and a rating of 5 means "Always" with the person demonstrating the specific behavior. The responses are assessed according to the following general criteria (adapted from Hyde and Allen's 1996 book):

- Scores in the range of 40 – 50 tend to mean severe stress from overload.
- Scores in the range of 30 – 39 tend to mean high stress from overload.
- Scores in the range of 20 – 29 tend to mean moderate stress from overload.
- Scores in the range of 19 and below tend to mean low stress from overload.

The goal for each individual or group should be to work with a moderate level of stress as that might be the ideal balance for the development of eustress or a little push to achieve deadlines toward one's personal and professional goals. Individuals who score in the high and severe levels or ranges of stress overload need to better balance their tasks, priorities, and different roles before their health is impacted negatively.

In today's fast paced world, ensuring that one is aware of potential stressors empowers one with the skills necessary to cope, which is essential to effectively manage stress. Managers and human resource personnel can use surveys or assessment tests as tools for employees or potential employees. While they should be used responsibly and objectively, these tests can assist in providing insight relative to the factors which persons in leadership positions should be aware of when it concerns employees. When applying for jobs, people can be asked to complete behavior or personality trait assessments to better place them within various positions. Managers should place these individuals in the position that seems most compatible with their skills, which would make for a smoother operation.

On a personal level, individuals can use assessment tests to make them aware of the areas in their life that they feel needs improvement. These surveys can be a kind of warning to alert people to curb their behaviors as they have potential to adversely affect their health. Personal knowledge of stressors in one's life can also help with family relationships. Sometimes, individuals may not be aware of how the stress can negatively affect their loved ones or those in immediate contact with them. But when one actually sits down and fills out these surveys then one is compelled to examine and analyze both one's lifestyle and behaviors. For example, managers and employees alike can use the Overload Stress Inventory to assess their stress perceptions on an annual basis for comparison and discussion purposes.

Stress Management Implications and Strategies

In simplest terms, stress is the opposite of relaxation. Both positive and negative aspects of life can be equally stressful. Stress comes from the external forces in one's life that pushes one's buttons and provokes extreme emotions. Although one commonly thinks of stress coming from the frustrations and low points in one's life, high points and achievements are stressful as well. Different stress management techniques may be needed for different situations because different stressors cause different responses. The literature provides at least three main approaches to better manage stress and they are categorized as: the action oriented approach, the emotionally oriented approach, and the acceptance oriented approach.

The action oriented approach, which is scientific in nature, is when one seeks to confront the problem causing the stress by changing the environment or the situation. People with superior decision making skills will excel the best with this approach. In this specific kind of approach, the problem creating the stress is identified. Identification of stress can be a bit complicated if there's a chain of reasons or stress creating factors, but once the source of stress is identified, it is almost half solved. In this approach, the identified problem is confronted directly.

The emotionally oriented approach is when one does not have the power to change the situation causing the stress. Instead, he or she can manage stress by changing one's interpretation and feelings towards it. For example, if you are at work and a new manager suggests how to deal with a situation and you do not agree with him/her, then you just have to adapt to his/hers management style and what is expected of you as an employee.

The acceptance oriented approach is when something has happened over which one has no power, no emotional control, and no focus except on surviving the stress. Death is an example of acceptance oriented stress management. Death is a difficult part of life that causes stress that one has no power or control over, except coping with the loss of a loved one, friend, or co-worker. A good way to handle this approach to stress management would be to take the time to grieve your loss.

The following are examples of different ways of dealing with stress (Stress management tips, n.d.):

1- *Take a deep breath* - Taking a deep breath or two will add oxygen to your system; this can almost instantly help a person to relax. The time you take during your breathing helps you to maintain self control of the in a stressful situation.

2- *Take time and smell the roses* – Often times, time is a factor in stress. When individuals do not manage their time properly stress is the end result. If we allow them, stressful events can build up, wall us in, and eventually stop us from enjoying the good things in life.

3- *Ask for help*, if needed - Some individuals try to deal with all of their stress such as work, family, and school on their own and never take the time to ask for assistance. Asking for assistance helps to relieve some of the stress that has and will build up from the stressors of everyday life. Asking for help also allows for the opportunity to have better time management.

Stress can manifest itself in many different areas of our life. School, work, and family can be considered the major areas of stress. For students, college is often viewed, at first, as a place away from the rules and regulation of parents, where they can be independent. "The American College Health Association cites stress as the number-one impediment to academic performance in its national college health assessment. Administrators at college counseling centers and support groups agree with those findings-stress is an almost unavoidable hurdle for students, with consequences that are significantly worse than a botched exam or a couple of missed classes" (Managing stress in school, n.d., para. 1). Effective stress management for college students will carry one a long way towards managing stress over one's lifetime. There are several techniques to handling and managing stress that come from education. Time management is a great way to eliminate stressors. Some suggestions to manage an individual's stress as a student is to have a calendar and write in their dates for assignments, projects, class schedule, and study time. Another way to eliminate stress is to always be prepared. Ways to avoid being unprepared are making sure one has sufficient paper, pens, and supplies, purchasing one's books ahead of time to avoid the normal rush at the bookstore or the possibility of a book shortage and getting a head start on one's assignments. It is also important to schedule in time for oneself to relax and have some fun. As a student, socializing is important and often times a way to relieve stress.

Stress on the job is common. "A recent American survey, published in the *Journal of Occupational and Environmental Medicine,* noted that for those working 12 hours a day, there was a 37% increase in risk of illness and injury in comparison to those who work fewer hours" (StressManagementTips, 2005-2009, para. 1). There are some jobs that by their very nature are more stressful than others. Jobs that entail twenty-four hour dedication, such as county jobs, can be stressful. Police officers and fire fighters, because they put their life on the line to save others, are usually stressed. Oftentimes, fire fighters and police officers partake in different stress management classes where they acquire several techniques to learn how to better manage stress. For those who work in an office and do not physically put their lives on the line, time management is often a source of stress. Today, some businesses have combined two or more traditional positions and have created one position that encompasses multitasking. Having to be responsible and complete several different tasks at one time for several different people can be very taxing and can lead to stress. Working with others on the job whose character, values and beliefs are different than yours can also lead to a source of stress. Crossing cross-cultural barriers on the job can be very trying if one is not properly trained how to handle them. Because of the number of hours many employees work per week, the job can easily become all-encompassing. Most people wake and get ready for work, drive to work, spend eight or more hours at work, and then drive home from work. Some ways to manage workplace stressors are:

1- Discipline yourself to wake and get ready, not for work, but for your day.
2- On the drive to work, listen to music, humor – anything that isn't related to work.
3- Take an alternate route to work. The change in scenery will help you stay alert to the road and keep your mind off the job.
4- Plan your work and work your plan. Devote every paid minute to your job. Deviate from your work plan only when absolutely necessary.
5- Take your allotted breaks. Remember: the opposite of stress is relaxation. Don't work through lunch or coffee breaks. This also means don't think or talk about work during your breaks.
6- Instead of coffee, drink water, juice, or electrolyte infused drinks. Dehydration often is the cause of fatigue. Coffee and soft drinks that contain caffeine may seem to "keep you going," but in reality they add to stress and do not keep your body hydrated (StressManagementTips, 2005-2009, para. 7).

As mentioned earlier, family life can be a source of stress and needs to be managed. Spousal relationships, children, and bills are all family stressors. Along with these mentioned stressors, family life can include both deaths and weddings. When you throw all of these topics in the mix of life, stress can manifest itself into one or all of these areas of family life. Some people start their day getting out of bed filled with stress. They then proceed to wake-up, cook breakfast, get dressed, get the kids dressed, feed the dog, walk the dog, drop the children off at school and get to work on-time. Often there is the same type of stressors still causing stress at the end of the day that was there when the day started. If one thing goes wrong in this scenario then the entire morning/evening could be thrown off.

Benefits and Challenges of Stress Management
Most people experience stress almost every day, and managing that stress is crucial to not burning oneself out. The right way to manage stress is one of the most important skills one can ever learn. Many people, unfortunately, wait until they are on

the verge of burning out before thinking about stress management. In her article, *Why Stress Management? Learn The Benefits of Stress Relief and Healthy Living*, Elizabeth Scott (2007) mentions that today, it does not always seem important to take on the practice of stress management before a worn-out body forces the issue. Developing healthy stress relieving habits do have many benefits and do pay off over time. Stress management helps take away some of the negative effects of stress as well as bring positive outcomes that contribute to one's overall well-being. Stress Management has its benefits and challenges, but the challenges one faces in managing stress are worth the beneficial outcome. Some benefits of stress management are one's health, looks, increased productivity, happiness, and stress levels (Scott, 2007).

Health is extremely important in one's life, and stress can easily lead to many poor health outcomes. Stress can lead to minor health problems such as headaches and gastrointestinal problems, but it can also lead to diseases in the long-run. Stress can have psychological effects such as depression and anxiety. It can also reduce the feeling of pleasure and accomplishment, which can affect relationships as well. Mental stress negatively affects the heart in several ways, which can later lead to heart disease. The website "about.com" provides evidence that stress management efforts can reduce the risk of heart problems by up to 75% in those with heart disease (Scott, 2007). Stress can also cause damage to one's immune system and make one susceptible to infections or cause many people to either lose or gain weight, which can lead to eating disorders. It can also lead one to alcohol substance abuse, which causes many damages to one's health. Effectively managing stress is extremely vital for one's health. Stress reduction leads one to better immune function, less illnesses and physical complaints, more energy, more relaxation, better sleep, better digestion, calmer mood, more focused, and more positive towards life.

Believing in oneself is important for self esteem. To some degree, everyone is worried about the way they look and are not satisfied if they are not where they want to be. Stress can have many affects on the way one looks, but these effects can be avoided by effectively managing stress:

> For example, taking care of your body by getting enough sleep can make you more productive and healthier, and can help you better manage stress, as well as avoid dark circles under the eyes and a poor complexion. Also, eating right can keep your blood sugar levels even, keeping your emotions in check and making you more resilient to stress, as well as helping you stay in your 'skinny jeans' or favorite tee-shirts from college. Getting regular exercise can help you blow off steam when you're frustrated and keep your body fit and toned (Scott, 2007).

These strategies are all ways that can make one healthier and look more attractive by effectively reducing one's stress.

Reducing stress can increase productivity by making one more focused. There are some stress relief habits that naturally make a person more productive. Elizabeth Scott (2007) mentions in her article that one can catch up on one's sleep and be more focused and productive by power napping, which helps one make a few hours of sleep stretch further. Being organized is beneficial because it helps an individual have more control of their life and allows them to be more productive in all aspects of their life. Limiting caffeine can even help them with reducing stress. It would improve their sleep and help them feel less stressed at the end of the day. Finally, Scott says that the right attitude is actually a habit that can be learned. Being an optimist can benefit one in many areas of life, helping one achieve more. Reducing one's stress and increasing one's productivity, and helps he/she allocate their time better within their workplace and family. This is helpful because, as previously mentioned, one's workplace and family are two big stressors in one's life.

Managing one's stress and having control of one's life brings more joy into one's life. People want to adopt some stress relievers if they want to enjoy life more and have fun come to them more easily. Such things as taking care of pets, listening to music, dancing regularly, working more laughter into life, maintaining a circle of friends, and having sex are all stress relievers (Scott, 2007). It is important to always remind oneself that one is never too busy to include these activities in one's lifestyle. Happiness and joy are very important for one's overall well-being. Learning to reduce stress effectively can help create more happiness in one's life and benefit one in the long-run.

One of the most beneficial outcomes of effectively managing stress is the decrease of one's stress levels. There are many stressors that cause stress in one's life, but managing them and avoiding the minor stressors can keep one's stress levels relatively low. The key advantage that leads to all of the aforementioned benefits of managing stress is lowering the amount of distress in one's life. There are stresses that can be avoided and there are some that naturally exist, such as death or cancer. If one can avoid the minor stressors that cause harm to the body, then it becomes easier to manage the unavoidable stressors. Having low stress levels can help one spend more time with friends and family and enjoy the good things in life. It can help one focus on the now, instead of the past or the future.

There are many benefits and challenges to effectively managing stress. George S. Patton was one of the most successful United States field commanders of any war (Potter, 2009). Potter believed that people need to "accept the challenges so that you can feel the exhilaration of victory" (2009, para. 1). Many things one does involves some sort of challenge, but how one manages the challenge is what allows one to overcome it and enjoy the benefits. Some of the challenges involved in effectively managing stress are accepting change, breaking bad habits, managing time, consistency/dedication, and motivation.

Change is something that can cause much stress and conflict among people in their everyday life. Managing stress involves dealing with whatever change may be causing the stress. Implementing change can be somewhat burdensome because it involves people and new ways of doing things, which makes it difficult. Change is challenging when dealing with managing stress because most people tend to resist changing. Two possible reasons for resistance to change can be the feeling of being controlled by the amount of stress, and the feeling of having too many things going on at once. Many people allow stress to accumulate because they like the feeling of always being in a rush, which makes it difficult for them to change the way they manage their stress. Accepting the change involved in managing stress differently may be difficult for some people; however, it is worth the change in the end because change can help one learn and grow.

Breaking bad habits can be a challenge in managing stress effectively. An example would be one wanting to quit smoking when stressed. To manage this stress, one needs to stop smoking and learn to use other methods, such as exercising or breathing techniques to handle stressors. Procrastination is one common bad habit that causes stress among many people. Benjamin Franklin once said, "Never leave for tomorrow that which you can do today" (Latumahina, 2007). Procrastinators find it difficult to break their bad habit of waiting until last minute because they do not realize that the key in managing stress is to avoid stress by doing what Benjamin Franklin said, not leaving things for tomorrow when you can do them today.

Time management is probably one of the most important challenges in managing stress. If people do not learn to manage their time efficiently, they may have a difficult time getting what they need done and/or accomplished, which may bring stress upon them. Managing one's time involves organization because it is important to learn how to divide appropriate time for each imperative situation in one's life. Time management may be challenging to some because if people do not manage their time efficiently, then they will not have the time to accomplish what they wish to accomplish, and they will become stressed out. Having a calendar and writing down every event, idea, situation, or errand they need to do can help them avoid the stress involved in forgetting to do something. A good way of managing their time is to look over what they need to accomplish the following day, every night before they go to sleep. This will better help people to manage their time and avoid whatever stress involved in not being able to control their own responsibilities.

Dedication and consistency to managing stress can be a challenge for many people. Sometimes, it can be difficult to dedicate people to do something because some believe that they do not have the time, and some lack the motivation. Motivation can be a challenge, because some people do not have enough motivation to be able to dedicate themselves to managing stress and being consistent in managing it. A common example would be someone who is usually stressed out and wants to begin yoga to relax and alleviate the stress they experience. If he/she does not set aside a specific time period to doing yoga, then it will be difficult to dedicate him/her to consistently going every week. Finding the motivation to get up and go to yoga can be difficult, but once he/she makes it a routine and stays consistent for at least a few months, then it will eventually become easier to dedicate to. Yoga is a form of exercise that people should dedicate some time to each week. It can help people manage their stress by relaxing and allowing their body to recuperate from the stress it has been through.

Stress has many effects on people and can be very difficult to learn to effectively manage. However, once people get through the challenges involved in managing stress, they can enjoy the benefits. Every situation one experiences in life involves a few challenges before being able to benefit from the results. Hans Seyle once said, "It's not stress that kills us, it is our reaction to it" (Hans seyle quotes, n.d.). The way people manage stress can help them learn how to react to it in a way that will not create more stress or harm their body. It can be difficult to surpass the challenges involved in managing stress but once people find the motivation then they will be able to enjoy the benefits involved, which will help them be consistent in managing their stress every day.

Summary

The symptoms of stress can be manifested in many different ways and to varying degrees, especially in times of economic depression. It is a fact that we are constantly bombarded by challenges relevant to our lives and lifestyles as well as our work environment. Stress itself is difficult to avoid. If left unchecked, its very existence can have serious and sometimes fatal effects. The links between increased stress levels and health have been well documented. The possible negative effects on one's relationships and family members are unmistakable. Moreover, the debilitating effects of stress on one's life can actually force them to become withdrawn and unsociable. They can no longer appreciate the simple things in life because they are consumed by what they feel are challenges that appear insurmountable. It is important to understand that while one may not be able to completely eliminate stressful events from one's life, it is one's perception of these events that will determine one's responses to them. Yes, stress management is not easy, but with time and effort, just like anything else in life, it can be achieved.

Learning how to take some time to relax and unwind on a regular basis is extremely important. It has been mentioned that time management and organization can alleviate a lot of stress in one's life. Not only will people benefit as individuals, but so will their loved ones and all those that they interact with. All of the effort put into learning to manage one's stress is worth the outcome. Allowing a certain degree of flexibility will also ease the burden in many areas. In the workplace, managers and others in leadership positions can invite experts to conduct workshops in the areas of stress management so that employees can learn and/or practice the skills necessary to balance all of the responsibilities. When people are equipped with these important skills, then they will be able to cope with the daily challenges. In essence, effective stress management is vital if one desires to lead a happy and healthy life.

The Overload Stress Inventory Survey

The Overload Stress Inventory, adapted from Hyde and Allen's conceptual analysis of overload (1996, pp. 29-30), is designed to provide a person the extent to which being overloaded with tasks and responsibilities might be a source of stress. It further clarifies a person's natural tendencies toward tasks and relationships. For each of the following questions in the inventory, select (or circle) an answer that best describes your agreement or disagreement regarding each statement. Higher scores indicate stronger tendencies toward those elements.

Stress Orientation Questions	Disagree..............Agree
1. I regularly take work home to finish in the evenings or weekends.	1 2 3 4 5
2. I have more work than it is possible to complete at a given time.	1 2 3 4 5
3. I have many important deadlines which I cannot always meet.	1 2 3 4 5
4. More often, I feel less competent on tasks than I think I should.	1 2 3 4 5
5. I do not always have enough time to do as good of job as I am capable of doing.	1 2 3 4 5
6. I am usually given more work than my current qualifications and skills.	1 2 3 4 5
7. Despite the fact that I am usually busy, I often fall behind schedule and deadlines.	1 2 3 4 5
8. Most of my tasks are usually too difficult and/or too complex to complete.	1 2 3 4 5
9. I have too many tasks and jobs needing done all at the same time.	1 2 3 4 5
10. There are many times that I feel overwhelmed by my tasks and assignments.	1 2 3 4 5
Add Total Score for "C" Inventory:	

Interpretation of Overload Stress Inventory:

Scores in the range of 40 – 50 tend to mean *severe* stress from overload. It might be best to take appropriate steps to prioritize and/or reduce the number of stressful tasks and activities you are currently handling.

Scores in the range of 30 – 39 tend to mean *high* stress from overload. Perhaps it is best to prioritize tasks and work on managing those that are direct causes of your stress.

Scores in the range of 20 – 29 tend to mean *moderate* stress from overload. These ranges mean that you might experience the impact of overload at times, but this is normal and tolerable level of stress. You are able to successfully control this level of work and/or overload.

Scores in the range of 19 and below tend to mean *low* stress from overload. Perhaps you have an appropriate number of tasks with properly designed deadlines. It may also indicate that you are managing your time effectively and you feel comfortable with your current workload and responsibilities.

CHAPTER SEVEN

7 – Values and Stress Research

W ith relative few studies exploring values in the Caribbean, this chapter examines similarities in the values and Type A stress behaviors of working adults in the developing countries of Belize and the Bahamas, and the developed countries of the United Kingdom and the United States. For value convergence, 30 of the 36 values of the developed and developing countries were similarly ranked most important, important or unimportant. For value divergence, the developed countries placed higher importance on the achievement and competition values freedom and independence and the developing countries placed higher importance on the safety and security values a world at peace, national security, forgiving, helpful, wisdom, health, and broadminded.

On the other hand, the developing countries placed equal importance on the achievement and competition value a sense of accomplishment, and higher importance on self-respect and ambition, and the developed countries placed higher importance on the safety and security value family security. The value system in Belize and The Bahamas were more similar (convergence) with the US as compared to the UK. Finally, Type A stress behaviors were higher in Belize and The Bahamas as compared to the US. Finally, the chapter provides a discussion of the meaning and implications of these findings for international business entrepreneurs, the limitations of the study, and makes recommendations for further research.

Convergence and Divergence of Values and Stress[2]

The globalization of the marketplace mandates that managers of companies operating around the world understand the values, attitudes and behaviors of their employees, managers, customers, and competitors. Deeply-held values tend to influence or drive ethical decision-making and ethical judgment of employees and managers across cultures and countries. As managers and employees throughout the world increasingly work with people from different cultures, do they modify their

---

[2] Published with permission of the authors from original source: Mujtaba, B.G., Murphy Jr., E.F., McCartney, T., Williams, A., Trumbach, A., Reid, J., Greenwood, R., Teeple, W., and Woodhull, M.D. (2009). An Investigation of Convergence and Divergence of Values and Type A Stress Behaviors among Respondents from the US, UK, Belize, and the Bahamas: What are the Implications for Multinational Entrepreneurs? *The Icfai University Journal of Organizational Behavior*, VIII (2), pp. 6-34.

values, attitudes and behaviors so they are more similar? Are values converging by becoming more similar? While Bailey and Spicer (2007) argue that "the identification of cultural similarities may be just as important as that of differences, since members of different societies need to build on common moralities and beliefs (values) when working together to meet common goals" (p. 1462), a vast number of research studies have a primary focus on differences across the cultures. A relatively neglected region in the cross-cultural literature is Belize and The Bahamas. The researchers could find no studies that focused on the values, attitudes and behaviors of working adults in Belize and The Caribbean. We filled this research gap by exploring whether there were cross-cultural value and Type A stress behavior similarities and differences between the developing countries of Belize and the Bahamas, and the developed countries of the UK (United Kingdom) and the US (the United States).

The chapter is laid out in five sections. First we present theory and hypotheses. Next we explain our research methodology and finish with a discussion of our main findings, followed by limitations and implications for management and future research.

Theory and Hypotheses

Are cross-cultural values and Type A stress behaviors more similar or different between the two developing countries of Belize and the Bahamas, and two developed countries of the UK and US? These topics are of extreme importance as companies develop global production processes, hire employees in the global marketplace, make ethical judgments, coach and motivate employee, and market their products globally (Bigoness and Blakely, 1996; Elkhouly and Buda, 1997; Neelankavil, Mathur and Zhang, 2000; Lenartowicz and Johnson, 2002; Lenartowicz and Roth, 2001; Triandis and Suh, 2002; Ryckman and Houston, 2003; Gustavo, 2004; McGuire et al., 2006). Our study expands the work of Murphy et al. (2007a) which explored values and Type A behaviors in the developed countries of the US, Hong Kong and Singapore as compared to the developing countries of Afghanistan, China, Colombia, Mexico, Philippines, and Thailand. We updated that research study with a new US population sample. Our study will add to the cross-cultural and practitioner literature concerning developing and developed countries because it will serve as a second study of similarities and differences between countries using the developed versus developing country constructs. Our study also contributes to the literature because no known studies have explored cross-cultural similarities and differences in values and Type A stress behaviors in Belize and The Bahamas, and even fewer have done so comparing the UK, US, Belize, and the Bahamas. This study addresses this research gap. The present study examines the values and Type A stress behaviors of working adults in two Caribbean developing countries (Belize and Bahamas) as compared to two western developed countries (US and UK).

How is culture defined? Based upon the early research of Rokeach, Hofstede, and more recently by Schwartz, Connor and Becker and Leung et al., we define culture as an interrelated set of values, attitudes and behaviors that form a sub-group, group, organization or nation's value system. Trompenaars and Hampden-Turner (1998) related that values, norms and institutions create a profile that allows the group, organization or society to be differentiated from other groups, organizations or societies. Schwartz (1999) stated that "culture at the national level attempts to capture the typical individual value priorities in a society" (p. 26). While Hofstede (2001) explained culture as the "software of the mind" (p. 2), Leung et al. (2005) explained culture as "values, beliefs, norms and behavioral patterns of a national group" (p. 357), and Jameson (2007) indicates that "culture transmits and inculcates knowledge, beliefs, values, attitudes, traditions and ways of life" (p. 199). Rokeach (1968, 1979), Connor and Becker (2003), Connor et al. (2006), Khilji et al. (2008a, b), Limthanakom et al. (2008), Mujtaba et al. (2008), and Murphy et al. (2007a, 2008a) related to us that culture consists of an interrelated set of values, attitudes and behaviors that are socialized early in life and form a value system.

Where does culture come from? Early research by Kluckhohn and Kohlberg suggests values and culture are socialized from the moment of conception, with socialization continuing until death. Children are socialized through their interaction in the environment, through the influence of families, friends, significant others, teachers, and organizations, as socialization teaches each offspring how to operate and succeed in society (Kluckhohn, 1951, 1962; Kohlberg, 1970). Rokeach indicated that we must infer people's values through their attitudes and behaviors and that all three form a culture, sub-culture, value system, personality, or value orientation type. What are values?

Rokeach (1986) defined a value as "a type of belief, centrally located within one's belief system, about how one ought or ought not to behave, or about some end stated of existence worth or not worth attaining" (p. 125). Rokeach's early research on values, attitudes and behaviors suggests that values are differentiated from attitudes and behaviors, because while we may have hundreds of thousands of behaviors, we only have several thousand attitudes, and only several dozen values. Rokeach defined attitudes as "a relatively enduring organization of beliefs around an object or situation predisposing one to respond in some preferential manner" (Rokeach, 1986, p. 112). Values are important because we can explore them in order to see how people might behave. Values form value schemas, value systems or value orientations and "are simultaneously components of psychological processes, of social interaction, and of cultural patterning and storage" (Rokeach, 1986, p. 17).

Rokeach related that values were the most important construct to study because first, "value seems to be a more dynamic concept since it has a strong motivation component as well as cognitive, affective and behavioral components." Second, while values and attitudes have been shown to impact behavior, attitudes only impact behavior, and values impact both attitudes and behavior. Finally, "the value concept provides us with a more economical analytic tool for describing and explaining similarities and differences between persons, groups, nations and cultures" (1986, pp. 157-158).

The instrument we have chosen to use in our research study is the Rokeach Value Survey (RVS). The RVS consists of 36 values which Rokeach stated were present in most societies. Although some societies will possess more values and some less than the 18 terminal and 18 instrumental values of the RVS, Rokeach felt that most societies will possess the values in the RVS, and as such, they can be used to explore similarities and differences across cultures and across most demographic sub-groups. While the terminal values are end-state of existence values are the most important goals in the lives of respondents, the instrumental values are the means-based values or the behavioral means respondents might use to obtain their terminal value goals

(Murphy, Gordon and Anderson, 2004). The terminal and then instrumental values are rank ordered in a hierarchy of importance separately from (1) most important to (18) least important, leading to what Rokeach called a value schema, value system or value orientation. Cross cultural research has shown that values and value systems differ in their hierarchy of importance in each society, and as previously mentioned, values have been shown to impact behavior.

Cross-cultural Research

As goods and services, capital, and know-how flow across borders (Leung et al., 2005) practitioners, managers and HRM managers must understand the values, attitudes, behaviors and culture of countries that they are doing business with. The global marketplace in the 21st century makes it imperative that we study cross-cultural similarities and differences in values, because values influence attitudes and Type A stress behaviors. An understanding of the values and Type A stress behaviors of employees, managers, practitioners, customers, and competitors in countries businesses are operating in throughout the world can give them an insight into how they can develop better world-wide customer relationships, develop better human resources programs, including stress reduction programs for their employees throughout the world, and how they can develop closer relationships and predict the behaviors of customers, competitors and employees operating in the global marketplace (Neelankavil, Mathur and Zhang, 2000; Hofstede, 2001; Lenartowicz and Johnson, 2002; Lyons, Duxbury and Higgins, 2005; Leung et al., 2005; Murphy et al., 2006; McGuire et al., 2006).

Culture and business environment of The Bahamas. It's better in the Bahamas" is a slogan adopted some years ago by the Bahamas Ministry of Tourism to advertise the cultural uniqueness of the beautiful, stable, history-rich, and productive small island-nation. The Bahamas is an archipelago of more than 700 islands and 2,400 cays that stretches 50 miles southeast from the tip of Florida to the southwestern coasts of Cuba and Hispaniola (Haiti and Dominican Republic). Each of these islands has a distinct character and unique qualities that appeal to a variety of people, such as tourists, developers, entrepreneurs, bankers, environmentalists, to name a few. It is also the "playground" of the "rich and famous," and it is alleged that between the months of November to April of any given year, the Bahamas has one of the highest concentration of wealth and celebrity in the world.

The original inhabitants of these islands were the gentle Arawaks (Luycan) Indians who migrated from Central America and other Caribbean islands, fleeing from the war-like, cannibalistic, Carib Indians, to find a simple way of life of peace and harmony. The American War of Independence had a profound effect on the Bahamas, as many Loyalists with their allegiance to the British Crown and grants of money and land in the Bahamas, moved to these islands with their trusted slaves. By 1789, the population of the Bahamas was nearly 12,000 people scattered among the various islands, with the population changing dramatically to a black majority. It is important to chart the development of the Bahamas in order to understand its present state by explaining the progression of the psycho-social stratification of the peoples of the Bahamas and the impact of the location, soil, water, and the political and economical factors that have played a role in its national determination. The proximity to the United States, the institution of slavery, and British colonialism were the "fuels" that propelled the development of the Bahamas. The system of slavery, which became very important economically to the colonizers of the Caribbean, was also established in the Bahamas, although it differed somewhat from U.S. and Caribbean slavery.

The socio-ethnic configuration of the Bahamas has played a significant role in the economic development of the Bahamas. It is this progression of cultures and world events that have shaped the political and economic decisions that have placed the country in an enviable position today. Although there may be traces of Arawak or Seminole Indian in the Bahamian population, the ethnic configuration used to be traditionally black (majority), white, and the "in betweens." The emancipation of the slaves in the Bahamas was the beginning of social, racial, and class differences of a British colonial system. At that time, over ninety percent of the Bahamian people were of African extraction. From a socio-economic viewpoint, class structures used to be: 1) foreign and local whites = upper class; 2) mixed race people = middle class (different shades of "high yellow" to browns); 3) black and poor white = lower class. At present, the ethnic population in the Bahamas is: 1) Black = 85%; 2) White = 12%; and 3) Asian and Hispanic = 3%. There have been significant increases in the population (contractors, workers, doctors, accountants, bankers, etc.) of East Indian, West Indian, Haitian, and Filipino descent. The literacy rate is 98.2%.

The Bahamas plays host to more than 4 1/2 million visitors each year, largely U.S. citizens since the Bahamas is very close geographically to the U.S., and Bahamians are very comfortable with U.S. culture and customs. Over the years, the Bahamas has projected stable government which is structured very much like Great Britain but with Bahamian "overtones." With the "number one" industry tourism, the need for modern accommodation and infrastructure has attracted developers and entrepreneurs from around the world. The encouraging laws, tax structure, and the potential of the "family islands," especially Grand Bahamas, Abaco, Eleuthera, Exuma, Andros, and others, provide an exciting climate for investment.

The Bahamas offers attractive features to the potential investor: a stable democratic environment, relief from personal and corporate income taxes, timely repatriation of corporate profits, proximity to the United States with extensive air and telecommunication links, and a good "pool" of skilled professional workers. The Government of the Bahamas welcomes foreign investment in tourism and banking, and has declared an interest in agricultural and industrial investments to generate local employment, particularly in white-collar or skilled jobs. Despite its interest in foreign investment to diversify the economy, the Bahamian government responds to local concerns about foreign competition and tends to protect Bahamian business and labor interests. As a result of domestic resistance to foreign investment and high labor costs, growth can stagnate in sectors which the government wishes to diversify. The country's infrastructure is best developed in the principal cities of Nassau and Freeport, where there are relatively good paved roads and international airports. Electricity is generally reliable, although many businesses have their own backup generators. In Nassau, there are two daily newspapers, three "weeklies," and several international newspapers available for sale. There are also six radio stations. Both Nassau and Freeport have a television station. Cable TV and satellite also are available locally and provide most U.S. programs.

The Bahamas has strong bilateral relationships with the United States and the United Kingdom, represented by an ambassador in Washington and High Commissioner in London. The Bahamas also associates closely with other nations of the Caribbean Community (CARICOM). The Bahamas has an ambassador to Haiti and works closely with the United States and CARICOM on political and migration issues related to Haiti. The Bahamas has diplomatic relations with Cuba, hosting a Cuban Ambassador and recently opening a Bahamian Consulate in Cuba. A repatriation agreement was signed with Cuba in 1996, and there are commercial and cultural contacts between the two countries. The Bahamas also enjoys a strengthening relationship with China and many other countries in Asia. However, the United States historically has had close economic and commercial relations with the Bahamas. The U.S. shares ethnic, cultural, and historical ties with Bahamians. The Bahamas is home to more than 30,000 American residents. In addition, there are about 110 U.S. related businesses in the Bahamas. In 2004, about 87% of the 5 million tourists visiting the country were Americans. As a neighbor, the Bahamas and its political stability are especially important to the United States. The U.S. and the Bahamian governments have worked together on reducing crime and reforming the judiciary.

Culture and business environment of Belize. Belize is a small democratic country (8,867 square miles) in Central America. It is bordered to the south and west by Guatemala, to the north by Mexico, and to the east by the Caribbean Sea. It got its independence from Great Britain in 1981. Belize's main industries are agriculture, light manufacturing, and tourism. The main exports are citrus concentrate, bananas, sugar, and sea foods. The tourism industry has grown considerably. Many tourists, especially Americans and Canadians, visit its barrier reef (the longest in the Americas and the second longest in the world), its tropical rain forests, and its many Mayan archeological sites. According to the most recent vegetation surveys, about sixty percent (60%) of Belize is forested, with only about twenty percent (20%) of the country's land subject to human uses (such as agricultural land and human settlements). Savanna, scrubland and wetland constitute extensive parts of the land. As a result, Belize's biodiversity is rich, both marine and terrestrial, with a host of flora and fauna. About thirty-seven percent (37%) of Belize's land territory falls under some form of official protected status. Although a number of economically important minerals exist in Belize, none has been found in quantities large enough to warrant their mining. These minerals include dolomite, barite (source of barium), bauxite (source of aluminum), cassite (source of tin), and gold.

As of July 2008, its population was estimated at 301,270 people (Belize: People, 2008). Belize is a multiracial country. About 34% of the population is of mixed Maya and European descent (Mestizo), 25% are Kriols (a mixture of European and African descendants), 15% are Spanish, about 10.6% are Mayan, and about 6.1% are Afro-Amerindian (Garifuna). The remaining population includes European, East Indian, Chinese, Middle Eastern, and North American groups, including Mennonites (Belize, 2000). Belize has a young population with 38.4 percent 14 years of age or less. It has 58.1 percent between the ages of 15 and 65, and 3.5 percent beyond 65 years. Its median age is 20 years. It birth rate is 27.84 births per 1000 and its death rate is 5.77 deaths per 1000. The population growth rate, estimated in 2008, was 2.207 percent per year. Most Belizeans are Christian (Roman Catholic 49.6%, Protestant 27% (Pentecostal 7.4%, Anglican 5.3%, Seventh-day Adventist 5.2%, Mennonite 4.1%,

Methodist 3.5%, Jehovah's Witnesses 1.5%), other 14%, and none 9.4%) (Belize, 2000). This Christian background influences the population's value systems for business. English is the official language in Belize, but 43 percent of the population speaks Spanish at home. (Belize: Language and Religion -*MSN Encarta Encyclopedia*). The literacy rate, defined as those 15 years and over who can read and write, was 76.9%.

Belize is a small, essentially private-enterprise economy. Tourism is the number one foreign exchange earner. This is followed by exports of marine products, citrus, cane sugar, bananas, and garments. Due to the government's expansionary monetary and fiscal policies, initiated in September 1998, GDP grew at an annual rate of 4% in 1999-2007. Economic growth was further stimulated with oil discoveries in 2006. Belize's major concerns continue to be the sizable trade deficit and unsustainable foreign debt. In February 2007, the government restructured nearly all of its public external commercial debt. This reduced interest payments and liquidity concerns. Poverty reduction continues to be a key concern. (CIA World Factbook, 2008). Belize's gross domestic product was $1.3 billion U.S. in 2007, or $3, 950 U.S. per capita. Its economic growth rate is 2.2 percent in 2007. Its exports in 2007 were $ 215 million U.S. f.o.b. and consisted of sugar, bananas, citrus, clothing, fish products, molasses, and wood. Its imports in 2007 was $321 million U.S. f.o.b and consisted of machinery and transport equipment, manufactured goods; fuels, chemicals, pharmaceuticals; food, beverages, and tobacco.

Belize also has strong bilateral relationships with the United States and the United Kingdom, represented by an ambassador in Washington and High Commissioner in London. Belize also associates closely with other nations of the Caribbean Community (CARICOM). Belize is a parliamentary democracy. Its laws are based on English laws. Its government has three branches, the Executive Branch, the Legislative Branch, and the Judiciary Branch. There are two main political parties, the People's United Party (PUP) and the United Democratic Party (UDP).

Research Hypotheses

Murphy et al. (2007a, b) investigated cross-cultural differences in values between developed and developing nations. The research results indicated many similarities or a convergence of values between the developed and developing countries as 14 of 18 terminal and 16 of 18 instrumental values were ranked similarly as most important, important or unimportant. This led to the development of the following research hypotheses:

Hypothesis One (H1): There are more similarities in the terminal values ranked most important, important or unimportant between developed and developing countries.

Hypothesis Two (H2): There are more similarities in the instrumental values ranked most important, important or unimportant between developed and developing countries.

Research has shown that developed countries will rank achievement, independence and competition values (*accomplishment, freedom, independent, responsible, self-respect* and *ambitious*) higher than developing countries; and developing countries will more highly value safety, tradition and conformity values (*a world at peace, national security, wisdom, self-controlled family security, health, broadminded, forgiving, helpful* and *loving*). Murphy et al.'s (2007a, b) findings were mixed, and indicated that working adults in developed nations like the US and UK more highly valued the terminal values *accomplishment, freedom*, and instrumental values *independent, responsible, forgiving, helpful* and *loving* as compared to developing nations. Their research results also indicated that respondents from developing nations will more highly value the terminal values *family security, health, a world at peace, national security, wisdom* and *self-respect* and instrumental values *ambition, broadminded, obedient* and *self-controlled*. We labeled the US and UK as developed countries as they had GDPs per capita of US ($45,800) and UK ($35,000), and The Bahamas and Belize as developing countries as they had GDPs per capita of Belize ($7,900) and The Bahamas ($25,000) (Country Facts, 2008). As a result of the literature review we developed the following research hypotheses:

Hypothesis Three (H3): Working adults in developed nations like the US and UK more highly values the terminal values accomplishment, freedom, and instrumental values independent, responsible, forgiving, helpful and loving as compared to developing nations.

Hypothesis Four (H4): Working adults in the developing nations will more highly value the terminal values family security, health, a world at peace, national security, wisdom and self-respect and instrumental values ambition, broadminded, obedient and self-controlled.

Hypothesis Five (H5): Respondents from the US will place higher importance on the terminal values accomplishment, freedom, and instrumental values independent, responsible, forgiving, helpful and loving as compared to Belize.

Hypothesis Six (H6): Respondents from the US will place higher importance on the terminal values accomplishment, freedom, and instrumental values independent, responsible, forgiving, helpful and loving as compared to the Bahamas.

Hypothesis Seven (H7): Respondents from the UK will place higher importance on the terminal values accomplishment, freedom, and instrumental values independent, responsible, forgiving, helpful and loving as compared to Belize.

Hypothesis Eight (H8): Respondents from the UK will place higher importance on the terminal values accomplishment, freedom, and instrumental values independent, responsible, forgiving, helpful and loving as compared to the Bahamas.

Hypothesis Nine (H9): Belize will place higher value importance on the terminal values family security, health, a world at peace, national security, wisdom and self-respect and instrumental values ambition, broadminded, obedient and self-controlled as compared to the US.

Hypothesis Ten (H10): The Bahamas will place higher value importance on the terminal values family security, health, a world at peace, national security, wisdom and self-respect and instrumental values ambition, broadminded, obedient and self-controlled as compared to the US.

Hypothesis Eleven (H11): Belize will place higher value importance on the terminal values family security, health, a world at peace, national security, wisdom and self-respect and instrumental values ambition, broadminded, obedient and self-controlled as compared to the UK.

Hypothesis Twelve (H12): The Bahamas will place higher value importance on the terminal values family security, health, a world at peace, national security, wisdom and self-respect and instrumental values ambition, broadminded, obedient and self-controlled as compared to the UK.

What is Type A Behavior and TABP?

According to Murphy et al. (2007a), the beginning of early research on Type A Behavior Pattern (TABP) was by Friedman and Rosenman (1974) who indicated that TABP is the behavior of a person that has an aggressive and untiringly demand to succeed on the job. This means they place higher importance on this desire to succeed than they do to their friends and families. It is the "work before all" attitude and its subsequent behavior. Type A behavior pattern is a form of work stress that can lead to what Menon and Akhilesh (1994) related can lead to "decreased motivation, lowered performance levels and mental and physical ailments" (1994, p. 13). More recently, Turnipseed and Turnipseed (1997) relate that TABP has shown relationships with physical and emotional exhaustion, depression, insomnia, and sometimes drug or alcohol abuse, and TABP can lead to job dissatisfaction and turnover (p. 180). Some of the characteristics of TABP include a time urgency, competitiveness, and ability to get more done in a short time than another employee or manager. Another interesting finding by Friedman and Rosenman is that people with TABP cannot stand to lose, and sometimes, they will compete to win games with young children and they might become very critical and impatient with their supervisors, employees and other managers (Bradstatter and Eliasz, 2001, p. 5). One of the most serious problems with the Type A personality is that some individuals develop coronary heart disease (CHD). For instance, Bradstatter and Eliasz (2001) reported that when Type A person cannot achieve their goals, they might display signs of frustration, anger, hostility and sometimes outright violence (p. 59), and Geen (1990) stated that TABP behavior respondents concealed their anger, and this pent up anger could lead to CHD (p. 193).

Not all TABP behavior is negative though. Many of the drive and competitiveness skills demonstrated by people with TABP are highly desired in managers and employees. What seems to happen is that some employees and managers use stress management techniques to control the negative behaviors, and they harness their TABP for success on the job (Mudrack, 2004).

In research exploring the characteristics of individuals classified as having TABP in the U.S., Type A behavior has been linked to higher levels of stress in blue collar workers (Evans, Palsane and Carrere, 1987), higher levels of occupational stress, job dissatisfaction and turnover (Ivancevich and Matteson, 1984), lower job performance (Jamal, 1985), and other negative health outcomes like CHD (Matteson and Ivancevich, 1982).

In cross cultural research, Kouichi et al. (2000, pp. 77-83) explored the relationship between TAFP and CHD indicators in a sample of 197 Japanese males. Their research results suggested that Type A and job strain together might induce coronary heart problems. In studies of Type A respondents and their children, Keltikangas-Jarvinen and Heinonen's (2003) studies suggested that children of parents with Type A behavior patterns were more likely to have TABP as adults, than the children of non-type A parents.

In Type A research studies on Canada, MacLennan and Peebles (1996) explored Type A stress behavior and health-related problems of 217 Canadian air traffic controllers, finding that Type A subcategories of time urgency, job dissatisfaction, and volatility were related to elevated health problems. Lavanco (1997) studied the relationship between TABP and burnout in Sicilian teachers and nurses, finding that the nurses' Type A behavior patterns were related to burnout and negatively related to their job satisfaction. Similarly, Catipovic-Veselica (2003) explored Type A behaviors in 1,084 Spanish workers, and suggested that health indicators implied numerous more health problems for Type A classified respondents as compared to those not classified as Type A personalities.

More recently, Murphy et al. (2007a, b) explored value and Type A behavior differences between developed and developing countries, finding that developing countries demonstrated higher levels of Type A behaviors as compared to developed countries. Their study suggested that developing countries do not have the banking, work and other associated support programs that are normally available in developed countries, and this contributed to the higher Type A stress behaviors of developing country respondents as compared to developed country respondents. As a result, we developed the following research hypothesis:

Hypothesis Thirteen (H13): Working adults in Belize will have higher Type A behavior scores as compared to working adults in the US.

Hypothesis Fourteen (H14): Working adults in the Bahamas will have higher Type A behavior scores as compared to working adults in the US.

Research Methodology
This study expands the research literature by exploring cross-cultural similarities and differences in RVS terminal and instrument values and Type A stress behaviors, using adult respondents from two Caribbean nations (Belize and the Bahamas) as compared to two western nations (US and UK).

Survey Instrument
We investigated cross-cultural similarities and differences in values using the RVS and in Type A stress behaviors using the Friedman and Rosenman (1974) Type A Personality Scale. We chose to use the RVS to measure values, because it is one of the easiest and most common instruments to use in value research (Rokeach and Ball Rokeach, 1989; Connor and Becker, 2003; Connor et al., 2006; Murphy et al., 2007a, b; Khilji, 2008a, b; Ruiz-Gutierez et al., 2008; Uy et al., 2008a, b). Our research has shown as compared to other value instruments, the RVS is much simpler and easier to use, is easier to statistically analyze, is a much shorter instrument, is easier to translate, and has shown its reliability and validity in a large number of cross-cultural research studies in the past 30 years (Connor and Becker, 2003; Murphy et al., 2007a, b; Khilji, 2008a, b; Ruiz-Gutierez et al., 2008; Uy et al., 2008a, b). Rokeach (1973, 1979) and Rokeach and Ball-Rokeach (1989) established reliability for the RVS using the test-retest reliability method, finding that for each of the 18 terminal values considered separately, from seven weeks to eighteen months later, test-retest reliability scores ranged from a low of .51 for *a sense of accomplishment* to a high of .88 for *salvation*. Comparable test-retest reliability scores for instrumental values ranged from .45 for *responsible* to .70 for *ambitious*. Employing a 14-16 month test interval, median reliability was .69 for terminal values and .61 for instrumental values.

We chose the Type A Scale because it has proven its validity and test-retest reliability in identifying individuals with High Type A personalities (Kunnanatt, 2003; Cunningham et al., 2004). Murphy et al. (2007a) explain that the Friedman and Rosenman scale asks a series of 24 questions that respondents rank as very typical of me (3), the statement is somewhat typical of me (2), and/or the statement is not at all typical of me (1). The scale allows us to produce mean scores for Type A Competitiveness, Life Imbalance/Work Involvement, Hostility/Anger, and Impatience/Urgency, and these are summed to produce a total Type A behavior score, with scores ranging from 0 to 72. Murphy et al. (2007a) and Whetten and Cameron (1998) explain that scores of 12 in Type A Competitiveness, Life Imbalance/Work Involvement, Hostility/Anger, and Impatience/Urgency, indicates high for that area. As such, we classified any individual who scored 48 for the sum of all four areas as high Type A, and individuals who scored below 48 were classified as low Type B.

Research Population

As part of larger studies exploring values, attitudes and behaviors in 17 countries, we administered the surveys in 2008 in the US and to working adults in Belize and the Bahamas. The UK sample was a sample we collected in 2006 and did not include the Type A behavior scale. We elected to use the UK sample because Belize and The Bahamas were prior colonies of the UK. The researchers chose adults who were working full or part-time because their values represent the values of working professionals in those countries.

As shown in Table 1a, the final sample consisted of 2,344 working adult respondents, 131 from Belize, 161 from the Bahamas, 1,052 from the UK and 1,000 from the US. The final sample consisted of 1,091 males (490 from UK, 39 from Bahamas, 62 from Belize and 500 from the US) and 1,253 females (562 from the UK, 122 from the Bahamas, 69 from Belize, and 500 from the US.

Table 1a – Demographic Information

	UK	Bahamas	Belize	US	Total
Male	490	39	62	500	1,091
Female	562	122	69	500	1,253
18-25 YOA	117	96	19	100	332
26-29	156	23	21	150	350
30-39	296	24	24	140	484
40-45	96	13	19	160	288
46-49	78	5	10	210	303
50+	309	0	38	240	587
Total	1,052	161	131	1,000	2,344

Statistical Analysis Techniques

Rokeach and Ball-Rokeach (1989), Connor and Becker (2003), Connor et al. (2006), Murphy et al. (2007a, b), Khilji (2008a, b), Ruiz-Gutierez et al. (2008), and Uy et al. (2008a) explain that the Rokeach Value Survey is a ranking instrument that produces non-normative data, data which must be analyzed first using non-parametric statistical techniques like the Kolmogorov-Smirnov Two-Sample Test for differences between the developed and developing countries and Kruskal-Wallis ANOVA median test for differences between the countries.

Table 1 Developed versus developing country cross cultural differences in values AND Type A Behavior

	Max Neg Differnc	Max Pos Differnc	Developed Mean(Rank)	Developing Mean(Rank)	S.Dev. Gp 1	S.Dev. Gp 2	Sign
COMFORT	-.071149	.035898	7.81(4)	8.22(7)	5.21	5.19	***
EXCITING	-.045693	.057596	10.53(13)	10.33(12)	4.41	4.68	***
ACCOMPL	-.076251	.038033	8.92(8)	9.05(8)	4.47	4.02	***
WP	0.000000	.165728	11.53(16)	9.27(9)	4.96	5.55	***
WB	-.005945	.280655	13.86(18)	11.93(16)	3.96	4.14	***
EQUALITY	-.102885	.012213	10.95(14)	11.65(15)	4.72	4.68	***
FAMSEC	-.105986	.058665	5.38(1)	5.39(2)	4.80	3.98	***
FREEDOM	-.085877	.063498	7.42(3)	7.58(3)	4.36	4.34	***
HEALTH	-.024393	.177604	5.76(2)	4.90(1)	3.95	4.26	***
INHARM	-.006234	.132628	10.15(11)	9.44(10)	4.77	4.61	***
MATLOVE	-.132557	.017545	9.31(9)	10.49(13)	4.89	6.11	***
NATNLSEC	-.062636	.056601	11.46(15)	11.44(14)	4.68	4.96	***
PLEASURE	-.037464	.098302	10.30(12)	9.96(11)	4.69	4.92	***
SALVAT	-.356735	0.000000	9.80(10)	14.20(18)	6.57	5.69	***
SELFRESP	-.040925	.072012	7.84(5)	7.69(4)	3.93	3.81	***
SOCREC	-.089117	.007892	12.68(17)	13.43(17)	4.56	4.00	***
TFRIEND	-.041517	.107979	8.16(6)	7.76(5)	4.51	4.16	***
WISDOM	-.017610	.125972	8.75(7)	7.94(6)	4.52	4.49	***
ABITIOUS	-.115008	.009522	8.68(7)	9.85(11)	5.08	5.22	***
BMINDED	-.040699	.115377	9.65(9)	8.72(7)	4.78	4.43	***
CAPABLE	-.027717	.047038	8.62(6)	8.24(4)	4.45	4.20	*
CLEAN	-.129728	0.000000	11.19(16)	12.41(17)	5.26	4.73	***
COURAGE	-.039873	.090382	9.86(12)	9.60(10)	4.86	4.64	***
FORGIVE	-.070759	.115999	10.45(14)	9.88(12)	5.31	4.79	***
HELPFUL	0.000000	.203207	10.00(13)	8.45(5)	4.88	4.52	***
HONEST	0.000000	.085062	5.12(1)	4.51(1)	4.52	3.90	***
IMAGINAT	-.022719	.089720	12.67(17)	11.94(16)	4.65	5.04	***
INDEPENT	-.113803	.027710	8.29(5)	8.87(8)	5.09	5.01	***
INTELLEC	-.127597	.049000	9.85(11)	10.47(13)	4.90	4.64	***
LOGICAL	-.202171	0.000000	9.73(10)	11.35(15)	4.58	4.85	***
LOVING	-.047047	.131794	8.02(3)	7.26(3)	5.28	5.16	***
LOYAL	-.140420	0.000000	8.24(4)	9.02(9)	4.78	4.87	***
OBEDIENT	-.130618	.002976	12.77(18)	14.02(18)	4.82	4.38	***
POLITE	-.015656	.265900	10.73(15)	8.53(6)	4.34	4.93	***
RESP	-.104668	.032308	6.82(2)	6.98(2)	4.17	4.21	***
SELFCONT	-.129401	.002955	9.56(8)	10.75(14)	5.05	5.12	***
TYPATOTA	-.286860	.010274	42.53	47.16	6.72	8.87	***
COMPTOTL	-.309422	0.000000	10.12	11.97	2.34	2.81	***
LIFIMTOT	-.096783	.028937	11.63	11.87	2.24	2.66	*
HOTILTOT	-.387501	0.000000	8.86	11.80	2.35	3.88	***
IMPATOTA	-.003711	.069812	11.78	11.51	2.69	2.64	n/s

Kolmogorov-Smirnov Test (us uk belize bahamas 10 25 08.sta)

Recent research by Schwartz and Bilsky (1987, 1990), Kamakura and Novak (1992), Lenartowicz and Johnson (2002, 2003), Murphy, Gordon and Anderson (2004), Connor and Becker (1994, 2003) and Connor et al. (2006), Murphy et al.,

(2007a, b, 2008a, b), Khilji (2008a, b), Ruiz-Gutierez et al. (2008), and Uy et al. (2008a) supports Rokeach's findings for statistical analysis of the RVS as ways to evaluate value systems.

Research Results

We first explored whether there were cross-cultural developed versus developing country similarities in values. The developed countries (US, UK) were coded as one and the developing countries (Belize, Bahamas) were coded as two. The developed versus developing countries served as the independent variables and values as the dependent variables. The Kolmogorov-Smirnov Two-Sample Test indicated statistically significant differences for 18 terminal and 18 instrumental values. Table 1 shows the means and rankings and standard deviations for the developed versus developing countries combined.

Working adults in the developed nations (US, UK) ranked as most important, important or unimportant 14 of 18 instrumental values as compared to the developing countries of Belize and The Bahamas, showing a convergence of values and allowing us to accept the hypothesis (**H2**) and reject the null.

Table 2 *Cross-cultural differences in terminal value rankings*

Terminal Values	US N=1,000	Belize N=131	Bahamas N=161	UK N=1,052	Kruskal-Wallis ANOVA H & Sign Belize/Bahamas	Kruskal-Wallis ANOVA H & Sign US/Belize/Bahamas	Kruskal-Wallis ANOVA H & Sign UK/Belize/Baha	Kruskal-Wallis ANOVA H & Sign All 4 Countries
Comfort	4	5	6	7				11.4 ***
Exciting	13	12	13	12	6.14 **	6.9 *	6.5*	9.6 ***
Accomplish	8	4	8	9	6.67 **	9.3 **	14 ***	14 ***
WP	16	13	9	8		28.9 ***		202 ***
WB	18	14	18	15	17.30 ***	48.8 ***	30 ***	341 ***
Equality	10	10	12	16	5.33 **	13.5 **	44 ***	72 ***
Fam Security	1	1	4	2	12.07 **	53.2 **	21 ***	65 ***
Freedom	3	6	7	4		23.1 ***	20 ***	37 ***
Health	2	2	2	1			78 ***	179 ***
Inn Harmony	16	7	10	10	12.14 ***	12.4 **	13 **	30 ***
Mature Love	9	11	14	13	5.01 *	19.2 ***	7.1 **	60 ***
Nat Security	15	18	15	14	19.57 ***	41.8 ***	46***	48 ***
Pleasure	12	16	16	11		34.3 ***	59 ***	68 ***
Salvation	10	15	1	18	67.7 ***	99.8 ***	444 ***	1,043 ***
Self-Respect	5	3	3	6	5.7 **	24.5 ***	27 ***	25 ***
Soc Recogn	17	17	17	17			7.0 **	29 ***
True Friend	6	8	11	3	6.75 **	47.1 ***	126 ***	102 ***
Wisdom	7	9	5	5	7.74 ***	18.4 ***	14.1 ***	54 ***

*= p<.05; **=p<.001; ***=p<.001

Working adults in developed nations (US, UK) more highly valued the instrumental value *independent* but *accomplishment, freedom, responsible* and *loving* were ranked equally by developed and developing countries, and *forgiving* and *helpful* were ranked more important by developing countries. As such, we could only partially accept **H3**.

Working adults in the developing nations (Belize, The Bahamas) more highly valued the terminal values *health, a world at peace, national security, wisdom* and *self-respect* and instrumental value *broadminded*. The developed countries ranked *family security, ambition* and *self-controlled* higher in importance, and both ranked *obedient* equally. As a result of these findings, we could only partially accept **H4**.

Working adults in the developed nations (US, UK) ranked as most important, important or unimportant 16 of 18 terminal values as compared to the developing countries of Belize and The Bahamas, showing a convergence of values and allowing us to accept the hypothesis (**H1**) and reject the null.

We then conducted Kruskal-Wallis ANOVA median tests with culture and the independent variable and values as the dependent variables between the UK, Belize and Bahamas, US, Belize and Bahamas, and Belize and Bahamas (Tables 2 + 3 show the ANOVA H and significance values).

Table 3 *Cross-cultural differences in instrumental value rankings*

Instrumental Values	US N=1,000	Belize N=131	Bahamas N=161	UK N=1,052	Kruskal-Wallis ANOVA H & Sign Belize/Bahamas	Kruskal-Wallis ANOVA H & Sign US/Belize/Bahamas	Kruskal-Wallis ANOVA H & Sign UK/Belize/Baha	Kruskal-Wallis ANOVA H & Sign All 4 Countries
Ambitious	7	2	1	12		28.2 ***	96 ***	164 ***
Broadminded	9	4	14	7	16.1 ***	14.2 ***	22 ***	68 ***
Capable	6	5	15	6	14.3 ***	26.2 ***	42 ***	47 ***
Clean	16	17	9	17	18.4 ***	20.6 ***	75 ***	115 ***
Courage	12	9	16	10	8.25 **	7.5 **	19 ***	20 ***
Forgiving	14	13	8	11	4.5 *	6.9 **	8.1 **	56 ***
Helpful	13	11	13	5			32 ***	157 ***
Honest	1	1	2	1	6.6 **	24.4 ***	56 ***	67 ***
Imaginative	17	15	18	16	18.2 ***	18.2 ***	21 ***	40 ***
Independent	5	7	3	9			17 ***	34 ***
Intellectual	11	6	11	13	6.35 **	9.6 **	38 ***	103 ***
Logical	10	12	17	15	17.4 ***	44.5 ***	20 ***	147 ***
Loving	3	8	5	3			29 **	121 ***
Loyal	4	10	7	8		14.1 **		40 ***
Obedient	18	18	12	18	39.9 ***	56.1 ***	142 ***	215 ***
Polite	15	14	10	4	8.1 **	26.3 ***	51 ***	275 ***
Responsible	2	3	4	2		18.7 ***	26 ***	26 ***
Self-control	8	16	6	14	13.1 **	16.1 ***	23 ***	83 ***

* = $p < .05$; ** = $p < .001$; *** = $p < .001$

Respondents from the US did place higher value importance as compared to Belize on the terminal value *freedom* and instrumental values *independent, responsible* and *loving*, but they did not for *accomplishment, forgiving* and *helpful*, allowing us to only partially accept **H5**.

Respondents from the US did place higher value importance as compared to the Bahamas for the terminal value *freedom* and instrumental values responsible and *loving*, but not for *accomplishment, independent, forgiving* and *helpful*, allowing us to only partially accept **H6**.

Respondents from the UK did place higher value importance as compared to Belize on the terminal values *freedom* and instrumental values *responsible, helpful* and *loving*, but not for *accomplishment, forgiving*, and *independent*, allowing us to only partially accept **H7**.

Respondents from the UK did place higher value importance as compared to the Bahamas on the terminal values *freedom* and instrumental values *responsible, forgiving, helpful* and *loving*, but not for *accomplishment* and *independent*, allowing us to only partially accept **H8**.

Belize did place higher value importance as compared to the US on the terminal value *a world at peace* and *self-respect* and instrumental values *ambition* and *broadminded*, but not for *family security, health, national security, wisdom*, and *self-controlled*, allowing us to only partially accept **H9**.

Respondents from the Bahamas did place higher value importance as compared to the US on the terminal values *a world at peace, wisdom* and *self-respect* and instrumental values *ambition, obedient* and *self-controlled*, but not for *family security, health, national security*, and *broadminded*, allowing us to only partially accept **H10**.

Belize did place higher value importance as compared to the UK for the terminal values *family security*, and *self-respect* and instrumental values *ambition* and *broadminded*, but not for *health, a world at peace, national security, wisdom, obedient*, and *self-controlled*, allowing us to only partially accept **H11**.

The Bahamas did place higher value importance as compared to the UK for the terminal value *self-respect* and instrumental value *ambition*, but not for *family security, health, a world at peace, national security, wisdom, broadminded, obedient*, and *self-controlled*, allowing us to only accept **H12**.

Belize did have higher Type A behavior scores as compared to working adults from the US, allowing us to accept **H13** (Table 4).

The Bahamas did have higher Type A behavior scores as compared to working adults from the US, allowing us to accept **H14** (Table 4).

Table 4 - Cross-cultural differences in Type A behavior

	US N=1,000	Belize N=131	Bahamas N=161	Kruskal-Wallis ANOVA H & Sign Belize/ Bahamas	Kruskal-Wallis ANOVA H & Sign US / Belize/ Bahamas
Type A Total	42.534	***52.038***	43.204	70.9***	158.0 ***
High Competitiveness	10.122	***12.763***	11.335	19.6 ***	140.0 ***
High Life Imbalance (Work Involvement)	11.634	11.793	***11.937***		
High Hostility or Anger	8.864	***15.221***	9.024	178.3***	324.0 ***
High Impatience or Urgency	11.789	***12.259***	10.906	18.2***	19.7 ***

*= p<.05; **=p<.001; ***=p<.001

Discussion

The researchers could find very little cross-cultural value research concerning Belize and The Bahamas, in fact, the researchers found no studies that explored values and Type A stress behaviors in Belize and The Bahamas. Hofstede (1980, 2001) surveyed respondents in The Bahamas, but did not discuss his research results in any known published documents. Since the majority of the research literature on cross-cultural values, attitudes and behaviors has focused on the differences with little attention paid to similarities between national cultures, we first explored developed versus developing country similarities in values, followed by explorations of the differences. This allowed us to extend the research results of Murphy et al. (2007a). As shown in Table One, value convergence is suggested by the result for the most important, important and least important values, and those whose rankings are equal. The values ranked one through five are considered the most important values, those ranked six through thirteen are considered important and those ranked fourteen to eighteen are considered unimportant. A total of 16 of the 18 terminal values were ranked most important, important or unimportant by both groups. For example, a comfortable life was ranked as most important four by the developed countries, but was also ranked an important seven by the developing countries. Other terminal values ranked slightly higher in importance by developed countries but slightly less important by developing countries were: *family security* (ranked 1 by developed and 2 by developing), *mature love* (ranked 9 by developed and 13 by developing). Other values were ranked slightly higher in importance by developing countries: *an exciting life* (ranked 12 by developing and 13 by developed), health (ranked 1 by developing and 2 by developed), *inner harmony* (ranked 10 by developing and 11 by developed), *pleasure* (ranked 11 by developing and 12 by developed), *self-respect* (ranked 4 by developing and 5 by developed), *true friendship* (ranked 5 by developing and 6 by developed), and *wisdom* (ranked 6 by developing and 7 by developed). Further, *a sense of accomplishment* was ranked equally (8) by both groups, freedom was ranked (3) by both groups, and *social recognition* ranked equally unimportant (17) by both groups. Finally, *a world at peace* (18 developed and 16 developing), and *national security* (15 developed and 14 developing) were ranked unimportant by both groups.

As shown in Table 2, value convergence is suggested by the result for the most important, important, and least important values, and those whose rankings are equal. A total of 14 of the 18 instrumental values were ranked most important, important or unimportant by both groups. First, there were some values that were ranked slightly more important by developed countries, but only slightly less important by developing countries: *ambitious* (ranked 7 by developed and 11 by developing), *independent* (ranked 5 by developed and 8 by developing), *intellectual* (ranked 11 by developed and 13 by developing), and *loyal* (ranked 4 by developed and 9 by developing). *Broadminded* (ranked seven by developing and 9 by developed), *capable* (ranked 4 by developing and 6 by developed), *courage* (ranked 10 by developing and 12 by developed), *helpful* (ranked 5 by developing and 13 by developed) were ranked slightly more important by developing countries, but only slightly less important by developed countries. Finally, *honest* was equally ranked most important (1) by both groups, *loving* (3), and *responsible* (2), and *obedient* was ranked equally unimportant (18) by both groups.

Working adults in the developed nations more highly valued the instrumental value *independent* but *accomplishment, freedom, responsible* and *loving* were ranked equally by developed and developing countries, and *forgiving* and *helpful* were ranked more important by developing countries (**H3**). This seems to indicate a convergence of values between the developed and developing countries, because *accomplishment, freedom, independent* and *responsible* are achievement, independence and competition values and *loving* is a safety, tradition and conformity value (Murphy et al., 2007a). We explored for difference between the two developed countries, the US and UK. The US ranked accomplishment, freedom, independent, much higher in importance than the UK, and responsible was equally ranked by the US and UK. This suggests that the US is more achievement oriented than the UK. Although the developing countries have colonial ties to the UK, we suspect the greater influence by the US because of its closer proximity and greater import/export ties. For instance, the CIA's (Central Intelligence Agency) country studies reports indicate that the US is a major import and export partner of Belize and The Bahamas, while the UK is only a major export partner of Belize, and is not a major import or export partner of The Bahamas (CIA, 2008).

Working adults in the developing nations more highly valued the terminal values *health, a world at peace, national security, wisdom* and *self-respect* and instrumental value *broadminded*. The developed countries ranked *family security, ambition* and *self-controlled* higher in importance, and both groups ranked *obedient* equally unimportant (**H4**). Once again, this seems to indicate a convergence of values between the developed and developing countries, because *ambition* is an achievement, independence and competition values and *family security* and *self-controlled* are safety, tradition and conformity values (Murphy et al., 2007a).

For value divergence between developed and developing countries in our study, the only real differences in rankings were for *a world at peace* which was an unimportant sixteen for developed countries and an important nine for the developing countries; *polite* which was an unimportant fifteen for developed and an important six for developing countries, *forgiving* which was an unimportant fourteen for developed an important twelve for developing countries; *salvation*, which was an important ten for developed and unimportant eighteen for the developing countries; *logical* was an important ten for developed and an unimportant fifteen for developing countries; and *self-controlled*, which was an important eight for developed and an unimportant fourteen for developing countries.

Table One further suggests differences between the developed and developing countries. The developed countries ranked the terminal values *a comfortable life, equality, family security, mature love,* and *salvation* and instrumental values *ambition, clean, independent, intellectual, logical, loyal,* and *self-controlled* higher in importance than the developing countries. The developing countries ranked the terminal values *an exciting life, a world at peace, a world of beauty, inner harmony, national security, pleasure, self-respect, true friendship,* and *wisdom* and instrumental values *broadminded, capable, courage, forgiving, helpful* and *polite* much higher in importance.

We expected the US and UK to place higher importance than Belize and the Bahamas on the terminal values *accomplishment* and *freedom* and instrumental values *independent, responsible, forgiving, helpful* and *loving* (**H5-H12**). The US and UK did rank *freedom, responsible,* and *loving* higher in importance than Belize and the Bahamas; the US ranked *independent* higher than Belize, but not higher than the Bahamas, and the UK ranked *independent* lower in importance as compared to Belize and the Bahamas; Belize and the Bahamas ranked *forgiving* and *helpful* higher than the US, the UK ranked *forgiving* and *helpful* higher in importance as compared to Belize and the UK ranked *helpful* higher in importance than the Bahamas. *Accomplishment* was ranked higher by Belize and the Bahamas. *Accomplishment* is an achievement, independent and competition value normally valued higher in importance by developed countries. In this case, respondents from Belize and the Bahamas ranked this achievement value higher in importance than the US and UK. Respondents from the Bahamas ranked another achievement, independent and competition value *independent* higher in importance than the US and UK. *Forgiving, helpful* and *loving* are safety, tradition and conformity values. The US and UK ranked the safety, tradition and conformity value *loving* higher in importance as compared to Belize and the Bahamas. Belize and the Bahamas ranked the safety, tradition and conformity values *forgiving* and *loving* higher in importance than the US, but the UK ranked *forgiving* and *loving* higher in importance than Belize and *forgiving* higher in importance than the Bahamas.

We predicted that working adults in Belize would have higher Type A stress behavior scores as compared to the US. The results (Table 4) indicated that working adults in Belize had Type A total scores of 52.038 compared to the US score of 42.534. Their scores for Type A competitiveness, life imbalance, hostility/anger and impatience/urgency were also higher than the US. Respondents from The Bahamas had a higher Type A stress behavior score of 43.204 as compared to the US score of 42.354. Working adults in The Bahamas had higher Type A competitiveness, life imbalance and hostility/anger, but US working adults had higher scores for Type A impatience (Table 4). Our results replicate Murphy et al.'s (2007a), as developing countries had high Type A total scores as compared to developed countries. Murphy et al. explain that working adults in developing countries don't have the training, health, education, banking, and other entrepreneurial and economic support systems available in developed countries, leading to their high stress in the workplace.

In order to add more meaning to the research results, we explored value differences between the US, UK, Belize, and the Bahamas, followed by a discussion of the similarities. We explored differences in country pairs in order to fully explore the value similarities and differences.

There were cross cultural difference in values for 18 terminal and 18 instrumental values. In order to highlight these differences we will explore the differences by which values were more important for each country. For terminal values, the US ranked *a comfortable life, freedom,* and *mature love* as significantly more important; Belize ranked *a sense of accomplishment, a world of beauty,* and *inner harmony* as more important; The Bahamas ranked *salvation* as more important, and respondents from the UK ranked *a world at peace, health, national security, pleasure,* and *true friendship* as more important. *An exciting life* was ranked and equally important twelve by respondents from Belize and the UK; *equality* was ranked an equally important ten and *family security* an equally most important one by respondents from the US and Belize; *self-respect* was ranked an equally most important three by respondents form Belize and The Bahamas; *social recognition* was ranked an equally unimportant seventeen by respondents from all four countries, and *wisdom* was ranked an equally most important five by respondents from the UK and Bahamas.

There were cross cultural differences for 18 of 18 instrumental values. US respondents ranked *logical* and *loyal* as more important; Belize respondents ranked *broadminded, capable, courage, imaginative,* and *intellectual* as more important; respondents from The Bahamas ranked *ambitious, clean, forgiving, independent, obedient* and *self-controlled* higher in importance, and UK respondents ranked *polite* and *helpful* as more important. *Honest* was equally ranked as one for US, Belize and

UK respondents, *loving* was equally ranked three by US and UK respondents, and *responsible* was equally ranked two by respondents form the US and UK.

Value convergence was demonstrated for values that were ranked most important or important across the four cultures. First, the terminal values *family security* and *health* and instrumental values *honest* and *responsible* were ranked most important (1 through 5) across the cultures and the terminal values *a world of beauty, national security* and *social recognition* and instrumental value *imaginative* was ranked unimportant (14 to 18) across the cultures. Next, the terminal values *a comfortable life, an exciting life, a sense of accomplishment, freedom, true friendship*, and *wisdom* and instrumental values *ambition, helpful, independent, intellectual, loving* and *loyal* were ranked most important (1 to 5) or important (6 to 13) across the cultures.

The divergence or major differences across the cultures for terminal values were that *a world at peace* and *inner harmony* were ranked unimportant by the US and important by Belize, The Bahamas and the UK; *mature love* was ranked unimportant by respondents from The Bahamas and it was important for the US, Belize and UK; *pleasure* was important for the US and UK but unimportant for Belize and The Bahamas, and *salvation* was unimportant for Belize and the UK and important for the US and The Bahamas. For major differences in instrumental values across the cultures, respondents from The Bahamas ranked *broadminded, capable* and *courage* as unimportant, but it was important for respondents from Belize, the US and UK; *clean* and *obedient* were only important for respondents from The Bahamas – this is understanding for the value of cleanliness related to the environment since the Bahamian government has been promoting the slogan of 'A clean, green and pristine Bahamas' over the past few years; *forgiving* was unimportant for respondents from the US and was important for respondents from Belize, The Bahamas and the UK; *logical* was unimportant for respondents from The Bahamas and UK, but important for Belize and the US; *polite* was not important for respondents from the US and Belize, and *self-controlled* was only important for respondents from the US and The Bahamas.

Conclusions and Limitations

The major contribution of this study is that it indicates that exploring similarities across cultures is just as important as exploring differences. For example, our study suggests a convergence of values across the developed and developing country cultural groups, in that, 30 of the 36 values were ranked most important, important, least important or were ranked equally between the developed and developing countries. Both groups ranked the terminal values *family security, freedom, health,* and *self-respect* and instrumental values *honest, loving* and *responsible* in their top five most important values. Both groups ranked the terminal values *a comfortable life, an exciting life, inner harmony, mature live, pleasure, true friendship* and *wisdom,* and the instrumental values *ambitious, broadminded, capable, courage, helpful, independent, intellectual, loyal,* and *polite* as important. Further, both groups ranked the terminal values *a world of beauty, equality, national security,* and *social recognition,* and instrumental values *clean, imaginative* and *obedient* as unimportant values. Both groups equally ranked *a sense of accomplishment, freedom, social recognition, honest, loving, obedient,* and *responsible.*

Further convergence is demonstrated when we compared our results to Murphy et al. (2007a). The terminal values *family security, health,* and *self-respect* and instrumental values *honest* and *responsible* were ranked most important and the terminal values *a world of beauty, national security* and *social recognition,* and instrumental values *imaginative* and *obedient* were ranked unimportant by working adults in the 7 developed and 7 developing countries of the Murphy et al. study and the 2 developed and 2 developing countries in our study. Similarly, the terminal value *a comfortable life* and instrumental values *independent, logical, loyal,* and *self-controlled* were ranked more important by developed countries in our study and the Murphy et al. study, and the terminal values *inner harmony,* and *wisdom* were ranked more important by developing countries in our study and the Murphy et al. study.

Managers and practitioners need to understand these similarities and differences because this knowledge will help them develop human resource management (HRM) policies that meet the needs of employees, will help them develop products that meet the needs of the different cultures in the global marketplace, will allow them to lead their employees in interactions with customers, and will allow them to develop marketing campaigns that emphasize the similarities across the cultures, but have a locally-developed cultural focus.

Our study confirmed Murphy et al.'s (2007a) findings that developing countries have higher Type A stress behavior scores as compared to developed countries. The developing countries face a higher risk for CHD because they must not only industrialize and compete in the global marketplace, but they must also bring their health, training and education systems into the 21st century. For instance, the World Health Organization (WHO) reports that "More than 60 percent of the global burden of coronary heart disease occurs in developing countries" (Who Surf 2, 2006: 46). Lifestyle and behavioral patterns (Type A behaviors), lack of access to health care and chronic stress lead to CHD and Type A stress behaviors (Murphy et al., 2007a; WHO, 2006; Who Surf 2, 2006). Our research results seem to support the WHO's findings because Type A stress behaviors were significantly higher in the developing nations as compared to the developed nations.

These findings are important because they support the World Health Organization's data which indicates that developing nations have higher incidences of death due to stress, lack of proper nutrition, and lack of education and training concerning the causes of chronic diseases like coronary heart disease. The developing countries must understand these finding so they can develop programs that provide government support, access to health care systems, and access to education and training programs and other macro institutions that allow respondents to decrease the quantity of Type A stress behaviors they possess.

As Murphy et al. (2007a) explain, "being able to identify the values, traits and characteristics exhibited by people with Type A behavior patterns are important for practitioners and managers to understand because research has shown that understanding the components of Type A behavior patterns can lead to positive behavioral and lifestyle changes, significantly reducing the risk for CHD" (p. 28). For example, developed countries have successfully reduced Type A stress behaviors through massive public educaAtion, training and public media programs to decrease deaths from chronic diseases like coronary heart disease by 70 percent from 1979 to the present (WHO, 2006; Murphy et al., 2007a). Developing countries need to develop similar programs in order to decrease Type A stress behaviors.

Rokeach (1973), Feather (1979), Triandis (1994) and Hofstede's (1980) early cross cultural studies indicated that Western nations placed higher importance on achievement-oriented, materialistic and competitive values like *a sense of accomplishment, a comfortable life, social recognition,* and *ambition,* while Latin American nations placed higher importance on the group-oriented or collectivist values *helpful, clean, polite, obedient,* and *self controlled,* and *capable.* More recent research by Neelankavil, Mathur, and Zhang (2000) indicated that American managers highly valued individualism, an achievement orientation and material prosperity, while Latin American nations valued group goals, interdependence, social hierarchies and cooperation, and Hofstede's research confirmed the higher individualism of western nations and more collectivist nature of Latin American and Caribbean countries.

These findings are important to understand, because they immediately give the practitioner, manager or marketer a point from which to start their relationship with Caribbean nations. For example, the terminal values *family security* and *health,* and instrumental values *honest* and *responsible* were in the top five values of importance (most important) across the sexes and cultures, and *a world of beauty* and *obedient* were ranked unimportant across the sexes and cultures. These results were very similar to Murphy et al.'s (2007a, b; 2008) studies of 7 developed and 7 developing nations. These values could serve as universal means that practitioners, managers and marketers can bring to the sub-cultural level in order to target the local culture and their values of importance. While managers and practitioners can use an understanding of these values to lead and motivate their employees and develop relationship with their trading partners, marketing managers can use these values as major themes for marketing or advertising campaigns, companies could be more effective with their marketing expenditures (DeMooij, 1998, 2004).

Practitioners, managers and marketers need to be aware of the fact that all the cultures felt having a prosperous life, making a lasting contribution at home and at work, having independence and free choice, having inner peace, having self-esteem, and close companionship were important goals in the lives of respondents and they would pursue those goals by being sincere and truthful, being self-reliant and self-sufficient and by being dependable and reliable. Practitioners and managers leading their employees and developing relationships with trading partners and marketers developing advertising campaigns would easily be able to develop international relationships by emphasizing how they and their companies will contribute to their trading partners or the cultures prosperity, making a difference or contribution at work, providing independence and free choice, freedom from inner conflict, will increase their self-esteem, and will provide companionship, and that they or their products are sincere and truthful, will provide self-sufficiency, dependability and reliability. Each of these goals or techniques can be used as broad areas of focus while still tailoring the relationship to the culture and situation and in the case of an advertising campaign, to the target market based on the psychographics, demographics, peculiarities of the culture involved and the situation (Triandis, 1994).

This study will also help practitioners and managers who supervise foreign nationals understand what motivates them (Mujtaba, 2008) and will help companies operating globally develop international human resources management strategies that not only meet company needs but also the cultural needs of their organizational members. Finally, by understanding values and culture companies should be able to achieve better performance outcomes and these outcomes should positively impact their profitability.

The limitations of this study include the research populations we used, as they were generally convenience samples of working adults from the capitals or major cities in each country. One of the major limitations of our study was the use of a two years old UK sample. Our US, Belize and The Bahamas samples were collected this for this study. We were forced to use a previous UK sample (Murphy et al., 2007a, b), and it did not include Type A behaviors. We presently have a fellow researcher in the UK collecting data using the RVS and Type A instrument to solve this limitation. Future research needs to compare our results to other studies of working adults throughout the world. Other studies of working adults need to be explored by public versus private occupation, by government versus military occupations, and further cross cultural research with college age respondents need to be conducted with this value orientation typology.

Another limitation is trying to compare our results to other studies published in the research literature. Many studies use the RVS but do not report the means and rankings for their populations, possibly due to the publishing constraints imposed by many journals. This makes comparison difficult. Further, many researchers are using only the terminal or instrumental values portions of the RVS, which does not allow for comparison studies using the entire RVS. We recommend that researchers using the RVS report the means, medians and rankings for each value and for each demographic variable studied, as they would allow future researchers to compare their results across the globe.

CHAPTER EIGHT

8 – EXERCISING THE FREEDOM TO CHOOSE

W e live in work environments that seem to be full of inevitable conflict, change and stress. While workplace conflict, change and stress cannot be eliminated they can and should be managed effectively in order to have a productive workplace. There are professionals and even managers who get frustrated and lose their temper over routine and non-routine issues. Such incidents can negatively impact the morale of the department and lead to much undue stress in the workplace.

While being frustrated, sad, and angry might be a reality of life in the twenty-first century workplace, this chapter provides a realistic perspective on how a person can be driven by emotions during a frustrating moment which can lead to health problems and undesirable outcomes. Based on personal experiences, the chapter provides suggestions on how stressful situations and interpersonal conflicts should be managed through effective people skills, such as the "inside-out-approach," and intrapersonal communication. By offering a model, the chapter emphasizes that instead of reacting based on the emotions during interpersonal conflicts, professionals should respond based on their predetermined personal or organizational values.

Understand and Manage Stress

Stress can easily become distress when it is negatively impacting your productivity and behavior in the workplace. Stress can be messy when it is not managed in a timely manner. Stress can sabotage a person's life if one allows it. What is sad is that many people do not realize that they are dealing with an excessive amount of stress on a daily basis. If one is not aware of his or her level of stress or stress-producing situations, then he or she cannot manage it in a timely manner. Furthermore, working professionals who take care of family members with various disabilities and those who are full-time parents, especially women, are more vulnerable to chronic forms of stress. In the case of most parents, the hands that rock the cradle are also likely to be cradling the kitchen appliances, the vacuum cleaner, the dishes, the telephone, monthly bills, and urgent deadlines. While some multi-tasking is doable, too much of it can cause distress. Excessive and chronic distress can result in personality changes, mood swings, being sick and tired all the time, experiencing or going into a depression, being forgetful, gaining weight, losing too much weight too fast, and an unhealthy immune system. Instead of allowing stress to become distress, busy professionals should understand the causes of stress and manage it before it turns into distress. Madeline A. Lewis (2009, p. 21) recommends that we make stress our friend by understanding it and keeping a close eye on it. Yes, befriending stress means making it work for you, not against you. Some of the ways to befriend and manage stress is to relax, have a positive attitude toward life and daily activities, take good care of your body by eating healthy foods, exercising, breathing deeply in every opportunity you get during the day, giving yourself positive and affirmative praises for the achievement of your goals, and by socializing and laughing as often you can. Children tend to naturally laugh hundreds of times throughout the day and adults should do the same. Deep breathing and laughing at good humor are things that we all can and should do to befriend and manage stress in today's competitive workplace.

The "Cat Kicking" Workplace[3]

We live in a *"cat kicking"* world and office conflicts and stresses should be effectively handled before employees leave for home. If office issues are not handled at work, then a person who is unfairly blamed or "kicked in the behind" by his or her colleagues at work is likely to take it out on other innocent people on the way home or in the house. Have you ever seen a person get mad and lose his or her temper over a minor concern or no issue whatsoever? In such cases, it is clear that there is something deeper that is causing the person's frustration and it has nothing to do with what is going on at the moment. For example, if you are walking in the park to get some exercise and the man coming from the opposite direction says "WHAT ARE YOU looking at?" in a loud and frustrated voice, then you know that your walk in the park is certainly not something that has angered him. There must have been something else that has angered him before this occurrence. Perhaps someone at the office unfairly blamed him for something that he did not even do. Or, maybe he was not given proper credit which he rightly deserves for quality work that he did do. However, now he is taking his frustrations out on others. He might even go home and get into a fight with his wife over a minor issue. Of course, the wife may not understand his anger and will feel sad because she works hard all day long just like him, comes home to take care of the family, and hopefully relax a little before the next day's hectic work schedule but instead gets blamed for no reason by her husband (who happens to be upset from what took place at his office). Now, the wife is upset and stressed…and she may take it out on the teenage children by yelling at them for no reason. The children will be unhappy because they are not clear on why the parents are mad at them when they have done nothing wrong. Thus, they will be unhappy and upset and may just end up taking out their frustrations by simply "kicking the cat" that is innocently walking by and looking for some affection. So, the anger that was

---

[3] Source: Mujtaba, B. G. (2008). Interpersonal Change through the "Inside-Out-Approach": Exercising the Freedom to Choose Our Responses during Conflict and Stressful Situations. *Ramkhamhaeng University (RU) International Journal*, Vol. 2(1), pp. 1-12.

caused at the office is now being passed on to others, and there is a snowball effect, even impacting the little cat in the house.

Being frustrated, sad, and even angry at times is a fact of life for most employees in the workplace at one time or another. However, instead of being driven by emotions, as adults, we need to realize and exercise our freedom to choose our responses for the circumstances that happen to us. Instead of responding based on the emotions of the moment, one can choose to respond based on his or her predetermined and clarified values. Consequently, mature human beings do not have to allow daily politics or other office "stuff" to make them angry. Mature individuals who exercise their freedom to choose can determine how, when, how long, and for whom to demonstrate their frustrations in a strategically fruitful manner. Good behavior begets more good behavior. Similarly, good deeds encourage more good deeds. Therefore, good behavior and good deeds are contagious. As Mahatma Gandhi once said, as role models, we all need to be the change that we desire from others. As it is commonly believed that the way others treat us is simply a mirror of our own actions, the "inside-out-approach" focuses on changing one's own conduct in order to attract others toward good deeds and appropriate behavior in the workplace.

Workplace Frustration

The reality of every workplace has been that there are many diverse personalities on each team and department. Perhaps it might be true that some people are more prone to be creative, innovative, opportunistic, or even problematic in the workplace than others based on diversity or homogeneity of their outlook on life. If a person sees the glass as "half full," then he or she is likely to have a positive outlook on life and might trust others by giving them the benefit of the doubt. On the other side, if a person is distrusting of people and believes that this world has scarce resources and opportunities then his or her outlook about the workplace might be that it is "survival of the fittest" in a "dog-eat-dog world," and you must do what you can to get ahead. Therefore, as an opportunistic individual, he or she might choose to get involved in unethical politicking or even backstabbing in a competitive workplace. Of course, regardless of whether the existence of such opportunistic behaviors and individuals are real or perceived, we do know that the true feelings of the "self-proclaimed victims" as well as their levels of stress are very much real. For example, a frustrated colleague once called during an evening crying, and saying that the secretary in her department is "from hell." When asked what is the real problem? she forcefully replied that "The secretary is the problem, not me." The secretary is a 66-year old accomplished woman who has supposedly been described as a "rude and mean old lady" by several people in the department. The secretary is supposedly the devil of the office, and she is ruining her days and evenings. Therefore, she should quit the job and work elsewhere. This colleague mentioned that she does everything right, and the obnoxious and rude secretary still complains to the boss about her performance and productivity. Furthermore, the colleague reiterated her perception of the issue that the problem is with the "rude" and egotistical secretary who was causing difficulties for everyone in the department by being friendly with the boss and passing on misinformation about each employee's overall performance. Such perceptions and feelings of frustration are real for many professionals in a competitive work environment. If such stresses and frustrations are not handled effectively, they can lead to minor or even major psychological and physiological health problems.

Dealing with Frustrations and Anger

When you think the problem is "out there" (with other people or the secretary), then that very thinking is the problem. The problem is this perception and allowing others (like the secretary) to make you upset. You can choose to ignore others (the secretary). On the other hand, you can choose to be friends with the secretary. And, you can choose to be pleasant to the secretary. The word "choose" has been purposely emphasized because, between the stimulus and response, human beings have the freedom to choose their attitude toward what others do. Between the stimulus and response, there exists the freedom to choose one's responses. Six hours after work, this colleague was at home and she was still "allowing" or choosing to allow what the secretary did during the day to make her night upsetting and miserable. She needs to realize that she can choose not to be upset by other people's actions, words, and behaviors hours after it happened. She needs to keep in mind that she truly has the "freedom" not to allow the secretary's statements to bother her for hours, nights, and days. In such events, she should step back, take deep breaths, relax for a few moments, and think about why she is being bothered. If it is over a minor issue, then she can choose to ignore it. If it is an issue that needs to be resolved, then she should plan to confront it in the right way at the next appropriate time before it becomes a bothersome issue that ruins her hour, day, or night.

Perhaps, one cannot control what the secretary does, or what one's parents do, but one can control his/her response to it. And, one can control his/her own attitude (i.e., being neutral, being happy, or being upset). Of course, being upset or angry does not produce many positive results....usually it is a wasted emotion, and it can be contagious when one is working with other people. So, this colleague could choose to ignore the secretary and focus on her job or personal goals in the department; and this will be a better use of her time. You will always get better results by exercising your "freedom" to choose. She can choose to quit her job and this might eliminate the problem or stress. However, regardless of the job or industry, there are always going to be some rude individuals with personalities similar to that of the secretary who is supposedly causing her chronic stress. While one can certainly choose to quit a job in order to get away from the real or perceived problem, a better option might be to simply confront the secretary and appropriately deal with the "real" or "perceived" challenges. It might be possible that the secretary is not really the problem. In that case, the employee needs to look in the mirror as everything she receives from others might simply be a reflection of her own behaviors! If this is the case, then she needs to change things from "an inside-out" approach. When she changes her behavior, she might notice that the world responds to her accordingly.

The "inside-out" approach requires recognizing and acknowledging that between the stimulus and response there exists a momentary opportunity when one can choose to act based on emotions or predetermined values. In other words, as visually demonstrated in Figure 8.1, one can respond reactively (based on emotions, feelings, and other variables surrounding the event), or one can respond proactively based on his or her values, goals and long-term strategic vision. Professionals that want to be respected by their customers, employees, colleagues, and superiors should remain cool and calm in stressful circumstances and strategically respond in a proactive manner to achieve their personal and organizational goals.

Figure 8.1 – The Stimulus-Response Model

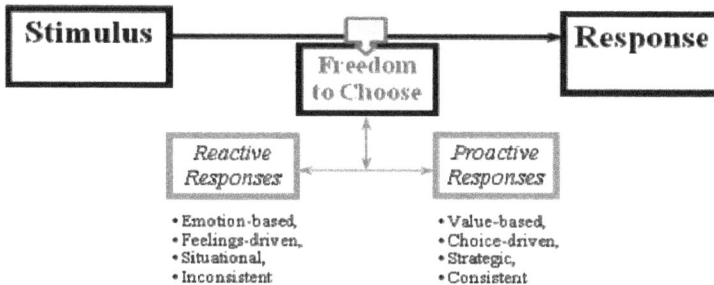

Avoid Being Angry or Upset

In today's competitive workplace, one cannot avoid the realities of being upset or angry at times. It is okay for a person to be upset, angry, or to even cry for a few moments when it is appropriate or when it helps one to feel better temporarily. But too much of it might not be good for one's health, nor will it produce better results. So, it is good to stay focused on the pre-determined goals and things that are under one's control (rather than wasting energy or crying about things that cannot be changed). If you get upset every now and then...this just means that you are a human being with emotions, wants, and desires. It is also a fact that all human beings want to be recognized for their contributions. Sometimes individuals allow other people's behavior to influence their "mood" during the hour, day, night, or even week. There is no reason to "allow" or permit other people to influence you negatively. Never allow anyone, including your superiors, to abuse you verbally or physically. Exercise your rights and know that you can choose, and you have the freedom to choose, your response and future actions. Choose your responses and actions based on your values and goals, not emotions.

It is best to keep in mind that the problem is usually not "out there" or with other people. Often times, the problem is our response to what happens to us. While we cannot always change what happens to us or when and how it happens, the good thing is that we can choose our response to what happens to us. Furthermore, we can alter our personal behaviors and conducts using the "inside-out-approach" in order to be the role models of how we want others to behave. Remember that "It is never the event that makes one feel or do anything—it is how we perceive, judge or evaluate it that makes a difference in the behavior or attitude." Every human emotion is a valid one; the key is how we manage or respond to it—be it appropriate, inappropriate, or indifferent. In every single emotional situation there is never just one way to think, feel, or act.

Be a Professional in the Workplace

Just like most employees, managers can also face complex challenges when it comes to behavior alignment in the workplace, especially when their personal values are in direct conflict with the department's expectations. Professionals must understand that there can be no question as to a manager's responsibility regarding fairness, diversity awareness, and being culturally competent in managing a diverse workforce or "rude" individuals. As a professional manager or agent of an organization, one must treat people with respect and dignity, and ensure that internal customers (associates and vendors) treat each other with respect and dignity. There can be no question as to a manager's responsibility regarding being culturally competent when managing a multicultural workforce or interacting with a diverse customer base. An effective and competent leader and manager must create and maintain an inclusive work environment for all employees by choosing to exercise the freedom to respond based on predetermined values.

As can be seen from the Personal Inclination and Alignment Model (Figure 8.2), managers have a right to receive training in the area of diversity and understand the organization's expectations regarding cultural competency and behavioral alignment. Similarly, when one's personal values and the departmental expectations are in conflict, managers can use professionalism to meet the organization's expectations and to achieve the goals of having a fair and an inclusive work environment where the natural externalities are teamwork, synergy, and a productive workforce.

Figure 8.2 – Personal Inclination and Alignment Model

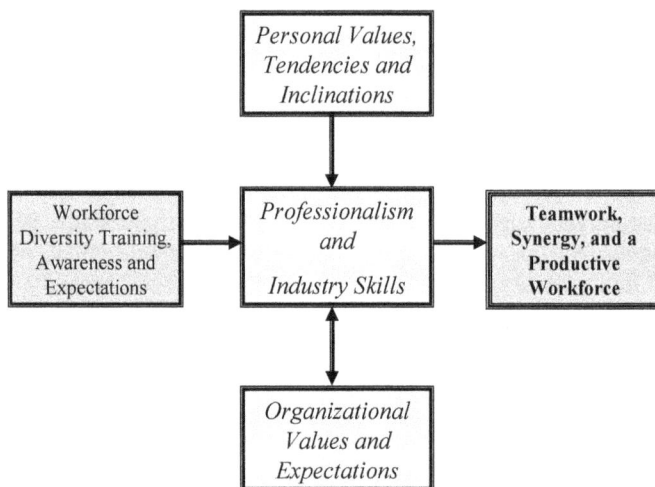

Today's associates come from diverse backgrounds and have a variety of experiences and personal values. Therefore, it is important to jointly discuss with everyone and emphasize the relationship between personal inclinations, professionalism, and organizational expectations as well as what to do if there is a conflict between one's personal values and the department's expectations. As taught to thousands of managers, the following definitions can be helpful in understanding this concept:

- *Personal inclinations* are responses based largely on personal feelings and values.
- *Professionalism* (or the bridge between personal inclination and organizational expectations) is about having the requisite skills and experiences in a particular field, industry and profession.
- *Personal alignment* is about adapting one's personal behavior to be compatible with the character and values of the organization. In such a case, one is not required to change his or her values; however, one must align his or her behavior in the workplace to meet the standards established or expected by the organization or agency.

For example, let us say that a manager, due to his or her personal inclinations tends to only believe in a marital relationship between a man and a woman, has attended a diversity workshop. As a result of this training or development, he or she does not have to change his or her personal values. However, since this manager or employee is a professional in his or her field, he or she is expected to behave according to the needed industry standards and expectations to treat each one of his or her employees and colleagues with respect and dignity regardless of their sexual orientation or personal inclinations. In other words, this employee or manager would need to use professionalism as a bridge between his/her own personal inclinations and the expectations of the company when the two are in conflict. Regardless of one's personal view or inclinations, professionals and managers are expected to behave within the law, industry or departmental policies, and the boundaries of fair and ethical treatment of all individuals in the workplace.

Professionalism also implies being focused on the facts of the situation. Effectively resolving conflicts and bringing a successful closure to stressful interpersonal incidents can speed up a team's progress toward achieving its purpose. When dealing with day-to-day conflicts, misconducts, and disagreements, one can use the 4-F model by clarifying and emphasizing the facts, feelings, future expectations, and following up when appropriate.

The 4-F model provides the facts and expects a change in behavior or the discovery of a new method or process. Discovering the right response in each changing moment requires having an open mind as well as an open heart to see new opportunities and the way things are, and then the way they can be. Change is a choice for learning, creativity, flexibility, and growth; and effective conflict management is the key to bringing about change in an efficient manner. Amid all the change, it is best to remember that flexibility allows one to stretch rather than shrink, and proactively welcoming and embracing change is about choosing a better or pre-determined future. Furthermore, choosing to be synergistic, while involving everyone in the stress and change management process, can transform a "personal" vision into a "professional" vision for everyone in the department or the organization. Being a professional in the workplace also means keeping good relationships with the people you meet and never burning your bridges as you may need to cross over them some day in the future.

Don't Burn Your Bridges[4]

Is "don't burn your bridges" an old wives tale; a myth or sound advice? "Don't burn your bridges" is a common place expression. What does it really mean? What is the metaphorical "bridge" they are referring to? How did you get there in the first place? What is the price you must pay and how can you avoid the inevitable bridge burning?

If you have ever been given the advice to "never burn your bridges" then it is safe to assume that you were in the midst of a conflict situation that was about to boil over. You were sharing your woes with a trusted colleague and contemplating telling someone else exactly what you thought of them. On hearing the advice from your trusted colleague, you may have rolled your eyes. After all you were in the midst of your tirade and ready to charge forward with righteous indignation. Of course you were going to burn your bridges because in that moment you were so convinced that YOU were right and the offender was wrong, that your sensible brain cells had temporarily abandoned you. The problem with this approach is that there are no winners. There is no turning back. If the military advances on a target and burns roads and bridges behind it to stop the enemy from following them, they have also closed off their own ability to retreat by the same path.

The "bridge" being referred to is not the relationship itself, but the road back to the relationship. If that road has been damaged the chances of you having the right to return to the relationship are limited if not impossible. People may forgive, but they rarely forget and you can never tell when you might need that individual again; or run into them when you least expect it and find that they are now in a position of power; power that has the ability to stop you from getting that next job, or contract, or acting part you most wanted. Most conflict occurs because of our socially constructed stories. Berger and Luckmann's classic work on *Social Constructions of Reality* speaks of relevancies and irrelevancies and the fact that we pick and choose how we design the stories in our heads. What is relevant to one person may not seem relevant to others and indeed they may not be able to find the same sense of drama in the situation (Berger and Luckman 1966). Perception is reality and when we tell ourselves that someone else is wrong we tend to find all kinds of ways to justify the righteousness of our story. It becomes our own personal drama and we can act it out in our heads, in our sleep and with anyone who will listen.

When we are in the midst of conflict drama we are not thinking straight and oftentimes our emotions are in charge of our decision making. The more we talk about our situation the more we can convince ourselves (and others) that we have been dealt an injustice. Another expression that comes to mind and seems inextricably linked is "loose lips sink ships." This expression is designed to discourage gossiping, but is equally valid for the person who is so wrapped up in their personal conflict drama that what they are about to say will sink them; if not today, surely at some time in the future. It might feel completely justified in the heat of the moment to "get it off your chest," give them a piece of your mind, and walk away, but before you do, stop and consider the possibility that you may cross paths at another time and place and wish you had not been so overzealous.

---

[4] Contributed by Helen Turnbul, Nova Southeastern University.

It is not easy, when you are in the midst of a tirade, to stop and tell yourself that there might be another point of view; that you might actually be wrong or that someone else has a different and equally valid point of view, but that is one of the skills necessary in order to avoid creating a train wreck. Imagine for a moment that you have burned your bridges with your boss by losing your temper and telling them exactly what you think of their rotten job and their equally dismal management skills. You leave the company, move to another city and promptly forget all about that unhappy time in your life. Five years later you have started your own business, are well on the way to becoming a successful entrepreneur and one of your consulting colleagues tells you about a fantastic contract opportunity and offers to set you up with the key decision maker. You are very excited at this prospect, until he tells you the name of the individual. Your heart sinks as you ask tentatively if this person used to work for your old company. Now you have a dilemma. You don't want to tell your colleague about your previous encounter and at the same time you now know you are not going to be considered for this contract. A bridge burned or damaged five years ago has come back to haunt you.

As a society we are inundated with media messages about heroes and victims whether in movies or the daily portion of Cable News. Aronson (1999) speaks of the phenomenon of "blaming the victim" and convincing ourselves that the victim deserved what he got. In a landmark study by Michael Kahn he allowed one group of college students to express hostility towards a fellow employee, and in the other group he asked them to withhold any expression of hostility. He was surprised to find that the group who withheld their hostility harbored less anger than the group who vented their anger. His experiment illustrated that when people are angry they often engage in overkill and the overkill produces dissonance (Aronson 1999, p. 268-269). Dissonance means that we feel conflict within ourselves. That conflict can sit dormant for many years and show up again when we are confronted with the person or the situation that first caused the conflict. Burning your bridges is just like eating too much sugar, it gives you short-term uplift, but in the long-term, it is not good for you. Instead of thinking how horrible the situation or the person has been to you, it might be best to leave the past behind and reflect about your life's important goals and be thankful of the opportunities you have received. Move on and leave the bridges exactly as you found them.

Reflecting on Life's Important Activities

Some people live a healthy life, and some people live a prosperous life. While others live a short life, a life full of suffering and hardships, and a life that is not so prosperous. It is a factual perception that we may not be able to change our destinies or things that happen to us in life; but we can change our actions and response to what happens to us in life. Success is not what you get in life, it is what you do with what you have and what you receive that makes you successful. So, all of us need to ask ourselves what am I becoming if I keep doing what I am doing right now? And, we need to ask ourselves, what do I need to become in order to get what I want in life? If you are not willing to become that person then you better change your "wants." Answering this question also helps create strong reasons for one's goals in life. Having strong goals are great motivators and knowing the reasons for wanting those goals are even more powerful motivators for action and eliminating procrastination.

The average person spends too much time on many mundane things on a daily basis because their urgency-driven world works that way. While that may be true for most of us in different stages of our lives, it is important that we take time to appreciate others and be thankful for what we have in life. Yesterday is the past; tomorrow is the future; and neither of these times can be of much use to us at the present time. However, our time right now is a gift called "present" and we should make the best use of it while we have it because once it is gone, it is gone forever and it becomes part of the past. Many teachers, mentors, and other writers have suggested the following guidelines with regard to time to help us focus on what is truly important in life.

1. Take time to think, for it is the source of growth, knowledge and power;
2. Take time to play, for it is the cistern (holding tank) of perpetual youth;
3. Take time to read, for it is the foundation of wisdom and understanding;
4. Take time to pray, for it is the greatest power on earth both psychologically and spiritually;
5. Take time to love and be loved, for it is what brings joy;
6. Take time to be friendly, for it is the road to happiness;
7. Take time to laugh, for it is the best lubricant;
8. Take time to give, for life is too short to be selfish; (We leave everything materialistic behind when we depart this world but our *faith*.) The only things that we take with us are things that we give away to help others who are less fortunate than us.
9. Take time to work, for it is the source and price of happiness and contribution to the society; however
10. Never take time to waste, for it is the road to failure and depression.

There is a wise statement about misuse of social time and it says: "great minds discuss ideas, average minds discuss events, small minds discuss people, and very small minds discuss themselves." There is no reason for anyone to waste time complaining about others. For busy managers, understanding the concepts behind the following terms is important in effective time management.

◊ *Murphy's Law*: What can happen, will happen. Take the time to plan and provide plenty of opportunities for activities that you want to happen in your life. Invite those activities and tasks that will drive your purpose of life and your mission in the right direction.

◊ *Pareto Law*: It states that 80% of the results flow from 20% of the activities. So, some activities have much more impact than others and we can call them "high leverage activities" or "big rocks."

◊ *Parkinson's Law*: It states that work expands to fill the time available to complete the job. The safeguard for this is to set realistic deadlines, to train people appropriately and trust them to do their jobs the right way and to be ethical about its completion.

◊ *True North*: The North Star at night helps pilots see the north direction. Faith, thinking, hope, and education are our true north star, our yardstick, our ruler, our inspector, and our guide, which can measure our effectiveness to see whether we are on the right path or not. So, organize your life and execute your actions around your priorities according to the mission and purpose of your life and that becomes the essence of time management.

Overall, remember that life is full of many special gifts and valued treasures that should be put first and must never be ignored. One must understand his or her beliefs and values. There's nothing that can help you understand your beliefs more than trying to explain them to an inquisitive child...so try it. If you can explain it to children then you are probably pretty clear on your beliefs, values and goals in life. When it comes to the clarity of one's goals, values, vision, and what inspires a person, Pete Goss (a sailor who successfully sailed around the world - alone) said:

> My parents taught me that I could do anything I wanted and I have always believed it to be true. Add a clear idea of what inspires you, dedicate your energies to its pursuit and there is no knowing what you can achieve, particularly if others are inspired by your dream and offer their help (Pete Goss, Sailor).

Everyone should take personal responsibility to make every day an inspiring day. Overall, remember that "The purpose of life is not to win. The purpose of life is to grow and to share. When you come to look back on all that you have done in life, you will get more satisfaction from the pleasure you have brought into other people's lives than you will from the times that you outdid and defeated them" said Harold Kushner, Rabbi and author.

Enlightened Perspective - from Andy Rooney

Several months ago in the early part 2009, the following insights were being distributed electronically about some very important lessons that are beneficial to us all. These statements were supposedly made by Andy Rooney about things that he has learned over the years:

1. That the best classroom in the world is at the feet of an elderly person.
2. That when you're in love, it shows.
3. That just one person saying to me, 'You've made my day!' makes my day.
4. That having a child fall asleep in your arms is one of the most peaceful feelings in the world.
5. That being kind is more important than being right.
6. That you should never say no to a gift from a child.
7. That I can always pray for someone when I don't have the strength to help him in some other way.
8. That no matter how serious your life requires you to be, everyone needs a friend to act goofy with.
9. That sometimes all a person needs is a hand to hold and a heart to understand.
10. That simple walks with my father around the block on summer nights when I was a child did wonders for me as an adult.
11. That life is like a roll of toilet paper. The closer it gets to the end, the faster it goes.

12. That we should be glad God doesn't give us everything we ask for.
13. That money doesn't buy class.
14. That it's those small daily happenings that make life so spectacular.
15. That under everyone's hard shell is someone who wants to be appreciated and loved.
16. That to ignore the facts does not change the facts.
17. That when you plan to get even with someone, you are only letting that person continue to hurt you.
18. That love, not time, heals all wounds.
19. That the easiest way for me to grow as a person is to surround myself with people smarter than I am.
20. That everyone you meet deserves to be greeted with a smile.
21. That no one is perfect until you fall in love with them.
22. That life is tough, but I'm tougher.
23. That opportunities are never lost, someone will take the ones you miss.
24. That when you harbor bitterness, happiness will dock elsewhere.
25. That I wish I could have told my Mom or Dad that I love them one more time before they passed away.
26. That one should keep his words both soft and tender, because tomorrow he may have to eat them.
27. That a smile is an inexpensive way to improve your looks.
28. That when your newly born grandchild holds your little finger in their little fist, that you're hooked for life.
29. That everyone wants to live on top of the mountain, but all the happiness and growth occurs while you're climbing it.
30. That the less time I have to work with, the more things I get done.

Understanding Wealth, Success and Love

Effective change, stress, conflict, and time management skills can make your life happier and more successful. With happiness and success comes love and wealth. An Afghan woman came out of her house and saw three older men with long white beards sitting in her front yard. She did not recognize them. She said "I don't think I know you, but you must be hungry. Please come in and have something to eat." "Is the man of the house home?" they asked. "No", she replied. "He's out." "Then we cannot come in," they replied.

In the evening when her husband came home, she told him what had happened. "Go tell them I am home and invite them in!" The woman went out and invited the men in. "We do not go into a House together," they replied. "Why is that?" she asked. One of the men explained: "His name is Wealth," he said pointing to one of his friends, and said pointing to another one, "He is Success, and I am Love." Then he added, "Now go in and discuss with your husband which one of us you want in your home."

The woman went in and told her husband what was said. Her husband was overjoyed. "How nice!" he said. "Since that is the case, let us invite Wealth. Let him come and fill our home with wealth!" His wife disagreed. "My dear, why don't we invite Success?" Their daughter-in-law was listening from the other corner of the house. She jumped in with her own suggestion: "Would it not be better to invite

Love? Our home will then be filled with love!" "Let us heed our daughter-in-law's advice," said the husband to his wife. "Go out and invite Love to be our guest."

The woman went out and asked the three men, "Which one of you is Love? Please come in and be our guest." Love got up and started walking toward the house. The other 2 also got up and followed him. Surprised, the lady asked Wealth and Success: "I only invited Love, Why are you coming in?" The old men replied together: "If you had invited Wealth or Success, the other two of us would've stayed out, but since you invited Love, wherever He goes, we go with him. Wherever there is Love, there is also Wealth and Success!" The author's wishes for you are as follows:

1. Where there is pain, I wish you peace and prosperity.
2. Where there is self-doubting, I wish you a renewed confidence in your ability to work through it.
3. Where there is tiredness, or exhaustion, I wish you understanding, patience, and renewed strength.
4. Where there is fear, I wish you love, and courage.
5. Where there is love, I wish it for you with wealth and success.
6. Where there is a challenge to decide, I wish you wisdom.
7. Where there are diverse individuals with various levels of "readiness" for doing the job, I wish you situational leadership skills.

Making a Difference through a Positive Attitude

Sometimes, the best way to reduce stress is to assist others and/or be involved in fighting for good causes to make a difference in some manner. Find your own way of making a difference as per your desires, means and abilities. For example, an elderly man was walking along the beach while making a difference. Spread across the entire beach were hundreds of starfish. A young boy noticed how the man kept throwing a starfish back into water, but didn't understand why. The young boy decided to ask the elderly man. As the young boy approached the elderly man, the young boy asked, "Sir, why are you throwing the starfish back in the ocean?" The elderly man replied, "Because they need to live in the water or else they will die." The young boy stood there thinking for a moment and then told the man, "Well, you can't pick all of these starfish up and throw all of them back. So what difference does it make?" The elderly man picked up a starfish held it to show the young boy and then said, "It matters to this one."

In this time of such a fast paced life, it is really easy to forget to slow down and remember how important each of us are and the difference we can make to people we may not even know. Reaching out can make a difference to someone and it may also make your day brighter. Yes, the little things can make a difference to you and others. Some people try to help others when they are hurt instead of trying to get revenge. As the following story demonstrates, helping others might be a good choice compared to seeking revenge.

Supposedly, three high school graduates, two men and a woman were walking in the desert when a rattlesnake, coiled in the dark, bit the woman. The two guys took off after the snake and eventually caught it and brought it back. Meanwhile the woman, left to deal with the venom, nearly died. The morale of this story is that at one time or another, life bites us all. The choice is the same in each case. We can spend our time chasing the snakes in our lives or deal with the poison. Professor William James of Harvard University said it long ago that "The greatest discovery of my generation is that a human being can alter his life by altering his attitude." Effective leaders and managers tend to have an attitude of caring instead of negativity and revenge.

The authors of this book emphasized that effective managers and leaders do what is right for them, their family and colleagues, and the society in general. In other words, effective managers, change agents, and problem solvers are ethical and great role models for everyone. Therefore, their conscience is usually clear and free of guilt. They understand that having a guilty conscience hinders one's progress and creates undue stress. They also understand that having a clear conscience due to the successful performance of one's duties with honor and integrity can greatly assist in being victorious in the race of life. Of course, with a clear conscience and a strong moral character, one will always be able to get up each time he or she falls and will eventually win the race of life with honor and integrity.

Johann Schiller, poet and historian, is quoted as having said that "Only those who have the patience to do simple things perfectly will acquire the skill to do difficult things easily." The key is to focus and make life-long priorities one's goals. Denis Waitley, author and speaker, said that "The reason most people never reach their goals is that they don't define them, learn about them, or even seriously consider them as believable or achievable. Winners can tell you where they are going, what they plan to do along the way, and who will be sharing the adventure with them." So, define your goals and then have the courage to go after it wholeheartedly. Maxwell Maltz said that "You must have courage to bet on your ideals, to take calculated risk, and act...Everyday living requires courage if life is to be effective and bring happiness." Make your dreams and pre-determined destiny come to fruition.

Mother Teresa created a destiny for herself because of the harmony in her thoughts, actions, habits, and character. The authors would like to end now with a powerful message from Mother Teresa. She is quoted as saying that "People are sometimes unreasonable, illogical, and self-centered; forgive them, anyway." She further stated:

1. If you are kind, people may accuse you of selfish, ulterior motives. Be kind anyway.
2. If you are successful, you will win some false friends and some true enemies. Succeed anyway.
3. If you are honest and frank, people may cheat you. Be honest and frank anyway.
4. What you spend years building, someone could destroy overnight. Build anyway.
5. If you find serenity and happiness, they may be jealous. Be happy anyway.
6. The good you do today, people will often forget tomorrow. Do good anyway.
7. Give the world the best you have, and it may never be enough. Give the world the best you've got anyway.
8. You see, in the final analysis, it is between you and your Creator. It was never between you and them anyway.

So be happy, be kind, be honest, succeed, and build your character one action and one day at a time. Live your life according to your priorities in a balanced manner while you have the opportunity to do so. If you can honestly perceive and believe a better state of being, then you are very likely to achieve it as well. So, do your best in all that you do, and know that you have done all that you could! The authors wish harmony in your thoughts, feelings, and behaviors so you can continue to "lead" through a strong character while leaving a great legacy. May you always have the hindsight to know where you have been, the foresight to know where you are going, and the insight to know when you are about to go too far!

Summary

A certain level of conflict is inevitable and a fact of life in today's diverse workplace. Therefore, everyone should gain the needed skills to effectively management interpersonal conflicts in a professional manner. Instead of complaining about interpersonal conflicts or blaming others for having a "rude" personality, one should reflect on the fact that a person can "choose" his/her responses, and thus does not have to allow other individuals like a rude person who is having a bad day, a politically motivated colleague, or an incompetent teammate to ruin his/her day, night, or week. Just because someone loses his or her temper during a frustrating moment does not mean that this person is "rude" or "mean" all the time. Furthermore, just because someone is older than you and near retirement age does not mean he or she is going to be "rude" or "mean" to his or her younger colleagues.

Take a few minutes and think of past events when somebody made you upset or angry, think of your responses to it, and plan on how you might respond differently in the future using the "inside-out-approach." Why waste a few moments of your day or night by being upset, sad, or angry over a nonissue. At times, there might be a few negative and opportunistic individuals who may try to make you feel angry, sad or bad...but you can choose not to fall into their trap. As a professional in the workplace, you can be smarter than them, and exercise your "freedom to choose" an appropriate response; and choose based on your values and goals. Most importantly, choose to be happy, and demonstrate a positive attitude regardless of others' intentions and actions!

EXERCISES

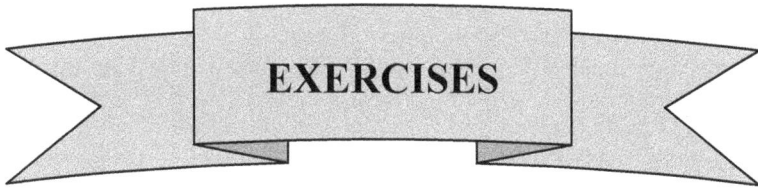

REFLECTION TOPICS FOR DISCUSSION AND RESEARCH

S tress and change management related research and exercises for reflection can serve as tools for self-assessment for the application of theoretical concepts and long-term learning. Read each of the following topics for research and follow its relevant directions or questions for further exploration and reflection.

If you are doing a formal presentation and writing of your findings in a research paper format, then you can follow the traditional headings of: Introduction, Literature, Study Methodology, Analysis and Results, Conclusions.

1 - Change and Conflict Management
Change is inevitable and part of life. Survey a group of 50 or more individuals about their views on change and conflict. You can explore how individuals respond to certain situations where change and/or conflict are involved. Document and discuss your results as relevant.

2 - Time Management
Time consumption is a necessity for people who are alive. Survey a group of 50 or more individuals about their views on time and time management challenges. You can explore how individuals respond to certain situations where they believe to have too many things to do but not enough time. Document and discuss your results as relevant.

3 - Personality Types
Everybody is different and demonstrates difference responses to specific situations. Survey a group of 50 or more individuals to determine their personality styles and how they respond to change, conflict or stress. Or, you can explore how these

individuals respond to certain situations where they believe to have too many things to do but not enough time. Document and discuss your results as relevant.

4 - Stress Reactions and the Freedom to Choose

Discuss stress and possible responses to such situations by answering the following questions:

1. What is the difference between positive stress (eustress) and negative stress (distress)? Discuss and provide workplace examples.
2. How is the "inside-out-approach" linked to role modeling? Can one change others by changing himself / herself first? Discuss.
3. What is the difference between reactive and proactive responses? Discuss and provide examples from the workplace.
4. Provide an example of a person who made you frustrated, angry, mad, or upset in the workplace, classroom, or in the community.
   - Describe the situation and discuss why this person made you mad, sad, or angry?
   - How did you handle the situation?
   - What will you do differently if this happens again?
5. How can professionals use their "freedom to choose" to effectively respond to emotionally-charged situations with colleagues or customers? Make a list of two to three practical recommendations?

5 - Anger and Conflict Management

According to Ramos and Sharma, anger is "a normal emotion one encounters when presented with an obstacle or difficulty in accomplishing a desired goal in a desired way in a desired time frame" (2007, p. 131). It is then noted that one can see the relationship between anger and conflict which is defined as "a situation involving anger between two or more people" (Ramos & Sharma, 2007, p. 131).

The conflict resolution survey was created so that individuals can rate their effectiveness using specific communication styles in resolving conflict which include:

1. Competing
2. Avoiding
3. Accommodating
4. Collaborating
5. Compromising.

The essence of effective conflict resolution is to work together without offending anyone or being offended. That being said, it is up to individuals to determine their respective resolution style and then perhaps work on either maintaining that style or learning a new one.

Survey a group of 50 people about anger and conflict management issues. You can explore how individuals respond to certain situations where conflict is involved. Document and discuss your results as relevant.

6 - Gender and Personality Types

Male and female are different. However, do they respond differently to stress, change and conflict. Survey a group of 50 or more individuals (males and females) to see if there are specific differences in the patterns of their responses. Document and discuss your results as relevant.

7 - Ethnicity and Personality Types

Cultures of different countries are different. Some people claim that cultures also socialize people to behave differently to different situations. Survey a group of 50 or more individuals from two different countries (cultures) to see if there are specific differences in the patterns of their responses. Document and discuss your results as relevant.

8 – Education and Change

More education should equal better decision-making and more effective responses to stressful and conflicting situations. Survey a group of 50 or more individuals with different educational backgrounds (i.e. high school graduate versus college graduates) to see if there are specific differences in the patterns of their responses. Document and discuss your results as relevant.

9 – Academic Concentration and Happiness

Happiness is a personal choice. At any time, one can choose to be happy or sad, mad or glad, good or bad, delighted or disappointed, etc. Others say that happiness is a state of mind. What do you think about happiness? What is it and how can one achieve it? Can a person's academic major tell you more about their state of mind or happiness level?

Survey a group of 50 or more individuals with different educational backgrounds (i.e. business versus education or medicine) to see if there are specific differences in the patterns of their responses. Document and discuss your results as relevant.

10 – What is Success?

Success is a process and not always a destination. You are here because you have achieved many milestones over the past years. Survey a group of 50 or more individuals to determine what success means to them and see if there are specific differences in the patterns of their responses (such as between males and females or younger and older respondents). Document and discuss your results as relevant.

11 – "New in Town" –Management and Worker Conflict Movie

In the Hollywood movie "*New in Town*," directed by Jonas Elmer, actors Renee Zellweger and Harry Connick Jr. play opposites each other in management and union capacities. The movie shows how Zellweger (playing Lucy Hill) adjusts to a new life when she is put in charge of the new plant in a small Minnesota town where she experiences a bit of a culture change. See the movie and reflect on the following questions:

1. How are the organizational cultures different between the headquarters and the plant in Minnesota?
2. What challenges are present for Lucy Hill as she takes over as the new plant manager? What are some of the stresses that she experiences?
3. What do employees think of the new plant manager who is sent from the headquarters?
4. What types of stress are the employees facing with the new plant manager?
5. What are some of the common management mistakes that the new plant manager made during the initial days?
6. What could the new plant manager have done to make the transition less stressful for herself and the employees during her initial transition?

References

Adams, S. M. (1999). Settling cross-cultural disagreements begins with "where" not "how". *Academy of management executive, vol.13* retrieved September 9, 2004 from EBSCO database.

Adler, N. (1983). A typology of management studies involving culture. *Journal of International Business Studies*, 14: 29-47.

Ahmed, S. A., and Rojas, J. (1998). *A comparative study of job values of North and South American business students.* Downloaded from the web on January 22, 2003, from: http://ww.sbaer.uca.edu/Research/1998/SRIBR/98sri230.txt.

Allport, G. W., Vernon, P. E., and Lindzey, G. (1960). *Study of values* (3rd ed.). Boston: Boston University Press.

Anderson, W. T. (1992). *Reality isn't what it used to be.* San Francisco: Harper and Row.

Andreason, A.W. & Kinneer, K.D. (2004). Bringing Them Home Again. *Industrial Management, 46* (6). Retrieved May 12, 2005 from ABI/INFORM Global.

Arango, L., Viveros, M. and Bernal, R. (1995), *Mujeres ejecutivas. Dilemas comunes, alternativas individuales.* Ediciones Uniandes, Ecoe Ediciones. Bogotá.

Arena, M. F. (2007) Los argentinos somos grandes fiesteros. http://www.minutouno.com/1/hoy/article/Los-argentinos-somos- fiesteros%5Eid_18690.htm, accessed September 28th., 2008

Arias-Galicia, F. (2005), Human resource management in Mexico. In M. Elvira and A. Davila, (Eds.), *Managing Human Resources in Latin America.* London: Routledge. 179-190.

Ariail, D. L. (2007). *Gender differences associated with the moral development and personal values of certified public accountants.* American Accounting Association, Research Conference, October 19-20, 2007, Philadelphia, PA.

Aronson, E. (1999). *The Social Animal.* New York, N.Y., Worth Publishers.

Ashford, B.E. & Humphrey, R.H. (1995). *Emotion in the workplace:* A reappraisal. Human Relations, 48(2), 97-125.

Association for Quality and Participation (AQP), 1995. *"The Spirit of Working Together."* The 17th Annual Spring Conference and Resource Proceedings. Pages 13- 100 are titled "Inspiring Change."

Aygun, Z. K., and Imamoglu, E. O. (2002). Value domains of Turkish adults and university students. *The Journal of Social Psychology*, 142(3): 333-351.

Aylesworth, A. B., Goodstein, R. C., & Kalra, A. Effect of archetypal embeds on feelings: An indirect route to affecting attitudes? *Journal of Advertising, 28*(3), 73-81.

Badaracco, J. L. (1997). *Defining moments: When managers must choose between right and right.* Boston: Harvard Business School Press.

Badaracco, J.L. (2001). *We Don't Need Another Hero.* Harvard Business Review, 78:8-92.

Babcock, P., (September 2005). A Calling for Change. *HR Magazine.* Pages 46-51.

Bailey, W., and Spicer, A. (2007). When does national identity matter? Convergence and divergence in international business ethics. *Academy of Management Journal, 50*(6): 1462-1480.

Beck, C. E. (1999). *Managerial Communication/ Building Theory and Practice.* Upper Saddle River, NJ: Prentice Hall. ISBN 0-13-849886-5

Beck, C. E (1985). *The Open Door Policy: Communication Climate and the Military Supervisor.* Retrieved March 31, 2005 from http://www.airpower.maxwell.af.mil/airchronicles/aureview/1985/may-jun/beck.html

Becker, B. W., and Connor, P. E. (1982). The influence of personal values on attitude and store choice behavior. In B. J. Walker, et al. (Eds.). *Educators' proceedings* (21-24). Chicago: American Marketing Association.

Belize People, 2008. Belize: People. *The World Factbook.* Central Intelligence Agency. Retrieved on 10, 09, 2008.

Belize, 2000. Housing and Population Census. Belize Central Statistical Office (2000).

Berger, P. L. and T. Luckmann (1966). *Social Construction of Reality : A treatise in the sociology of Knowledge.* London, England, Pelican Books Ltd.

Bigoness, W. J., and Blakley, G. L. (1996). A cross-national study of managerial values. *Journal of International Business Studies*, 27(4): 739-752.

Bond, M. H. (1994). Finding universal dimensions of individual variation in multicultural studies of values: The Rokeach and Chinese value surveys. In B. Apuka (Ed.),*New research on oral development: Moral development a compendium* (385-391). NY: Garland Publishing.

Bond, M. H. and Smith, P. B. (1996). Cross-cultural social and organizational psychology. *Annual Review of Psychology*, 47: 205-220.

Brett, Jeanne M, Goldberg, S. & URY, William L. (1988). *Getting Disputes Resolved: Designing Systems to Cut the Costs of Conflict.* Jossey-Bass, San Francisco

Bradstatter, H. and Eliasz, A. (2001). *Persons, situations, and emotions: An ecological approach.* Oxford; New York: Oxford University Press.

Braithwaite, V., and Law, H.G., (1985). Goal, mode and social value inventories. *Personality and Individual Differences.*

Bruschini, A. (2007), Trabalho e gênero no Brasil nos últimos dez anos, available at: http://www.fcc.org.br/seminario/BRUSCHINI.pdf, (accessed October 21, 2007).

Buela, A. (1990), *El Sentido de América*, Buenos Aires, Ed. Theoría, 1990, 56.

Cannon, Walter. B. (1932). *The Wisdom of the Body.* W.W. Norton, New York.

Capozzoli, T. K. (1999, November). Conflict resolution–a key ingredient in successful teams. *Supervision*, 60(11), 14. Retrieved September 10, 2004 from EBSCO database.

Catipovic-Veselica, K., Amidzic, V., and Buric, D. (1995). Type A/B behavior and eight basic emotions in 1084 employees. *Psychological Reports*, 76: pp. 1019-1024.

Cavico, F. J. & Mujtaba, B. G. (2009). *Business Ethics: The Moral Foundation of Leadership, Management, and Entrepreneurship (2nd edition).* Pearson Custom Publications. Boston, United States.

Cavico, F. & Mujtaba, B. G., (2008). *Legal Challenges for the Global Manager and Entrepreneur.* Kendal Hunt Publishing Company. United States.

Cavico, F. J. (2003). The Tort of Intentional Infliction of Emotional Disctress in the Private Employment Sector. *Hosftra Labor and Employment Law Journal.* Vol. 21, No. 1.

Chatman J, Jehn K (2000). The influence of Proportional and Perceptual Conflict Composition on Team Performance. *International Journal of Conflict Management* , 11, #1 pgs. 56-73.

Chhokar, J. S., Brodbeck, G. C., & House, R. J. (2007). *Culture and leadership across the world: The GLOBE book of in-depth studies of 25 societies.* Mahwah, NJ: Lawrence Erlbaum.

Chusmir, L. H. Koberg, C. S., and Mills, J. (1989). Male-female differences in the association of managerial style and personal values. *Journal of Social Psychology*, 129, 65-78.

Chumsir, L. H., and Parker, B. (1991). Gender and situational differences in manager's values: A look at work and home lives. *Journal of Business Research*, 23, 325-335.

Chuvala, B. (2001). Small business faces big challenges. *Fairfield County Business Journal*, 40(43), 19. Retrieved February 19, 2005, from EBSCOhost database.

CIA (2008). *Country studies.* www.cia.gov.

CIA World Factbook, 2008. Retrieved on November 27, 2008 from: https://www.cia.gov/library/publications/the-world-factbook/geos/bh.html).

Cileli, M., and Tezer, E. (1998). Life and value orientations of Turkish university students. *Adolescence*, 33(129), 219-228.

Clarke, C. & Lipp, Douglas (1998). Conflict resolution for contrasting cultures. *Training & Development.*

Cohen, R. *Negotiating Across Cultures: Communication Obstacles in International Diplomacy.* Retrieved on May 5, 2005 from the following URL: http://www.colorado.edu/conflict/peace/example/cohe7517.htm

Conflict Management skills. Retrieved Feb. 3, 2002 from: www.extension.unr.edu/CommDevBrd/CFLTMGMT.htm

Conflict Management Technique. Retrieved Jan. 31, 2002 from: www.col-ed.org/cur/misc/misc 33.txt.

Conflict Resolution Basics. Retrieved Feb.13, 2002 from: http://www.ivysea.com/pages/ctl297_2.html

Conner, Daryl R., 1992. *Managing at the speed of change: how resilient managers succeed and prosper where others fail.* Villard Books. New York.

Connor, P. E., and Becker, B. W. (1994). Personal values and management: What do we know and why don't we know more? *Journal of Management Inquiry,* 3(1), 67- 73.

Connor, P. E., and Becker, B. W. (2003). Personal values and decision-making styles of public managers. *Public Personnel Management, 32,* 155-181.

Connor, P., Becker, R., Moore, L., & Okubo, Y. (2006). Public-sector managerial values: United States, Canada and Japan. *International Journal of Organization Theory and Behavior,* 9(2): 147-173.

Country Facts (2008). *Country facts.* November 15, 2008, from www.cia.gov

Covey, S. R. (1995). *Principle-centered leadership.* New York: Simon & Schuster.

Crum, T. F., (1987). *The Magic of Conflict: Turning a Life of Work into a Work of Art.* Touchstone; Simon and Schuster.

Cunningham, J. B., Lischeron, J., Koh, H. C. and Farrier, M. (2004). A cybernetic Framework linking personality and other variables in understanding general Health. *Personnel Review,* 33(1): 55-80.

Davidson, Jeff (1997). *The Complete Idiot's Guide to Managing Stress.* Alpha Books. New York, NY.

Davis S.M. (1970), U.S. Versus Latin America business and culture, *Harvard Business Review,* page. 88

Definition of stress. (2002, March 22). Retrieved February 13, 2009, from medicinenet.com Web site: http://www.medterms.com/script/main/art.asp?articlekey=20104

D'Eugenio, D. P., (August 2005). *Transitional and Change Management: Assessment Application and Achievement.* Lecture Series Guest speaker at Nova Southeastern University on August 10, 2005.

Deems, Richard S., (1995). *Making Change Work for You: How to Handle Organizational Change.* American Media Publishing. American Media Incorporated.

DeMooij, M. (1998). *Global marketing and advertising: Understanding cultural paradoxes.* Thousand Oaks, CA: Sage Publications.

DeMooij, M. (2004). *Consumer behavior and culture: Consequences for global marketing and advertising.* Thousand Oaks, CA: Sage Publications.

deVaus, D. and McAllister, I. (1991). Gender and work orientation: Values and satisfaction in Western Europe. *Work and Occupation,* 18, 72-93.

DiDomenico, N. & Mujtaba, B. (October 2004). *Tempered Radicals: The Leadership Style for Making Changes Quietly.* The Association on Employment Practices and Principles. Published in the AEPP Proceedings, Pages 86-91.

Discipline without Punishment. A CRM Learning Video. 2215 Faraday Avenue. Phone: (800) 421-0833. Also made available by the Performance Systems Corporation: The Walk the Talk Company. Retrieved on 10, 06, 2005 from: http://www.crmlearning.com/product.cwa?isbn=111472V

Dio, D. L., Saragovi, C., Koestner, R. M., and Aube, J. (1996). Linking personal values to gender. *Sex Roles: A Journal of Research,* 34(9-10): 621-630.

Drafke, Michael (2006). *The Human Side of Organizations, 9th Edition.* Pearson/ Prentice Hall, Upper Saddle River, New Jersey 07458

Duffy, J. A., Fox, S., Punnett, B. J., Gregory, A., Lituchy, T., Monserat, S. I., Olivas-Lujan, M. R., Santso, N. M. B. F., and Miller, J. (2006). Successful women of the Americas: The same or different? *Management Research News,* 29(9): 552-572.

Duke's Fuqua School of Business. *Management Communication.* Retrieved on June 6, 2005 from the following URL: http://www.fuqua.duke.edu/faculty/areas/manageme.../management_communication_area.htm

Eaton, T. V. and Giacomino, D. E. (2000). Personal values of business students: Differences by gender and discipline. In B. Schwartz (Ed.), *Research on Accounting Ethics,* (7): 83-102. Oxford, UK: Elsevier Science, Ltd.

Eaton, T. V. and Giacomino, D. E. (2001). Personal values of business students: Differences by gender and discipline. *Research on Accounting Ethics,* 7: 83-102.

Edstrom, KRS, (1993). *Conquering Stress: The Skills You Need to Succeed in the Business World.* USA, Barron's: A Business Success Guide.

Elias, Marilyn (2009). Mental stress spirals with economy. *USA TODAY,* March 12, 2009. Retrieved on March 12, 2009 from: http://www.usatoday.com/news/health/2009-03-11-stress-poll_N.htm

Ellis, Albert; Harper, Robert (1975). *A Guide to Rational Living.* N. Hollywood: Melvin Powers, Wilshire Book Company.

Ellis, Albert; Harper, Robert (1979). *A New guide to Rational Living.* Prentice Wall, Englewood Cliffs, N.J.

Elkhouly, S. M. E., and Buda, R. (1997). A cross-cultural comparison of value systems of Egyptians, Americans, Africans and Arab executives. *International Journal of Commerce and Management*, 7: 102-199.

England, G. W. (1974). *The manager and the man.* University of Minnesota Press.

England, C. W. (1975). *The manager and his values: An international perspective from the U.S., Japan, Korea, India and Australia.* Ballinger, Cambridge, MA.

Evans, G., Palsane, M. and Carrere, S. (1987). Type A behavior and occupational stress: A cross cultural study of blue collar workers. *Journal of Personality and Social Psychology*, 52(5): 1002-1007.

Eysenck, Hans. J. (1988). Health's Character. *Psychology Today.* Pgs. 28-35.

Fawcett, C. (2008). *Latin American youth in transition: A policy paper on youth unemployment in Latin America and the Caribbean.* Labor Markets Policy Briefs Series, Social Development Division, Inter-American Development Bank.

Feather, N. T. (1979). Values, expectancy, and action. *Australian Psychologist*, 14, 243-260.

Feather, N. T. (1982). Reasons for entering medical school in relation to value priorities and sex of student. *Journal of Occupational Psychology*, 55, 119-128.

Feather, N. T. (1984). Masculinity, femininity, psychological androgyny, and the structure of values. *Journal of Personality and Social Psychology*, 47(3): 604-620.

Feather, N. T. (1999). *Values, achievement and justice: Studies in the Psychology of Deservingness.* New York: Academic/.Plenum Publishers.

Fisher, Roger, Kopelman, Elizabeth & Schneider Andrea (1996). *Beyond Machiavelli.* Penguin Press, New York

Fitzpatrick, J., Liang, S., Feng, E., Crawford, D., Sorell, G., and Morgan-Fleming, B. (2006). Social values and self-discourse: A comparison of Chinese native, Chinese resident (in U.S.) and North American spouses. *Journal of Comparative Family Studies*, 37(1): 113-121.

Freud, S. (1950). *Collected Papers.* (Ed.), edited by Jones, E. New York.

Friedman Jack P., (2000). Dictionary of Business Terms. 3rd Edition. (New York: Barron's Educational Series).

Friedman, M; Rosenman, R. (1974). *Type A Behavior and your Heart.* Fancett, Greenwich, Conn.

Frydenberg, E. Lewis. R., Kennedy, G., Ardila, R., Frindte, W., Hannoun, R. (2005). *Journal of Youth and Adolescence,* 32(1): 59-67.

Fujita, A. (1999). *Personal values of Japanese business managers.* Business Forum, 1/1/1999. Downloaded June 26, 2006, from www.highbeamresearch.com.

Garcia-Gonzalez, J. (2002). Latin American youth. *Advertising and Marketing to Children*, Jan-Mar 2002. 17-24.

Geen, R. G. (1990). *Human aggression* (Mapping Social Psychology Series), Milton Keynes: Open University Press.

Geller, Judith B. (1994). *A Manager's Guide to Human Behavior.* Fourth edition. American Management Association.

Gibson, J; Ivancevich, J.M. Donnelly J.H. Jr. Konopaske, R. (2005). *Organizations: Behavior, Structure, Processes.* McGRaw-Hill/Irwin-12th edition, New York, N.Y.

Greenberg J.S. (1993). *Comprehensive Stress Management.* Brown & Benchmark, Dubuque, IA.

Gustavo, C. (2004). Religiosity, values and horizontal and vertical individualism-collectivism: A study of Turkey, the U.S. and the Philippines. *The Journal of Social Psychology*, 12/1: 1-25.

Hage, J., & Powers, C. H. (1992). *Post industrial lives: Roles and relationships in the 21st century.* Newbury Park, CA: Sage.

Hans selye quotes. (n.d.) Retrieved February 18, 2009, from Brainy Quote Web site: http://www.brainyquote.com/quotes/authors/h/hans_selye.html

Hart, A. (2007, March 1). *7 Leading causes of stress.* Retrieved February 13, 2009, from http://ezinearticles.com/?7-Leading-Causes-of-Stress&id=473303

Health Library (2009). How vulnerable are you to stress? (1999-2006). Retrieved February 11, 2009, from Internet Health Library Web site: http://www.internethealthlibrary.com/sq/stress/stress-assess.htm

Herbig, P. (2005). *Cross Cultural Negotiations Lecture 2. The Importance of Thinking Globally.* Tri-State University. Retrieved on June 4, 2005 from the following URL: http://www.tristate.edu/faculty/hergig/pahccn2.htm

_____, P. Cross *Cultural Negotiations Lecture 3. 'The Incredible Shrinking World'.* Tri-State University. Retrieved on May 4, 2005 from the following URL: http://www.tristate.edu/faculty/hergig/pahccn3.htm

_____, P. Cross Cultural Negotiations Lecture 5: 'How to Succeed in negotiations without really trying. Tri-State University. Retrieved on May 4, 2005 from the following URL: http://www.tristate.edu/faculty/hergig/pahccn5.htm

_____, P. Cross Cultural Negotiations Lecture 12: 'How do we agree? Let me count the ways.' Tri-State University. Retrieved May 4, 2005from the following URL: http://www.tristate.edu/faculty/hergig/pahccn12.htm.

Hersey, Paul and Campbell, Ron (2004). Leadership: A Behavioral Science Approach. ISBN: 0-931619-09-2.

Hoeken, H., Brandt, C. V. D., Crijns, R., Dominguez, N., Hendriks, B., Planken, B., and Starren, M. (2003). International advertising in Western Europe: Should differences in uncertainty avoidance be considered when advertising in Belgium, France, the Netherlands, and Spain? Journal of Business Communication, 40(3): 195-205.

Hofstede, G. (1980). Culture's consequences: International differences in work-related values. Beverly Hills, CA: Sage Publications.

Hofstede, G. (1997). Cultures and organizations. The software of the mind. New York: McGraw;Hill.

Hofstede, G. (2001). Cultures consequences: Comparing values, behaviors, institutions and organizations across nations (2nd Ed). London, Sage Publications.

Hofstede, G. (2003). Geert Hofstede Cultural Dimensions. Retrieved on October 9th 2004 from ITIM website: http:// geert-hofstede.com/hofstede_united_states.shtml

Holder, W. (2002). " Why Change Efforts Fail." Refresher Publications, Inc.

Holmes, Thomas. H; Rahe, Richard, H. (1907). The Social Readjustment Rating Scale. Journal of Psychosomatic Research. 11:213-18.

Hyde, D. and Allen, R. (1996). Investigations in Stress Control, 4th Edition. Pearson Custom Publishing - United States.

Holton, Bil and Cher, (1992). The Manager's Short Course. John Wiley & Sons. See the section on welcoming change.

Hyde, D. and Allen, R. (1996). Investigations in Stress Control, 4th Edition. Pearson Custom Publishing; United States. ISBN: 0-8087-0161-4.

Gibson, J, Ivancevich, John M, Donnelly James & Konopaske, R. (2006). Organizations: Behavior, Structure, Processes, 12th Edition. McGraw-Hill/ Irwin, New York N.Y.

Impact Factory. Communication Skills. Retrieved on June 6, 2005 from the following URL: http://www.impactfactory.com/p/effective.communication_skills.html

Inglehart, R. and Carballo, M (1997), Does Latin American exist? (And is there a Confucian Culture?): A global analysis of cross-cultural differences. Political Science and Politics, 30 (1), 34-47: 127-138.

International Congress on Stress. Retrieved on October 12, 2005 from: http://www.sterss.org/cong.htm

Ivancevich, J. M., and Matteson, M. (1984). A Type A-B person-work environment interaction model for examining occupational stress and consequences. Human Relations, 37: 491-513.

Jamal, M. (1985). Type A behavior and job performance: Some suggestive findings. Journal of Human Stress, 11(2): 60-68.

Jameson, D. A. (2007). Reconceptualizing cultural identity and its role in intercultural business communication. The Journal of Business Communication, 44(3): 199-221.

Johnson, T. M. (1999). Are the effects of age and gender changing the personal values of Japanese executives. Business Forum, January 1, 1999. Downloaded from the web on September 27, 2005, from www.highbeamresearch.com

Johnston, C. S. (1995). The Rokeach Value Survey: Underlying structure and multidimensional scaling. The Journal of Psychology, 129(5): 583-597.

Johnson, G., & Leavitt, W. (2001). Building on Success: Transforming Organizations through an

Jones, G & George J. (2003). Contemporary Management (3rd ed.) New York: McGraw-Hill Irwin.

Judson, Arnold (1991). Changing Behavior in Organizations: Minimizing resistance to Change.

Judy, R., & D'Amico, C. (1997). Workforce 2020: Work and workers in the 21" century. Indianapolis, IN: Hudson Institute.

Juran, Joseph M. (1989). Juran on Leadership for Quality. Macmillan Inc. See "Rules of the Road" for Handling Resistance In the Work Place.

Kahle, L. R. (1983). Social values and social change: Adaptation to life in America. New York: Praeger.

Kahle, L. R., Beatty, S. E., and Homer, P. (1986). Alternative measurement approaches to consumer values: The List of Values (LOV) and Values and Life Style (VALS). The Journal of Consumer Research, 13(3), 405-409

Kamakura, WE. A., and Novak, T. P. (1992). Value-system segmentation: Exploring the meaning of LOV. The Journal of Consumer Research, 19(1): 119-132.

Kasamatsu, A; Hirai, T (1966). *Studies of EEG's of Expert Zen Mediators*. Folia Psychiatric Neurological Japonica 28:315.

Kawasaki, K. (1994). Youth culture in Japan. *Social Justice*, 21(2): 185-205.

Keirsey, David (2002). *The Four Temperaments*. Advisor Team: Harness the Power of Personality. Retrieved on February 13, 2002 from: www.col-ed.org/cur/misc/misc 33.txt.

Keltikangas-Jarvinen, L., and Heinonen, K. (2003). Childhood roots of adulthood hostility: family factors as predictors of cognitive and affective hostility. *Child Development*, 74(6): pp. 1751-1768.

Kent, S., (September 2005). Happy Workers Are the Best Workers. *Wall Street Journal*, September 6, 2005, p A20.

Khilji, S. E., Mujtaba, B., Greenwood, R. A., Murphy E. F. Jr., Chaturvedi, S., Christoforou, P. T., Ruiz,-Gutierrez, J. A., Olivas-Lujan, M. R., Luk, D. M., Madero, S., Monserrat, S. I. L., Santos, N. M. B. F., Teeple, W., Uy, A. O. O., and Woodhull, M. D., and. (2008a). *A cross-cultural investigation of religious affiliation differences in personal values across 11 countries and six regions*. AIB 2008 Annual Meeting, June 30-July 3, 2008, Milan, Italy. *Selected as one of Best Papers in Proceedings*.

Khilji, S. E., Murphy E. F. Jr., Mujtaba, B., Greenwood, R. A., Ruiz,-Gutierrez, J.A., Olivas-Lujan, M. R., Luk, D. M., Madero, S., Monserrat, S. I. L., Santos, N. M. B. F., Uy, A. O. O, Woodhull, M. D., and Teeple, W. (2008b). *Intergenerational value change: A Cross cultural empirical test*. Eastern Academy of Management Meeting, May 14-17, 2008, Washington, D.C.

Kiger, P. J. (2004). Workforce Management: 83 (12) pg 30.

Kim, C. W. and Mauborgne, R. (August 1997). Fair Process: Managing in the Knowledge Economy. *Harvard Business Review*. Pages 65-66.

Kluckhohn, C. (1951). The study of values. In D. N. Barrett (Ed.), *Values in transition*. Notre Dame, IN: University of Notre Dame Press.

Kohlberg, L. (1970). *Stages in the development of moral thought and action*. New York: Holt, Rinehart and Winston.

Kotter, John P., 1990. A force for change: How leadership differs from management. Free Press publication.

Kotter, John P. and Schlesinger, Leonard H.(1979). Choosing Strategies for Change. *HBR*, Page 111. March/April issue.

Kono, S., Arai, H., Koyanagi, S., Hiyamuta, K., Doi, Y., Kawano, T., Nakagaki, O., Takada, K., Nii, T., Shirai, K., Ideishi, M., Arakawa, K., Mohri, M., and Takeshita, A. (2000). Job strain, Type A behavior pattern, and the prevalence of coronary heart disease in Japanese working men. *Journal of Psychosomatic Research*, 49(1): 77-83.

Kouichi, Y., Liu, Y., Kodama, H., Sasazuki S., Washio, M., Tanaka, K., Tokunaga, S.,

Kreitner, R. & Kinicki, A. (2003). Organizational Behavior (6th ed.). The McGraw-Hill Companies. Retrieved September 30, 2004, from Publisher Web site: http://www.mhhe.com/kreitner.

Kreuter, Eric A. (1993). Why Career Plateaus are Healthy (CPA in Industry). Retrieved September 10th 2004 from http://www.nysscpa.org/cpajournal/old/14522934.htm

Kunnanatt, J. T. (2003). Type A behavior pattern and managerial performance: A study among bank executives in India. *International Journal of Manpower*, 24(6): 720-734.

Laukaran VH, Winikoff B, Myers D. (1986). The impact of health services on breastfeeding: common themes from developed and developing worlds. In: Jeliffe A, Jeliffe E, eds. *Advances in International Maternal and Child Health*. 121-128.

Latumahina , D. (2007, March 8). Time quotes: 66 best time management quotes. Retrieved February 13, 2009, from Life Optimizer Web site: http://www.lifeoptimizer.org/2007/03/08/66-best-quotes-on-time-management/

Lavanco, G. (1997). Burnout syndrome and Type A behavior in nurses and teachers in Sicily. *Psychological Reports*, 81, pp. 523-528.

Lazarus, Richard. S. (1966). *Psychological Stress and the Coping Process*. McGraw-Hill Book Co, New York.

Lazarus, Richards (1984). Puzzles in the Study of Daily Hassles. *Journal of Behavioral Medicine* 7: 375-389.

LeBaron, M, (2005) *Culture-Based Negotiation Styles*. Beyond Intractability.org. Retrieved on May 4, 2005 from the following URL: http://www.beyondintractability.org/m/culture_negotiation.jsp?nid

Lenartowicz, T., and Johnson., J.(2002). Comparing managerial values in twelve Latin American Countries: An exploratory study. *Management International Review*, 42(3): 279-307.

Lenartowicz, T. and Johnson, J. P. (2003). A cross-national assessment of the values of Latin America managers: Contrasting hues or shades of gray. *Journal of International Business Studies*, 34: 266-281.

Lenartowicz, T., and Roth, K. (2001). Does subculture within a country matter? A cross-cultural study of motivational domains and business performance in Brazil. *Journal of International Business Studies*, 32(2): 305-320.

Leung, K., Bhagat, R. S., Buchan, N. R., Erez, M., and Gibson, C. B. (2005). Culture and international business: Recent advances and their implications for future research. *Journal of International Business Studies*, 36(4): 357-380.

Levine, J. W., Ranelli, C. J., and Vale, R. S. (1974). Self-evaluation and reaction to a shifting other. *Journal of Personality and Social Psychology*, 29, 637-643.

Lewis, M (2002). The Last Taboo. *Fortune*, October 28, pp. 137-44.

Lewis, A. M. (Winter 2009). Is stress sabotaging your life? Make stress your life. *Balance: Personal Growth for Women*, 10(1), pp. 20-21.

Limthanakom, N., Lauffer, W., Mujtaba, B. G., and Murphy, Jr. E. F. (2008). The Ranking of Terminal and Instrumental Values by Working Professionals in Thailand, Singapore and the United States: What is Important and How Do They Impact Decision-Making? *International Business and Economics Research Journal*, 7(4): 45-60.

Lirio, P, Lituchy, T., Monserrat, S., Olivas Lujan, M.R, Duffy, J.A, Fox, S., Gregory, A Punnett, B.J.,.Santos, N.M.B. (2007), Exploring career-life success and family social support of successful women in Canada, Argentina and Mexico, *Career Development International* Vol. 12 (1): 28-50.

Lord, J. (1998). The Quote Center. Retrieved October 1, 2004, from Web site: http://www.appreciative-inquiry.org/AI-Quotes.htm.

Lovell, P.A. (1994), Race, Gender and Development in Brazil. *Latin American Research Review*, 29(3): 7-35.

Lyons, S., Duxbury, L., and Higgins, C. (2005). Are gender differences in basic human values a generational phenomenon? *Sex Roles: A Journal of Research*, 53(9-10), 763-775.

MacLennan, R. N, and Peebles, J W E. (1996). Survey of health problems and personality in air traffic controllers. *International Journal of Aviation Psychology*, 6(1), pp. 43-55.

Matteson, M., and Ivancevich, J. (1982). Type A and B behavior patterns and health symptoms: Examining individual and organizational fit. *Journal of Organizational Medicine*, 24, 585-589.

Management in Education, 17(2), 9. Retrieved September 30, 2004, from EBSCOhost database.

Managing Stress in School Part I & II. (n.d.) Yahoo Education online. Retrieved February 14, 2009, from http://education.yahoo.com/college/essentials/articles/grad/managing-stress-2.html

Markham, Ursula (1993*) How to Deal With Difficult People*, Thorsons, London

Mattock, John. (Ed.). (2003). *Cross Cultural Communication; the essentials guide to international business.* (New rev. ed 2.). London ; Sterling, VA.

Maultsby, Maxie (1984). *Rational Behavior Therapy.* Prentice-Hall, Inc. Englewood Cliffs, N.J.

Maxfield, S. (2004), Modifying best practices in women's advancement for the Latin American context, *Women in Management Review,* Vol. 20, No.4, 2005 249-261

Mayer, J.D. & Salovey, P. (1993). *The intelligence of emotional intelligence. Intelligence.* 17, 433-442.

McCartney, T; Neville, M. (1998). The Therapeutic Learning Process as Effective Modality in Coping with Addictions. *OD intervention*, Bahamas Oil Refining Corporation, Freeport, Grand Bahamas.

McCartney, T. (2007). *The Professional Development Process in Managing Self, Others and Organizations.* Unpublished Manuscript, Nova Southeastern University, Ft. Lauderdale, Florida.

McGuire, D., Garavan, T. N., Saha, S. K., and O'Donnell, D. (2006). The impact of individual values on human resource decision-making by line managers. *International Journal of Manpower*, 27(3): 251-273.

Medicinenet.com, (2009). Viewed on February 13, 2009 from: http://www.medterms.com/script/main/art.asp?articlekey=20104

Meglino, B. M. (1998). Individual values in organizations: Concepts, controversies and research. *Journal of Management*, May-June 1998. Downloaded from the web on December 22, 2002, from www.findarticles.com.

Menon, N. and Akhilesh, K. B. (1994). Functionally dependent stress among managers. *Journal of Managerial Psychology*, 9(3): 13-22.

Meyerson, D. (2001). *Radical Change, the Quiet Way.* Harvard Business Review, 79:9-92.

Miller, L. H. (2004). Stress: The different kinds of stress. Retrieved February 20, 2009, from American Psychological Association Web site: http://www.apahelpcenter.org/articles/article.php?id=21

Mills, H. (2008, June 26). Types of stressors (eustress vs. distress). Retrieved February 11, 2009, from mentalhelp.net Web site:
http://www.mentalhelp.net/poc/view_doc.php?type=doc&id=15644&cn=117
Mindtools. (1995-2008). What stress is... definitions. Retrieved February 12, 2009, Web site:
http://www.mindtools.com/stress/UnderstandStress/StressDefinition.htm
Mitroff, Ian I., (2005). *Why Some Companies Emerge Stronger and Better from a Crisis: Seven Essential Lessons for Surviving Disaster*. AMACOM.
Mohebbi, Rayka; Derlatka, Karen; Watson, Lweis; and Suskind, Raphael, (2004). *Cultural and Ethical Conflicts in the Workplace: How to Control and Minimize Them*. Project submitted for "Managerial Communication and Ethics." October 6th 2004.
Moncur, Michael. (1994-2004). The Quotations Page. Retrieved Feb 6, 2005, from www.thequotationspage.com.
Monserrat S.I.- Lluna H.E. (2000). Argentina's Development: democracy, economy and system law. *International Newsletter*, California State University, San Bernardino.
Monserrat, S., Lassaga, G., and Dannunzio, D. (2006), Argentina: returning to its glorious past. In B. J. Punnett; J. A., Duffy; S., Fox; A. Gregory;T. R. Lituchy; S. I. Monserrat; M. R. Olivas-Luján; and N. M. B. F. Santos (Eds). *Successful Professional Women of the Americas: From Polar Winds to Tropical Breezes*. Cheltenham, UK: Edward Elgar.
Mujtaba, B. (2006). *Cross Cultural Change Management*. ISBN: 1-59526-568-6. Llumina Press, Tamarac, Florida. Website: www.Llumina.com
Mujtaba, B. G. (2008). *Coaching and Performance Management: Developing and Inspiring Leaders*. ILEAD Academy Publications; Davie, Florida, USA. ISBN: 978-0-9774211-4-5.
Mujtaba, B. G. (2007). *Cross Cultural Management and Negotiation Practices*. ILEAD Academy Publications; Florida, United States. ISBN: 978-0-9774211-2-1.
Mujtaba, B. G. (2007). *Workplace Diversity Management: Challenges, Competencies and Strategies*. ISBN: 1-59526-548-1. Coral Springs, Florida.
Mujtaba, B. G. and Cavico, F. J., (2006). *Age Discrimination in Employment: Cross Cultural Comparison and Management Strategies*. BookSurge. ISBN: 1-4196-1587-4. Available through amazon.com.
Mudrack, P. E. (2004). Job involvement, obsessive-compulsive personality traits and workaholic behavioral tendencies. *Journal of Organizational Change Management,* 17(5): 490-508.
Murphy, E. F. Jr., and Anderson, T. (2003). A longitudinal study exploring value changes during the cultural assimilation of Japanese student pilot sojourners in the United States. *International Journal of Value Based Management*, May 2003, 16(2), 111-129.
Murphy, E. F. Jr., Gordon, J. D., and Anderson, T. (2004). An examination of cross-cultural age or generation-based value differences between the United States and Japanese. *Journal of Applied Management and Entrepreneurship*, 9(1), 21-48.
Murphy, E. F. Jr., Gordon, J. D., and Mullen, A. (2004). A preliminary study exploring the value changes taking place in the US since the September 11, 2001 terrorist attack on the World Trade Center in New York. *Journal of Business Ethics, 50* (1), March 2004, pp. 81-96.
Murphy, E. F., Jr., Greenwood, R. and Lawn-Neiborer, L. J. (2004). *Sex differences and similarities in cross-cultural values and internet marketing attitudes between the United States, Japan and United Kingdom*. Paper presented at Southern Academy of Management Meeting, Dallas Texas.
Murphy, E. F. Jr., Greenwood, R. A., Ruiz-Gutierez, J. A., Manyak, T. G., Mujtaba, B., and Uy, O. O. A. (2006). *Generational value changes: Their history and a cross-cultural empirical test*. Presented at National Academy of Management Meeting August 11-17, 2006, Atlanta, Georgia.
Murphy, E. F. Jr., Chaturvedi, S., Greenwood, R. A., Ruiz-Gutierez, J. A., Khilji, S. E., Olivas-Lujan, M. R., Luk, D. M., Manyak, T. G., Mujtaba, B., Madero, S., Santos, N. M. B. F., Uy, A. O., and Woodhull, M D. (2007a). *An investigation of Type A behavior pattern and personal values: A cross-cultural study between developed and developing countries*. Academy of Management Meeting, Philadelphia, PA, August 3-8, 2007.
Murphy, E. F. Jr., Chaturvedi, S., Greenwood, R. A., Ruiz-Gutierez, J. A., Khilji, S. E.,Olivas-Lujan, M. R., Luk, D. M., Manyak, T. G., Mujtaba, B., Madero, S., Santos, N. M. B. F., Uy, A. O., and Woodhull, M D. (2007b). *The values of males and females in the east and west: Are they diverging or converging?* Academy of Management Meeting, Philadelphia, PA, August 3-8, 2007.
Murphy, E. F. Jr., Greenwood, R. A. Chaturvedi, S., Ruiz-Gutierrez, J. A., Khilji, S. E., Olivas-Lujan, M. R., Luk, D. M., Manyak, T. G., Mujtaba, B., Madero, S., Santos, N. M. B. V. F., Uy, A. O. O. Monserrat, S. I., Wodhull, M. D., Christoforou, P. T., and Teeple, W. (2008). *The values of*

males and females in the east and west: Are they becoming more similar or different? Academy of Management, August, 2007, Philadelphia, PA. (In Press) Journal of Sex Roles.

Murphy, E. F. Jr., Greenwood, R. A., Ruiz-Gutierez, J. A., Manyak, T. G., Mujtaba, B., and Uy, O. O. A. (2006a). *Generational value changes: Their history and a cross-cultural empirical test.* Presented at National Academy of Management Meeting, Atlanta, Georgia.

Murphy, E. F. Jr., Greenwood, R. A., Ruiz-Gutierez, J. A., Manyak, T. G., Mujtaba, B.and Uy, Ol. O. A. (2006b). *Work and family: An exploration of work-family conflict and family-work conflict in work and home roles.* Paper presented at the Academy of Management Meeting Atlanta, Georgia.

Murphy, E., Jr., Snow, W., Carson, P., and Zigarmi, D. (1997). Values, sex differences and psychological androgyny. *International Journal of Value-Based Management,* 10, 69-99.

Murphy, Jim (1994). *Managing Conflict at Work.* American Media Publishing.

Musser, S. J., and Orke, R. A. (1992). Ethical value systems: A typology. *The Journal of Applied Behavioral Science,* 28(3): 348-362.

Myers & Briggs Foundation, 2008. Retrieved on March 30, 09 from: (www.myersbriggs.org/my-mbti-personality-type/mbti-basics/isable-briggs-myers.asp

Nadler, David A.; Shaw, Robert B.; Walton, A. Elise, and Associates, (1995). Discontinuous Change: Leading Organizational Transformation. Jossey-Bass Publication.

Neelankavil, J. P. Mathur, A., and Zhang, Y. (2000). Determinants of managerial performance: A cross-cultural comparison of the perceptions of middle-level managers in four countries. *International Business Studies,* 31(1): 121-130.

Obot, I.(1988). Value systems and cross-cultural contact: The effect of perceived similarity and stability on social evaluations. International Journal of Intercultural Relations, 12, 363-379.

Oddou, G.R & Mendenhall, M.E. (1991). Succession Planning for the 21ˢᵗ Century: How Well Are We Grooming Our Future Business Leaders? *Business Horizons.* Retrieved May 10, 2005 from Business Source Premier.

Offermann, L. R. & Hellmann, P. S. (1997). Culture's consequences for leadership behavior: National values in action. Journal of Cross-Cultural Psychology, 342-351.

Olesen, Erik, (1993). 12 Steps to Mastering the Winds of Change. Peak Perfomers Reveal How To Stay On Top In Times Of Turmoil. Rawson Associates, a ⬚ofstede of Macmilllan Inc.

Olmstead, J. W. (2006). Personal & work life stressors self-assessment questionnaire. Retrieved February 11, 2009, Web site: http://www.lifeonbalance.com/file_manager/files/docs/Life %20On%20Balance% 20%20Personal%20Life%

Ornstein, R; Sobel, D. (1987). *The Healing Brain: A new Perspective on the Brain and Health.* Semon & Schuster, New York.

Page, Susan, (2005). *On Security, Public Draws Blurred Lines.* USA Today, August 4, 2005.

Patten R. (2004, September/October). From implicit to explicit: Putting corporate values and personal accountability front and centre. *Ivey Business Journal Online, p. H1.*

Payne, N, (2005) *Cross Cultural Negotiations. Everoft.com.* Retrieved from the following URL:http://developers.eversoft.com/article/business/negotiation/cross-cultural-negotiations.shtmlTucker, M., Benton, D & McCarthy (2002). *The Human Challenge* (7ᵗʰ ed). New Jersey: Prentice Hall

Phalet, K., and Schonpflug, U. (2001). Intergenerational transmission in Turkish immigrant families: Parental collectivism, achievement values and gender differences. Journal of Comparative Family Studies, 32(4): 489-499.

PNUD (2003). Informe sobre desarrollo humano. Ediciones Mundi- Prensa. New York. *Cheltenham, UK: Edward Elgar.*

Political Database of Americas available on line (2008). Website: http://pdba.georgetown.edu/Elecdata/Arg/pres07.html, Accessed September 28th., 2008

Potter, J. (2009). Biography of General George s. Patton Jr. Retrieved February 26, 2009, from General George S. Patton Jr. Web site: http://www.generalpatton.com/biography.html

Princeton Study. (1989). *Student Stress Lowers Immunity.* Brain Mind Bulletin. 14:17

Pritchett, P. and Pound, R. (2005). *A Survival Guide to the Stress of Organizational Change.* Reviewed in 2005.

_____, P. (1993) *Culture Shift. The Employee Handbook for Changing Corporate Culture.* Pritchett & Associates, Inc. Dallas, Tx.

_____, P. and Pound, R. (1993) *High-Velocity Culture Change: A handbook for managers.* Pritchett & Associates, Inc. Dallas, Tx.

_____, Price. New Work Habits For A Radically Changing World: 13 Ground Rules for Job Success In the Information Age.

_____, Price and Pound, Ron (1990). Change: The employee handbook for organizational change. Reprinted in 1993. 8th. Ed.

Ralston, D., Gustafson, D., Elsas, P., Cheung, F. and Terpstra, R. (1992). Eastern values: A comparison of managers in the U.S., Hong Kong and PRC. *Journal of Applied Psychology*, 77: 664-671.

Ralston, D., Thang, N., and Napier, N. (1999). A comparative study of the work values of North and South Vietnamese managers. *Journal of International Business Studies*, 30(4): 655-670.

Robbins, Stephen P. (2005). *Organizational Behavior*. Pearson/Prentice Hall, Upper Saddle River, New Jersey.

Rogers, C. R., & Roethlisberger, F. J. (1952). Barriers and Gateways to Communication. *Harvard Business Review.*

Rokeach, M. (1968a). *Beliefs, attitudes, and values: A theory of organization and change*. San Francisco: Jossey- Bass Inc.

Rokeach, M. (1973). *The nature of human values*. New York: Free Press.

Rokeach, M. (1979). *Understanding human values: Individual and societal*. NY: Free Press.

Rokeach, M. (1983). *Rokeach value survey*: Form G. Palo Alto, CA: Consulting Psychologists Press.

Rokeach, M. (1986). *Beliefs, attitudes and values: A theory of organization and change*. San Francisco, CA: Jossey-Bass Publishers.

Rokeach, M., and Ball-Rokeach, S. J. (1989). Stability and change in American value priorities.*American Psychologist*, 44, 775-784.

Romas, J., & Sharma, M. (2010, 2007). *Practical Stress Management: A Comprehensive Workbook for Managing Chang and Promoting Health*. San Francisco: Benjamin Cummings / Pearson.

Ruiz-Gutierrez, J. (2005). *Change and organizational demography: The case of 30 Colombian companies*. Paper presented at the annual meeting of the Academy of Management, HI.

Ruiz-Gutierez, J. A., Monserrat, S. I., Olivas-Lujan, M. R., Madero, S., Greenwood, R. A., Murphy, E. F. Jr., and Santos, N. M. B. F. (2008). *Personal values and attitudes towards women in Argentina, Brazil, Colombia an Mexico: A cross-cultural investigation*. The Business Association of Latin American Studies (BALAS) Conferences, April 23-25, 2008. University of Los Andes, Bogota, Colombia.

Ryckman, R. M. and Houston, D. M. (2003). Value priorities in American and British female and male university students. *The Journal of Social Psychology*, 143(1): 127-138.

Salovey, P. & Mayer, J.D. (1990). *Emotional intelligence. Imagination, Cognition, and Personality.* 9(1990), 185-211

Schein, Edgar (1983). *Inter-group Problems in Organizational Development: Theory, Practice, Research 3rd Edition*. Wendell French, Cecil Bell and Robert Zawacki Business Publications

Schiemann, W. (1992). *"Why Change Fails" Across the Board*. April, 1992.

Schwartz, S. H. (1992). Universals in the content and structure of values: Theoretical Advances and Empirical Tests in 20 Countries. *Advances in Experimental Social Psychology*, 25, 1-65.

Schwartz, S. (1999) A theory of cultural values and some implications for work. An *International Review, Applied Psychology, Special Review*. The International Association of Applied Psychology.

Schwartz, S. H. and Bilsky, W. (1987). Toward a universal psychological structure of human values. *Journal of Personality and Social Psychology*, 58: 878-891.

Schwartz, S. H., and Bilsky, W. (1990). Toward a theory of the universal content and structure of values: Extensions and cross-cultural replications. *Journal of Personality and Social Psychology*, 58: 878-891.

Schwimmer, Lawrence D. (1993). The Art of Resolving Conflicts in the Workplace. Kantola Productions, 55 Sunnyside Ave. CA. 94941 (Video).

Schooler, C. (1996). Cultural and social structural explanations of cross-national psychological differences. *Annual Review of Sociology*, 22: 323-350.

Scott, E. (2007, November 7). Why stress management? Learn the benefits of stress relief and healthy living. Retrieved February 13, 2009, from About.com Web site: http://stress.about.com/od/understandingstress/a/why_stress_man.htm

Scott, E. (2007). The Low-Stress Healthy Lifestyle Quiz, Are you under Too Much Stress? Retrieved March 01, 2009 from: http://stress.about.com/od/selfknowledgeselftests/a/lifestylequiz.htm

Sekaran, U. (1983). Methodological and theoretical issues and advances in cross-cultural research. *Journal of International Business Studies*, 14: 61-73.

Seyle, Hans (1956). *The Stress of Life*. McGraw-Hill Books Co., New York.

Seyle, Hans (1974). *Stress without Distress*. J.B. Lippincott, New York.

Sfeir-Younis, A. (2002). The spiritual entrepreneur. *Reflections, 3*(3), 43-45. [Society for Organizational Learning and the Massachusetts Institute of Technology].

Shelton, C. D., & Darling, J. R. (2004). From Chaos to Order: Exploring New Frontiers in Conflict Management, Organization Development Journal, Chesterfield: Fall 2004. Vol. 22, Issue. 3; pg 22, 20 pgs. Retrieved September 9, 2004 from ProQuest database.

Siegel, Barry (September 2005). The Business Case for Recruitment Process Outsourcing (RPO): How outsourcing can improve your company. HR Florida Review, Vol. 4, No. 2.

Sikula, A. F. (1973). The values and value systems of governmental executives. Public Personnel Management, January-February 1973: 16-22.

Sims, Randi (2006). Stress Management Concepts and Practices. Retrieved on April 04, 2006 from: http://www.nova.edu/~sims/smmpover.html

Singh, B. R. (2002, June). Problems and possibilities of dialogue across cultures. Intercultural Education, 13(2), 215. Retrieved September 10, 2004 from EBSCO database.

Spera, S. and Lanto, S., (1997). Beat Stress with Strength: A Survival Guide for Word and Life. Park Avenue: an Imprint of JIST Works, Inc.

Sternberg, E.N. (2000). The Balance Within. W.H. Freeman & Co. New York.

Stone D.; Johnson R., Stone-Romero F., Hartman M. (2005) A comparative study of Hispanic-American and Anglo-American cultural values and job Choice preferences. Management research. The Journal of the Iberoamerican Academy of Management. Vol 4, No1 Winter.

Stress facts. (1996-2000). Retrieved February 15, 2009, from the health resource network Web site: http://www.stresscure.com/hrn/facts.html

Stress Management Tips (2005-2009). Stress management in the workplace. Retrieved February 12, 2009, from http://www.stressmanagementtips.com/workplace.htm

Stress Management Tips. (2005-2009). Stress Management Tips online. Retrieved February, 13, 2009, from http://www.stressmanagementtips.com/tips.htm

The Basics of Conflict Resolution: Interpersonal Problem-solver Series. Retrieved Feb. 13, 2002 from http://www.ivysea.com/pages/ct0200_1.html

The Stress Management Handbook, 1995. A Guide to Reducing Stress in Every Aspect of Your Life. Sixty-Minute Training Series. National Press Publications.

Thomas, Karen (2005). Teen People Select Young and Powerful. USA Today, August 4, 2005.

Thomas, K. L. and Kilman, R. H. (2007). Thomas Kilman Conflict Mode Instrument. Mountain View, California, CPP, Inc. Retrieved on March 25, 2009 from: http://susanpack76.googlepages.com/CONFLICT_RESOLUTION_QUIZ.pdf.

Ting-Toomey, S. (2005). Cultural barriers to Effective Communication. Conflict Research. Consortium. Retrieved on June 04, 2005 from the following URL: http://www.colorado.edu/conflict/peace/problem/cultrbar.htm

Tihanyl, L., Griffith, D. A., and Russell, C. J. (2005). The effect of cultural distance on entry Mode choice, international diversification, and MNE performance: A meta-analysis. Journal of International Business Studies, 36(3): 270-280.

Triandis, H. C. (1994). Theoretical and methodological approaches to the study of collectivism and individualism. In U. Kim, H. C. Triandis, C. Kagitcibasi, S-C.Choi, and G. Yoon (Eds) (1994). Individualism and collectivism: Theory, methods and applications. Cross-cultural Research and Methodology Series, Volume 18, Sage Publications.

Triandis, H.. C. and Suh, E. M. (2002). Cultural influences on personality. Annual Review of Psychology, 2002, pp. 133-150.

Trompenaars, F. and Hampden-Turner, C. (1998). Riding the waves of culture, 2nd ed, McGraw-Hill.

Turnipseed, D. S., and Turnipseed, D. L. (1997). A bi-cultural analysis of the cost of caring: Nursing burnout in the U.S. and Philippines. Career Development International, 2(4): 180-188.

Twin, A. (2003, Dec). 2003's Biggest Losers. CNN Money. Retrieved March 30, 2004 from http://money.cnn.com/2003/12/12/markets/yir_biglosers03/.

Uehara, A. (1986). The nature of American re-entry adjustment and the perception of the sojourn experience. International Journal of Intercultural Relations, 10, 415-438.

University of Virginia. Management Communication. Retrieved on June 6, 2005 from the following URL: http://www.darden.virginia.edu/faculty/fac_mc.htm

USA Today, (2005). How U.S Divorce Rate Compares. August 4, 2005.

Verspejc, M.A. (1989). The Ten Most Frequent Causes of Stress in the Work Place. Industry Week (pg. 19, 20). New York.

Virovere, A., Kooskora, M., & Valler, M. (2002). Conflict as a tool for measuring ethics at workplace. Journal of Business Ethics. Dordrecht: August 2002. 39 (1/2), 75. Retrieved September 22, 2004 from ProQuest database.

Walton, S. and Huey, J. (1992). Made in America. New York: Doubleday.

Ward, C., and Searle, W. (1991). The impact of value discrepancies and cultural identity on psychological and socio-cultural adjustment of sojourners. *International Journal of Intercultural Relations*, 15, 209-225.

Weber, J. (1990). Managerial value orientations: A typology and assessment. *International Journal of Value Based Management*, 3(2): 37-54.

Weber, J. (1993). Exploring the relationships between personal value and moral reasoning. *Human Relations*, 36: 435-364.

Wein, Harrison (2000). *A Report Firms the NIH World on health*. NIH Office of communications and Public Liaison. Retrieved on October 10, 2005 from: (http://www.nih.gov/news/wordonHealth/oct2000/story01.htm)

Whetten, D. A., and Cameron, K. S. (1998). *Developing management skills* (4th Ed). Addison-Wesley Educational Publishers (pp. 84-85).

WHO (2006). *Core health indicators*. WHO Statistical Information System. Retrieved August 8, 2006, from http://www3.who.int/ whosis/ corcore. selectprocess.cfm?strISO3_select=SGP&strIndicat...

WHO Surf 2 (2006). Surf 2: Country profiles. World Health Organization. Retrieved November 12, 2006 from http://www.who.int/ncd_surveillance/infobase/ web/surf2/ontry_list.html

Williams, W.M. & Sternberg, R.J. (1988). *Group Intelligence: Why some groups are better than others.* Intelligence, 12, 351-377.

Wikler, Y. (2001). 7 days in September. *Kashrus Magazine. 22*(2), 20-21. Retrieved February 19, 2005, from EBSCOhost database.

Wolin, L. D. (2003). Gender issues in advertising: An oversight synthesis of research: 1970-2002. *Journal of Advertising Research*, 43(1): 111-125.

Yerkes, L. A., & Decker, C. (2003). *Beans: Four principles for running a business in good times or bad.* San Francisco: Jossey-Bass.

Author Biographies

Bahaudin G. Mujtaba is a Department Chair and an Associate Professor of Management. As a corporate manager and trainer, he has worked in management development, human resources, and improvement systems departments for over sixteen years.

Bahaudin's areas of research include ethics, diversity management, stress management, and cross-cultural management practices. He has published articles nationally and internationally in peer-reviewed academic journals. And he has authored and coauthored over sixteen books

Timothy McCartney is a Distinguished Professor of Management and Paul Hersey Chair in Leadership and Organizational Behavior at the H. Wayne Huizenga School of Business and Entrepreneurship, Nova Southeastern University, Ft Lauderdale, Florida. He is a Clinical Psychologist and also an Organizational Development Consultant, facilitating seminars, workshops and advising national and multinational companies in the Caribbean and worldwide. Dr. McCartney was educated in the Bahamas. USA, Switzerland, Jamaica, England, and France where he obtained a Doctorate in Clinical Psychology, "tres honorable! (Suma_cum_ laude") He has received many awards and citations for his contribution to psychology and mental health from national and international communities. He has obtained "Excellence in Teaching Awards" and was named "Students Choice" Professor of the Year, 2008/2009.

Dr. Bahaudin G. Multaba
Nova Southeastern University
3301 College Avenue
Fort Lauderdale, Florida 33314
Phone: (954) 262-5000
Email: mujtaba@nova.edu

Dr. Timothy McCartney
Nova Southeastern University
3301 College Avenue
Fort Lauderdale, Florida 33314
Phone: (954) 262-5000
Email: mccartne@nova.edu

Index Table

Cats in the Cradle: By Harry Chapin

A child arrived just the other day,
He came to the world in the usual way.
But there were planes to catch, and bills to pay.
He learned to walk while I was away.
And he was talking 'fore I knew it, and as he grew,
He'd say, "I'm gonna be like you, dad.
You know I'm gonna be like you."

And the cat's in the cradle and the silver spoon,
Little boy blue and the man in the moon.
"When you coming home, dad?" "I don't know when,
But we'll get together then.
You know we'll have a good time then."

My son turned ten just the other day.
He said, "Thanks for the ball, dad, come on let's play.
Can you teach me to throw?" I said, "Not today,
I got a lot to do." He said, "That's ok."
And he walked away, but his smile never dimmed,
Said, "I'm gonna be like him, yeah.
You know I'm gonna be like him."

And the cat's in the cradle and the silver spoon,
Little boy blue and the man in the moon.
"When you coming home, dad?" "I don't know when,
But we'll get together then.
You know we'll have a good time then."

Well, he came from college just the other day,
So much like a man I just had to say,
"Son, I'm proud of you. Can you sit for a while?"
He shook his head, and he said with a smile,
"What I'd really like, dad, is to borrow the car keys.
See you later. Can I have them please?"

And the cat's in the cradle and the silver spoon,
Little boy blue and the man in the moon.
"When you coming home, son?" "I don't know when,
But we'll get together then, dad.
You know we'll have a good time then."

I've long since retired and my son's moved away.
I called him up just the other day.
I said, "I'd like to see you if you don't mind."
He said, "I'd love to, dad, if I could find the time.
You see, my new job's a hassle, and the kid's got the flu,
But it's sure nice talking to you, dad.
It's been sure nice talking to you."
And as I hung up the phone, it occurred to me,
He'd grown up just like me.
My boy was just like me.

And the cat's in the cradle and the silver spoon,
Little boy blue and the man in the moon.
"When you coming home, son?" "I don't know when,
But we'll get together then, dad.
You know we'll have a good time then."

www.ingramcontent.com/pod-product-compliance
Lightning Source LLC
Chambersburg PA
CBHW020401100426
42812CB00001B/148